Monitoring Children
An Evaluation of the Assessment of Performance Unit

Monitoring Children

An Evaluation of the
Assessment of Performance Unit

Caroline Gipps and Harvey Goldstein

Heinemann Educational Books · London

Heinemann Educational Books Ltd
22 Bedford Square, London WC1B 3HH
LONDON   EDINBURGH   MELBOURNE   AUCKLAND
HONG KONG   SINGAPORE   KUALA LUMPUR   NEW DELHI
IBADAN   NAIROBI   JOHANNESBURG
EXETER (NH)   KINGSTON   PORT OF SPAIN

British Library Cataloguing in Publication Data

Gipps, Caroline
    Monitoring children.
    1. Great Britain. *Department of Education and
    Science. Assessment of Performance Unit*—History
    and criticism
    I. Title   II. Goldstein, Harvey
    371.2'7'0942   LB2838

    ISBN 0–435–80345–X

Typeset by Inforum Ltd, Portsmouth
Printed in Great Britain by Biddles Ltd, Guildford, Surrey

Contents

Appendices 6–9

These appendices are available separately from the Institute of Education. Please write for details to the Department of Mathematics, Statistics and Computing, Institute of Education, University of London, Bedford Way, London WC1H 0AL.

Acknowledgements

This research project was funded by the Social Science Research Council whose support is gratefully acknowledged. However, the views expressed in this report are not necessarily those of the Social Science Research Council.

Many people have helped in the production of the report. The other members of the project team, Tessa Blackstone, Stephen Steadman and Barry Stierer have been invaluable in providing comments on drafts. Denis Lawton, Jack Wrigley, Harold Rosen, Helen Simons, Roy Macleod and Alec Penfold have provided valuable help as members of the project steering group. Deborah Head produced the chronology and helped with Chapter 5 while Jenny Read typed, retyped and organised the manuscript. Finally we should like to put on record the extensive contribution of Bob Wood who was the Senior Research Officer from January 1980 until August 1981.

Our thanks also go to all the people who were interviewed, to those who attended a seminar to discuss a draft of this report, and to the people who sent in comments on the draft. Last, but not least, our thanks go to the DES/APU personnel who so generously gave their time and allowed us free access to documents.

Preface

Following a seminar on accountability and education held at Cambridge in September 1977 the Social Science Research Council decided to commit £200,000 to research on accountability, the money to be allocated and progress overseen by a panel operating under the auspices of its Educational Research Board. Slightly less than half the funds were awarded to a team at the London University Institute of Education to carry out a three year project with two main tasks:

(1) to evaluate the work of the Assessment of Performance Unit (APU) with the Department of Education and Science;

(2) against a background of a suspected increase in testing by local education authorities (LEAs) popularly attributed to talk of falling standards, to investigate the uses LEAs make of standardised tests, focusing particularly on monitoring schemes.

What follows is our report on the APU. Briefly, the APU is a monitoring unit in the DES which commissions surveys of attainment in mathematics, language, science and modern languages. The unit has two bodies, the Consultative Committee and the Statistics Advisory Group, to advise it on general research and survey matters, and steering groups to advise the monitoring teams. At an earlier stage there also existed a Co-ordinating Group but this has been disbanded. When we refer in the text to the APU we are referring to the DES-based secretariat, including the head or heads of the Unit. The various committees, groups and monitoring teams are always referred to directly rather than being subsumed under APU as an umbrella team. In writing this report we have had access to all (save a very few) APU committee papers and minutes as well as APU personnel. Like others, we have had access to all the published material on the APU – publicity leaflets, reports etc, but we have not had access to draft reports or the work of the teams of unpublished test items. Nor have we been given access to any information on schools or LEAs involved in the APU's testing programme.

As well as reading minutes and documents we have interviewed 46 people involved at some time or another with the APU, and we are most grateful for the time that these people gave us. We also held a seminar on 21 April 1982 to discuss with interested parties a draft version of this report. Twenty four people, past and present members of the APU, its committees, groups and monitoring teams as well as academics, attended the seminar. Their comments, many of which have been incorporated into the final report, were most constructive and helpful. We have listed the names of people interviewed in Appendix 4 and the seminar participants in Appendix 5.

There are problems associated with working largely from minutes: it is axiomatic that more was said than recorded and that the discussion was livelier and sometimes more fraught than appears from the minutes. We know this from our discussions with members of the APU committees, and wherever possible we have attempted to indicate the flavour of such debates. We have been helped considerably in this respect by the interview material and comments from the seminar participants. Though we do not refer directly to anyone interviewed* – which may make it seem that the information has been underused – we should stress that the interview material has been a constant referent in shaping our understanding of the history of the Unit and in clarifying the problems facing those whose job it was to make decisions about the paths along which the APU was to go. We in no way underestimate the enormous task facing those involved in developing a system of national assessment. This task is not made easier by the staffing policy in Government departments such as the DES, since those who had the original idea for the APU and wrote the terms of reference were not those who wrote the blueprint, and those who wrote the blueprint were not those who had to effect the assessment programme. It is a truism to say that the Unit has no collective memory, and in a very real sense this has been at the root of some of the criticisms that outsiders have had of the APU; those observers who do have a (collective) memory wish to hold the Unit to its original promises more than the Unit itself would like, or is capable of. For example, though it may be well understood within the DES that the APU is a long-term project and will take many years to come 'on stream' this was never made really clear to outsiders and in some quarters has resulted in a disappointment that the APU has not 'delivered the goods'.

This report is an elucidation of the APU and as such is largely an historical account, though we do offer an assessment and critique of its work. It became clear to us quite early in our research that a detailed history was necessary since this is the only way in which the

_____

* We have a fully referenced copy of this report on our files

current role of the APU can be understood fully. We should make it clear that we have written this report from the standpoint of researchers. This perspective necessarily informs our attitudes towards and evalution of events. In particular we have chosen to regard the APU exercise as a research venture, to which standard ground rules should apply.

The report starts with a descriptive account of what the APU is, what it does and how it was set up. The second chapter deals with underachievement and includes a commentary on the Educational Disadvantage Unit, and the proposed study of West Indian children's performance. Chapter 3 outlines the work of the Consultative Committee and the Co-ordinating Group while Chapter 4 deals with the work of the Statistics Advisory Group. Chapter 5 deals with the work of the monitoring teams and their steering groups for maths, language and science. Chapter 6 discusses the APU's relationship with other bodies. Finally, Chapter 7 is a critical assessment of the APU with suggestions for the future. The first and last chapters stand on their own and can be read together by those who do not wish to go more deeply into the work of the committees, groups and teams. Appendix 1 consists of a brief chronology of the APU up to the beginning of 1982 when this report was written.*

Though we have not evaluated in detail the product of the research teams' work – that is the test material – we have commissioned critiques of the APU reports so far and these are given in Appendix 8. The views in these critiques are those of the authors who are themselves experienced in the areas they write about. We commissioned these critiques because we felt that our readers, as well as having a description and assessment of the APU, should also have some independent evaluation of its products. We have not been able to evaluate the test material itself because it is not available.

Why have we decided to write our report on the Unit at this stage rather than at the end of our project? The work of the APU research teams has been extended until well beyond the life of this project so that our report could not constitute a final analysis. Nevertheless, we have now had reports from the maths, language and science teams, so that in these areas there have been several surveys. Furthermore, the end of 1981 and the start of 1982, following the seminar on monitoring change over time in June 1981, was a time of decision making within the DES over the Unit's future direction. It seems appropriate, therefore, to write our assessment of the Unit's work now, at the time of their own internal reassessment.

---

* A detailed chronology, including press cuttings, is provided in Appendix 9, available separately from the Institute of Education

1 An Overview of the Assessment of Performance Unit

I Structure and Function

The APU is a unit within the Department of Education and Science. It is headed* by a senior Inspector (HMI) Mr Arthur Clegg (Staff Inspector) who is the Professional Head and a civil servant Miss Jean Dawson (Assistant Secretary) who is the Administrative Head. They report to an Under-Secretary and ultimately to the Permanent Secretary and Ministers at the DES. The Unit oversees the surveying of performance in maths and language at ages 11 and 15, science at 11, 13 and 15 and (shortly) first modern foreign language at 13. The Unit is also considering the feasibility of monitoring in the area of technology and possibly aesthetics.

The actual test development is contracted out to the National Foundation for Educational Research (NFER) for maths, language and modern language and to Leeds University/Chelsea College, London, for science. The surveying is carried out by the Monitoring Services Unit of the NFER which handles sampling, school contacts and test dispatch for all the teams. Each of the test development teams has a steering group to advise them, and these groups are composed of teachers, advisers, researchers, lecturers and HMI, all of whom are nominated by the DES. These steering groups have been through two stages. First they were *working groups* which came up with a blueprint for action. Once the research/monitoring team was appointed and the test development was under way they became *steering groups*.

There have been exploratory working groups, all chaired by HMI attached to the APU, pursuing the feasibility of monitoring in personal-social, aesthetic, physical and technological areas. The first three groups reported in 1981 and were then wound up. A decision on aesthetic monitoring awaits the outcome of further development work and it has been decided not to monitor physical or personal-social development.[1] The DES has commissioned for the APU a survey of schol practice in design and technology and the Unit is awaiting the outcome of this survey before taking any decision on monitoring in this area.

* In January 1983.

There is also a Statistics Advisory Group made up of DES, NFER and outside statisticians and researchers, which advises the Unit on technical aspects of its work.

Above all these groups and teams sits the Consultative Committee with approximately 30 members, of whom about two-thirds are appointed by teacher and LEA associations. The remainder are nominated by the Secretary of State to reflect the views and interests of parents, industry, commerce and the wider field of education including universities and educational research. Others, drawn from the HMI and DES, attend meetings as assessors or as members of the Unit; the chairman is an academic. Thus the Consultative Committee is the only group fully representative of outside interests. Its role was defined in an early APU publicity leaflet as one of examining the broad outlines and priorities that are proposed for the Unit's work and bringing its influence to bear on them.[2] The most recent leaflet says more succinctly that it 'advises the Secretary of State about the work of the Unit as a whole.'[3]

There also used to be a Co-ordinating Group which, as its name implies, co-ordinated the work of the various groups and reported to the Consultative Committee. Of the 17 members, ten were HMI or DES personnel and one was from the NFER, while the remaining six were chosen by the DES from schools, colleges, universities and LEAs. The group was disbanded in February 1980. The overall structure of the Unit and its associated groups is outlined in Diagram 1.

The Unit's terms of reference are:

To promote the development of methods of assessing and monitoring the achievement of children at school, and to seek to identify the incidence of underachievement.

The tasks laid down are:

(1) to identify and appraise existing instruments and methods of assessment which may be relevant for these purposes.

(2) to sponsor the creation of new instruments and techniques for assessment, having due regard to statistical and sampling methods.

(3) to promote the conduct of assessment in co-operation with local education authorities and teachers.

(4) to identify significant differences of achievement related to the circumstances in which children learn, including the incidence of underachievement, and to make the findings available to those concerned with resource allocation within government departments, local education authorities and schools.[4]

A History of the APU

The APU was announced in 1974 and began to come to the attention of educationists in 1975, with the publication of a paper 'Monitoring Pupils' Performance'[5] by Brian Kay who was the first head of the Unit.

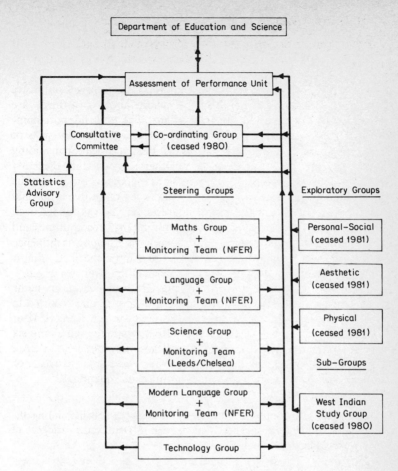

Diagram 1   The structure of the APU and its associated groups

In order to throw light on how the APU was set up it is useful to consider the educational and political climate in Britain in the early to mid 1970s. The following brief account of this climate does not seek to provide the kind of theoretical perspective which would be supplied, for example, by a socio-historical analysis. Rather, we have summarised the issues which achieved public prominence and hence determined the flavour of public debate.

The educational context in which the APU was set up
The prime reason for the emergence of the so-called Great Debate and the accountability movement in the 1970s was an increasingly questioning attitude among commentators, and sections of the general public too, towards the outcomes of the maintained education system.

The reorganisation of secondary education in the 1960s and early

1970s resulted in the decline of the 11+ test which signified to some the end of quality control in primary education. For over 40 years, the 11+ had had a powerful effect on primary schools, focusing attention on maths, English and reading. With comprehensive schools the need for the 11+ diminished and the primary schools were freed from its constraints. This liberation and the impact of the Plowden Report on primary education[6] gave a boost to the child-centred approach and widened the curriculum for this age group. At the same time the movement towards progressive primary education was associated with a good deal of popular concern about falling standards. Critics of the progressive movement were not slow to suggest that children were entering secondary school with poorer attainment in maths and English. There was no conclusive evidence to substantiate this, but the ending of the 11+ served to strengthen the hand of those who advocated a system of regular national assessment.[7]

This is not to say that there had not been surveys of attainment in the past; the NFER had carried out regular reading surveys for the DES from 1948 to 1964. These showed that during the 16 years of the surveys there had been an advance of 17 months in the reading age of 11-year-olds and 20–30 months for 15-year-olds.[8] Though there was much argument over the signifiance of this advance, the reading surveys had the effect of reassuring the public and the teaching profession that reading standards were not falling. The next NFER reading survey was not carried out until 1970 and it was unsatisfactory for a number of reasons, including poor response rate and unsatisfactory tests.[9] The findings, however, were interpreted as meaning that although standards had not fallen they had ceased to rise, and this was greeted by critics of progressive education as evidence of deterioration in the maintained sector.

Following this reading survey, the criticisms surrounding it and general concern over standards of literacy, a committee was set up in 1972 under the chairmanship of Sir Alan Bullock. The role of this committee was to consider all aspects of the teaching of English and how arrangements for monitoring the general level of attainment in this area could be introduced or improved. The report of the committee[10] gave fuel to the argument for better regular testing. Its first recommendation was for a system of monitoring, employing new instruments to assess a wider range of attainments.

Primary education took on a higher profile in 1975 with the William Tyndale affair. Parents of children in the William Tyndale Junior School in Islington (part of the Inner London Education Authority) complained about the quality of education their children were receiving under the 'progressive regime' of the head and his deputy. An enquiry, headed by an eniment QC, was set up and as a result the head and several staff were sacked, an unprecedented step in this country.[11] The shock waves following this decision spread throughout the education system. The result was that many LEAs interpreted both the William Tyndale affair and the Bullock Report as providing clear signals to start thinking about setting up their own local testing programmes to provide information on standards in the basic skills, which in many cases had been missing since the end of the 11+.

When the rapid growth of the education system in the 1960s and early 1970s started to slow down, people both inside and outside education began to consider questions of quality.[12] In 1976 Prime Minister Callaghan gave a speech at Ruskin College, Oxford. In this speech he suggested that education should be more accountable to society and that a general consideration of educational issues should be opened up to give the non-professionals a chance to have their say. 'We spend £6 billion a year on education so there will be discussion.'[13] There seems to have been some concern that education had fallen too much into the hands of the professionals, and behind the invitation for them to take part in this discussion there was felt to be a suggestion that the professionals had some explaining to do.[14] This call met with approval from much of industry and the general public and the ensuing discussion, including a series of semi-public meetings organised by the DES, was termed the Great Debate. The response from the world of education was hostile, based partly on a genuine fear that the Great Debate would lead to something like the popularly held view of the American version of 'accountability through testing', and partly on opposition to 'education for industry'.

The concept of accountability in education became prominent in the United States in the late 1960s when there was an economic crisis precipitated by the Vietnam war. This crisis led to cuts in government spending and resulted in the adoption of procedures to allocate the remaining slender resources. Accountability procedures had their roots in the 'scientific management' movement in which testing had played a central role by providing the data by which efficiency could be judged. Thus the testing of pupils was linked closely with accountability in the US and that link has been maintained in this country. As an example of this, the DES in their 1977 Green Paper *Education in Schools* linked the APU into the growing accountability framework: 'Growing recognition of the need for schools to demonstrate their accountability to the society which they serve requires a coherent and soundly based means of assessment for the education system as a whole, for schools and for individual pupils'.[15]

Thus the APU can be seen as a response to general concern over standards and to the specific recommendations of the Bullock Report. Although the APU was not the direct result of a press for accountability,

both because it came into being before the Great Debate got off
the ground and because its work was not explicitly informed by those
concerns, it did start coming to the public's attention at a time when
accountability was becoming an issue. In addition to the public debate
it is clear that monitoring had also been under discussion within the
DES for some years previously. In the late 1960s several strands came
together which were to encourage, within the DES, an interest in
national monitoring. First, there was an increasing interest in sub-
jecting the education system to systematic study of its objectives and
evaluation of its achievements. As early as 1968 an internal DES paper[16]
suggested a wide-ranging testing programme as one means of assessing
the pay-off from educational investment, and the area of maths was
given specific attention.

At the same time there was increasing discussion about trends in
educational standards. Critics of the reorganisation of secondary education were claiming that standards would fall[17] and there was also
concern about 'underachievement' of particular groups, especially
ethnic minorities. While the NFER reading surveys were available,
there was little information in other areas, especially mathematics.
There also seems to have been an increasing concern around 1970 that
the DES (as distinct from the HMI) was excluded from involvement
with the educational curriculum, despite funding the system and
ultimately being held accountable for it. Since the Schools Council and
the teachers themselves retained most control over the curriculum,
DES involvement with testing presented itself as a means of obtaining a
direct evaluation of the performance of the system and consequently a
means of achieving some say in curriculum content.

These strands came together in 1970 with the setting up under the
DES planning branch of a working group on the measurement of
educational attainment (WGMET).[18] It consisted of two administrators, two HMIs and four academics: the Professor of Education at
Bristol University and research consultant to the DES; the Director of
Studies and Head of the Research Group at the Schools Council; the
Director of the ILEA Research and Statistics Division; and the Deputy
Director of the NFER. The working group reported at the end of 1971,
and although seen by various people its recommendations were not
formally discussed by a policy group until the end of 1973. We shall
discuss its technical recommendations in Chapter 4, but its main conclusions were that 'regular measurements of educational attainment
are desirable', that 'measurement is feasible', should 'be done by
sampling' covering 'the main educational stages and school subjects'
and should be 'a partnership between testing bodies, the Schools
Council, LEAs and the DES'. The group recommended an early start
and, arising from this, a feasibility project at the NFER (Tests of

Attainment in Mathematics in Schools) was commissioned by the newly formed DES Policy Group B in 1972. This project then became the precursor to the APU maths monitoring programme. In 1974 an interim report from the project indicated that large scale maths monitoring was clearly feasible and could be undertaken by the NFER.

The Bullock Committee had a monitoring subcommittee which included two administrators, one HMI, two NFER representatives and four educationists and academics. One of the academics had also been a member of the 1970 group (WGMET), and the report of that group was referred to explicitly in the subcommittee's minutes, so that this subcommittee can be seen as a continuation of the DES interest in monitoring. The outcome of its discussions formed Chapter 3 of the Bullock Report.[19] The recommendations there went much further than the 1970 group's report and strongly recommended a national system of monitoring using 'light sampling' and 'item banking' techniques, both of which it was felt could overcome 'curriculum backwash' problems. The report, in its preface, pointed out that the evidence available to it did not allow unequivocal statements to be made about trends in performance and it attached great importance to a monitoring system which could throw light on the problem.

Thus by the end of 1974 there had been a strong series of recommendations in favour of national monitoring in the areas of maths and reading. A feasibility project in maths had been encouraging, and the NFER had been closely involved in all the discussions and indicated clearly its willingness and ability to carry out any monitoring programme.

An intimation that the APU was on its way came in April 1974 in a speech by the then Secretary of State for Education, Mr Reg Prentice, to the National Association of Schoolmasters' conference.[20] In August of the same year came the first official announcement in the White Paper *Educational Disadvantage and the Educational Needs of Immigrants.*[21] This paper announced the setting up of an Educational Disadvantage Unit (EDU) within the DES, the purpose of which was to influence the allocation of resources in the interests of those suffering from educational disadvantage which, given the focus of the White Paper, was generally understood to mean ethnic minority groups (see Chapter 2 for details of the EDU). The EDU was to develop, *in conjunction with the APU*, criteria to improve identification of this educational disadvantage. It was in an annexe to this paper that the APU's terms of reference and tasks were set out formally for the first time. It is these that APU officials have always considered to be their brief, while the notion of improving criteria to identify educational disadvantage seems to have been forgotten and indeed has never been mentioned in any material produced by the APU.

The political context

Althoug the APU is not identified exclusively with any major political party, and has been little exploited by them, nevertheless party politics are relevant to its continued operation. As we outlined earlier in this chapter, the early 1970s were a time of growing public concern over standards and a move towards increased accountability in education. The period which immediately preceded the establishment of the APU was one of fluctuating fortunes for the major political parties and of increasing economic pressure upon Britain.

The changes were rapid and dramatic between 1972 and 1975 and could not have been anticipated by those whose responsibility it was to govern education. In the last quarter of 1972 the DES, under the then Secretary of State for Education Mrs Thatcher, produced a White Paper, *Education: A Framework for Expansion*,[22] which outlined DES long-term thinking. There was to be expansion of higher education, mainly, but not exclusively, through polytechnics and technical colleges rather than residential universities, and increased stress was to be laid on the provision of free nursery school education for children from three years old. Though concerned with expansion, the White Paper heralded the end of an era of expansion and liberalism. The tone was optimistic, for 1972 had been the year of North Sea Oil, but inflationary pressures soon increased. In September 1973 Lord Rothschild, head of the Government's 'Think Tank', suggested in a public speech that by 1985 Britain would be one of the poorest European nations. In 1973 two events precipitated crisis. The OPEC countries quadrupled the price of their oil and the coal miners, mindful of their successful 1972 strike, banned overtime working to put pressure upon the new government pay limits. The Conservative government declared a State of Emergency on 13 November 1973 and the nation moved into the 'three-day week'. In February 1974 the miners declared a national strike and the scene was then set for the announcement of a general election on the theme of 'Who rules Britain?'

The election brought a very slender majority for Labour, the settlement of the miners' claim, and an end to the State of Emergency in March. The election result also meant that it was Reg Prentice, the new Labour Secretary of State for Education, who in August 1974 announced the establishment of the Unit which was to become known as the APU. In the announcement and the press release[23] the emphasis was on the problem of underachievement. In October of the same year a second general election returned the Labour party to office, this time with an absolute, although precariously small, majority over all the other parties.

It is easy to appreciate, against such a sequence of events, that in the general public consciousness there should be greater calls to account at all levels. The need to save energy, to be efficient and to increase productivity had been brought to the forefront of people's minds. There were also major constraints upon increasing public expenditure. Education was no exception, so that when the Bullock Report was published in February 1975 the implementation of the remedial measures recommended in the report was deferred by the government for reasons of economy. Educational expenditure was now being examined critically along with every other part of government spending.

Later events, in 1975 when the William Tyndale school enquiry was opened and in 1976 when Prime Minister Callaghan made his Ruskin College speech, served to sharpen that scrutiny and to focus attention upon the potential of the APU for monitoring the system. At this point the APU became politically useful: the Labour Government was able to say that they *were* concerned about standards, since they were finding out about them and not racing to conclusions. The Conservative party too, thought the APU might be a useful body and in its 1979 election manifesto the very brief section on education was dominated by reference to the APU:

> We shall promote higher standards of achievement in basic skills. The Government's Assessment of Performance Unit will set national standards in reading, writing and arithmetic, monitored by tests worked out with teachers and others and applied locally by education authorities.

Since the Conservative party came to power there has been no suggestion, as yet, of reducing the APU's budget nor of using the APU to set national standards. Thus the APU has survived successive governments – as indeed it was no doubt designed to do by the DES civil servants – because both parties could see a use for it. Both parties have acknowledged the importance of the 'standards' issue, albeit from different viewpoints, and both see it as a lever for allocation of resources. The key reason for its acceptability to both parties was, however, that it came at the time of a call for more consumer control over education.

What the APU says about itself
The APU's public face is best observed in the publicity leaflets and public statements that it has put out. Throughout them all runs a thread of concern over standards and a justification of the decision to aim for surveys of attainment. Thus in 1975 Kay wrote in his cross-curriculum article:[24]

In recent years there has been a growing interest in the assessment of pupils' performance at school, related in the minds of many people to some anxiety about standards. This interest and concern is felt not only by teachers but by politicians and administrators, employers and the general public.

In 1976 the first of the Unit's publicity leaflets explained:[25]

THE PROBLEM
Everyone wants to raise educational standards. But how do we know what the educational standards are? How do we measure standards in education? How can we monitor progress?

There is not enough information available at present. There is plenty of hearsay, hunch and opinion. There are plenty of tests about but there are many important things these tests don't attempt to measure. And most of them are designed to give information about individuals, not to paint a picture of pupils' achievements nationally.

The last ten years have seen changes in school organisation and curriculum. We need to be able to monitor the consequences for children's performance in school. We need to know how our schools are serving the changing needs of children and society.

and continued:

WHAT IS THE APU DOING?
The first task of the APU is to identify and define standards of performance pupils might be expected to achieve through their work at school.

Next, it has to find generally acceptable ways of measuring and assessing pupils' achievements against these standards and to decide at what ages assessment could be done.

To do this the APU has to look at the existing techniques for measurement and, where there are no suitable techniques already, to get new ones developed and tested.

The APU will not carry out this development work itself. It will sponsor work by research groups and keep in close touch with their progress. Only when ways have been devised of measuring at least some of the most important goals of education can a start be made on monitoring performance.

The following year's leaflet[26] expanded on the need for a national assessment of standards:

There has always been a substantial amount of testing of one kind or another in our schools, initiated either by heads, individual teachers or local education authorities. However, little of this activity is co-ordinated. Procedures, actual tests and the conditions in which they are used vary widely; it is neither possible to compare the results nor to put them together to give a national picture of performance.

Thus, at present, there are few national facts and figures available on which to base significant statements about standards in schools. We need such information not only to describe the current position but also to record changes as they occur.

And the same year (before surveying had begun) the Unit's head wrote in the *Times Educational Supplement* with perhaps premature optimism:

As subsequent surveys are conducted, changes in the national picture may be identified and described. Also it should be possible to accumulate parts of the data and make some more accurate statements later. Trends in the data . . . will help to show where small in-depth follow-up studies are needed.[27]

The most recent APU leaflet (1980) made this point again and enlarged on it in an even more optimistic vein:

As the years go by the APU's monitoring programme will produce increasingly accurate and useful data. It will trace changes in performance; it will draw attention to features which will give cause for satisfaction as well as concern; it will identify areas in which further detailed study will be warranted. Above all, it will contribute to the background against which decisions about resources are taken and promote the basis for a genuine and informed debate about educational standards.[28]

Though the APU was set up with a brief to monitor underachievement, it is concern over standards, the need for knowledge about national trends and the need to co-ordinate testing activity which have been given at various times by the APU itself as explanations of its role. These were also the predominant concerns of discussions in the early 1970s. These concerns were of course timely, given the climate of accountability and debate over standards, and this may well explain the Unit's focus. The move away from the original brief must, however, have been encouraged by the realisation that assessing underachievement was no easy task (see Chapter 2).

Carrying out annual monitoring surveys of performance was certainly one way of dealing with the APU's brief. But as the DES assessor on the Consultative Committee pointed out in 1978 the Unit's terms of reference did not limit them to this. The Unit was required to promote the development of methods of assessing and monitoring achievement and there were a variety of ways in which this could be done.[29] The Unit could indeed have aimed straight at underachievement by doing in-depth research studies, but chose not to. Instead it has pursued the tasks in the order that they were written, leaving underachievement to the last.

Dissenting Voices

As we have described, within the government in the early 1970s there was a concern with underachievement and the performance of ethnic groups, as well as a concern over falling standards and accountability in education. However, given the climate at the time when the APU was set up, it is reasonable to suppose that any proposal to monitor standards nationally would have been strongly resisted by the teaching profession which was feeling under attack. Assessing the needs of disadvantaged children, on the other hand, can be considered less threatening professionally and so the announcement of the APU, presented as part of a programme for dealing with disadvantage and underachievement, created little dissent among educationists.

Why then did dissent appear later? What led up to the publication in 1979 and 1980 of several articles criticising the APU and its likely effects? These are interesting questions for, as sociologists like Broadfoot[30] have argued, in the past the efficiency of assessment has been the main area of concern, not its purpose and effects. With the advent of the APU, however, this has changed, for the criticisms have centred on its wider effects – indeed some observers reject the idea of national monitoring altogether as educationally harmful[31] – although the efficiency of the programme has also been questioned.[32]

The first reason for dissent was that by 1975 it had become clear that the APU was not aiming to assess underachievement and disadvantage as originally announced, but was going to become a full scale national assessment programme concerned with standards. Though few observers believed that the more extreme aspects of the American accountability-through-testing model would come into play in this country, when the APU showed that it aimed to monitor standards there was some concern that it was intended as an instrument to force accountability on schools and therefore teachers. Though ostensibly concerned with children's standards, this was interpreted as dealing with teachers' competencies. However, by adhering to the principle of light sampling with only a small number of children tested at any time and the names of children and schools unknown to researchers, there is no way in which the results can be used to judge individual schools or teachers.

The next concern, however, was that the APU might encourage LEAs to indulge in 'saturation' or 'blanket' testing with a view to making judgements about the effectiveness of institutions. The 1977 Green Paper suggested that tests suitable for monitoring in LEAs were likely to come out of the work of the APU. In 1978 LEAs were urged to wait for this test material but, if they could not wait, to monitor using only a light sample of children.[33] Against this advice, many LEAs introduced their own blanket testing system whereby they tested every child in the target age group rather than the 10 per cent recommended by the DES. To what extent these LEA testing programmes have been used as agents of accountability is an area that we have explored as part of our research on LEAs and will be reported elsewhere. However, our findings can be summarised briefly as showing that though blanket testing is widespread, the uses to which results are put do not look nearly as harsh as many teachers had feared. Nevertheless, there is still some concern in this area.

The second big worry expressed about the APU was its effect on the curriculum. Is it possible to have a national system of assessment and not to affect the curriculum in some way? In order to develop test items it is necessary to take a model of the curriculum. Will this model then become the dominant model for the curriculum? Some critics viewed the whole exercise as an attempt to gain control of the curriculum and there was certainly concern in some quarters that the APU was an attempt by the DES to bring in an assessment-led curriculum.[34]

The way that a national monitoring system might bring about an assessment-led curriculum is essentially an indirect one, by which the APU's curriculum model would provide a framework for local authority assessment and thereby a means of introducing a core curriculum.[35,36] The pressure on LEAs to monitor standards has already been discussed, and the danger envisaged lay in the possibility that through 'item banking' procedures and in particular the Local Education Authority and Schools Item Bank (LEASIB) project at the NFER it would be possible to link local testing programmes to the APU's national monitoring programme. (For an account of LEASIB see Chapter 4). APU findings would then provide a baseline of performance and a core of items from which LEAs would be able to develop their own tests and examine the performance of their pupils. Thus the range of APU items would provide the common core of a national curriculum. As it happens there are technical problems associated with item banking and it is now apparent that LEAs will not have access to APU tests via LEASIB (see Chapter 6). The direct use by LEAs of APU test items is currently being discussed and while it is still some way off, this link would tend to accentuate the fears described.

As for direct impact on the curriculum, an impact which the APU has always been keen to play down – hence its adoption of light sampling and matrix sampling techniques – a quote from Burstall and Kay's report of their US trip (see later) indicates that the APU was not totally innocent of designs on the curriculum:

The interests and involvement of those bodies, such as the subject associations, need to be engaged so that they will take advantage of its findings and use them to further desirable curriculum developments.[37]

The view that the APU was a Trojan horse to introduce an assessment-led curriculum has recently been considered too simple an analysis.[38] And as our researches show, though high-level DES concern about their lack of say in the curriculum had some part to play in setting up the APU, as did the concern over the performance of immigrant groups, if its full history is taken into account the APU can be seen as the continuation of early discussions within the DES about national monitoring. This argument is supported by the close relationship of the APU's work to the recommendations made by the working group (WGMET) in their 1971 report.

Deciding what and how to monitor
The Unit's terms of reference are:

To promote the development of methods of assessing and monitoring the achievement of children at school, and to seek to identify the incidence of underachievement.

These terms of reference and the job of developing a system of national assessment were handed over to the Unit's first head in mid-1974 and he spent the next year pondering how to carry out this enormous task. A paper written in July 1974 stated his early views on the Unit's underachievement brief:

The APU is concerned with all pupils and with underachievement at every level of ability, but initially it should devote particular attention to underachievement among the pupils with whom the APU is mainly concerned.[39]

Given the political climate at the time, however, and public concern over standards and their alleged decline it must have seemed eminently reasonable to concentrate on the assessment and monitoring of standards, particularly since this was what the DES intended. From this point on underachievement was a lost cause, for the programme became geared to general monitoring and not to seeking ways of exploring the underachievement problem (see Chapter 2).

Questions facing the head of the Unit over *how* to monitor seemed fairly straightforward in the sense that there already existed the Bullock suggestion of surveying using light sampling and the American example of matrix sampling (see Chapter 4). Regular surveys using light sampling methods had been recommended in the Bullock Report, in order to reduce the chance of 'backwash' effects on the school curriculum. Matrix sampling and anonymity meant that no assessment of individual schools or pupils would be possible, while light sampling meant that curriculum impact would be minimal since so few children in any one school would be tested.

Questions over *what* to monitor were not quite so straightforward. In June 1975 Kay published an article which, as the first to come out of the Unit, can be viewed as a declaration of intent. This oft-quoted paper[40] expounded the APU philosophy which, briefly, was that a cross-curriculum model was to be used for developing the assessment tools, and that six lines of development were to be pursued within this cross-curricular model: verbal, mathematical, scientific, ethical, aesthetic, and physical. Kay acknowledged that these lines of development could not be isolated from a context of knowledge, and stressed that the monitoring programme should cover a broad spectrum of educational objectives. The objectives of the monitoring programme should be made clear, the methods adopted should be appropriate to those objectives and the interpretation of findings should be a strictly professional matter. The first three lines of development pointed to testing in the traditional areas of maths, English language and science. Thus far it was relatively straightforward but as for the other three lines of development, opinions ranged widely over whether it was feasible or even desirable to attempt to assess these. Consequently, discussions about monitoring in these areas occupied much of the Unit's and the committees' time.

Outside involvement in the APU's decision making started with the Co-ordinating Group which began meeting in October 1975 while the Consultative Committee, whose task was to oversee the work of the Unit, did not meet until April 1976 – that is ten months *after* the seminal cross-curriculum paper was published and the work of the Unit was already under way. One early critic[41] has viewed this delay as a deliberate move to allow the DES personnel involved to decide on the main thrust of the Unit's work without the 'embarrassment of a consultative group'. The Unit's view, however, seemed to be that this quiet period before the setting up of the Consultative Committee was necessary in order to make decisions on what *should* be assessed before the experts came in and said what *could* be assessed. Our own interpretation is that the Co-ordinating Group was a working group, with members able to advise on technical issues, and was therefore needed straight away, while the Consultative Committee was essentially a legitimating group which the APU was obliged to have but which was not vital at a very early stage.

It seems clear that there was very little outside consultation at this crucial early stage, i.e. from August 1974 to June 1975. Kay consulted internally with HMI but there was no attempt in this first year to go outside the DES or NFER to consult with researchers or academics, or to produce a conceptual analysis of what underachievement meant. The period after the cross-curriculum article and before the start of monitoring (i.e. June 1975 to May 1978) was not without outside consultation, however, and saw the establishment of the Co-ordinating Group, Consultative Committee and Statistics Advisory Group. In March 1976 Brian Kay and Dr Clare Burstall (a member of the Co-ordinating Group and the Deputy Director of the NFER), visited America to see what lessons could be learned from state monitoring programmes and the American National Assessment of Educational Progress (NAEP). This trip came before the final decision was made within the DES to have a monitoring programme and the reason for the visit was to help make such a decision. First, they discovered that monitoring on a large scale using light sampling was indeed feasible; there had been a big question in the DES over whether it was or not. Secondly, NAEP had run into serious problems because it had no teachers participating on the planning committee. This finding re-inforced the need for the Consultative Committee. Finally, and perhaps most importantly, Burstall and Kay learned that one of NAEP's biggest problems was that the data were not utilised by decision makers and politicians. This was because there had been no dialogue between NAEP and the administrators and politicians in Washington over plicy issues. The message for the APU was this: if there was no clear statement of policy issues on which information was wanted the Unit could not expect results which related directly to those issues.

The lesson for the APU is, we feel, clear . . . On the one hand, it needs to ensure that its findings are of interest and concern to the teacher . . . because of what can be said of the overall pattern of education. On the other hand, it must seek to obtain a clear statement of what sort of information is required by decision makers.[42]

The plea for forward planning could hardly have been made more clearly. It came from the head of the Unit and the person with overall responsibility for much of the test development, and yet it was ignored. There was no list of policy questions produced until June 1981, five years after the American visit, although some attempt was made by the Co-ordinating Group to discuss 'Planning Decisions' at their 1979 conference. The Unit's apparent failure to concern itself with forward planning forms a major theme of this book and we shall return to it repeatedly.

In 1978 there was a second APU-sponsored visit to the US by Tom Marjoram, head of the Unit, and Professor Paul Black, Director of the Science Team at Chelsea. In their report they made a rather plaintive comment about the breadth of the American national assessment pro-gramme particularly in the aesthetic areas of the curriculum. This had been achieved without raising objections from teachers or parents.

What is more, NAEP now collects without apparent difficulty or resistance far more background information than we propose in the APU surveys and their attitude assessments seem more detailed than our own.[43]

The ethical (later called personal–social development) exploratory group was set up in 1976. The monitoring of personal and social development had been a contentious issue from the start and feelings about it in the Consultative Committee ran high: in 1977 one member walked out of a meeting in which the proposal was discussed. In the end the decision was made that monitoring in this area should not go ahead (for a detailed treatment of this issue, see Chapter 3). Exploratory groups for aesthetic and physical development were set up in 1977. They reported as working groups in July 1981 and were wound up, with subsequent decisions to postpone consideration of monitoring in the former and not to monitor in the latter. A seventh line of development – technological – was added to the original list and a subgroup was set up in 1979 to consider this. Its report formed the basis of the discussion document *Understanding Design and Technology*[44] but by late 1982 no decision had been made on whether to go ahead with monitoring. A West Indian study group – to discuss the feasibility of investigating performance (and underachievement) of children of West Indian origin – was set up at the beginning of 1980 and reported at the end of that year. The decision to investigate the feasibility of a separate assessment of the performance of West Indian pupils was the result of anxiety in the education world about the so-called 'underachievement' of black pupils. In early 1981, however, the decision was taken not to go ahead with this assessment (see Chapter 2).

Monitoring in maths began in 1978 and in language in 1979. Both the maths and language monitoring teams were based at the NFER. Science monitoring – based at Leeds University and Chelsea College, London – began the following year and first modern foreign language monitoring (again based at the NFER) will start in 1983. Thus assessment in four 'traditional' curriculum areas is, or is about to become, under way while the more obviously cross-curricular areas have either been dropped or await a decision.

The adoption of the cross-curriculum model seems to have been a defence against the accusation that the APU was going to concentrate only on the 'basic' subjects, with the danger of encouraging a restricted curriculum. Nevertheless, the early choice of areas for monitoring soon led people away from cross-curricular thinking, as did having only specialists for the subject under discussion on the working groups. The early choice of subject areas (maths and language) seems to have been inevitable, given the Bullock Report and the TAMS project at the NFER. It is, in any case, questionable whether the cross-curriculum model was ever a workable proposition given that schools organise their teaching into subjects and that test development has always tended to follow this pattern. Once the teams began developing test items the plan to assess performance in various lines of development across the curriculum seems to have slipped out of view.* The only way to maintain the appearance of cross-curricularity was by increasing the number of areas to be assessed from those first commissioned. Even so,

*This is perhaps understandable in view of the pressures of test development. However, the teams have met at their own instigation to discuss cross-curricular items.

in 1977, the decision to set up a programme of science monitoring was not taken without demur because it was not clear how it fitted the cross-curriculum model. It went through because enough people in the APU and on the Consultative Committee were convinced that assessment of scientific processes genuinely could be cross-curricular. In the same year, the suggestion to assess modern languages was put forward and this was even more difficult to sustain within a cross-curricular model; but the proposal was accepted with the result that, by the end of 1977, the original cross-curriculum model was in disarray and now lies in ruins.

Nevertheless, long after those decisions were made in 1977, the cross-curriculum model was still a topic for discussion. The Co-ordinating Group held a conference in May 1979 and one of the issues they discussed was the cross-curriculum model. It was pointed out then that the model had two flaws. First, not all school subjects contain all six lines of development prominently, but it was felt that 'this is quite irrelevant and should cause no concern whatsoever'.[45] Secondly, the existing programme did not cover all the important areas so that others had to be added.

Was the cross-curriculum model an albatross around the Unit's neck? Apparently not, for the conclusion at the conference was that the original grounds for adopting the model were no less valid than they had been, though it had become obvious that the six lines of development were rather an oversimplification.[46] Our view is not that the model has been an albatross but rather that it was a useful idea for the planning stage and a necessary part of the Unit's desire to be seen as a valuable assessment programme rather than a narrow, back-to-basics movement. However, as the practicalities of test development and surveying have taken over and areas for monitoring have been adopted and dropped, the model has not really held up.

Discussion of Objectives

At no point has there been much public discussion of the APU's objectives, and this has contributed to the concern shown by some educationists over the Unit's role. True, there are terms of reference and associated tasks, but these are vague and give little idea of what the monitoring is actually for. To quote one critic:

Unless the objectives of monitoring are made very clear the objectives of both the monitoring and the total work of the Unit will remain something of a mystery. Under these circumstances mistrust easily becomes exaggerated, and commentators will inevitably speculate over the supposed real purpose of the Unit.[47]

In Kay's cross-curriculum article no mention was made of underachievement or disadvantage. The emphasis instead was on standards and their change over time. In 1976 the 'Yellow Book'[48] (a confidential DES memo) referred to the Unit as dealing with the first task by setting up a monitoring system in maths (following on from development work at the NFER), in reading and the use of language (following on from the Bullock Report) and making a start in science. There was again no mention of disadvantage or what the monitoring might be for. In January 1977[49] Kay wrote a programme of work which discussed each of the tasks in turn. Here the intention to look at trends in performance levels was put forward, as well as the possibility that the APU would make assessment materials available to LEAs. The DES documents *Educating our Children* and *Education in Schools*, both published in 1977, briefly mentioned the APU. Both referred to its role in developing a national monitoring system to provide information on standards. There was some mention of policy makers but no discussion of what policy questions might be answered by the APU's work. Publicity materials produced by the APU between 1977 and 1980 carry on in much the same vein: the APU's role was to monitor in order to provide information on standards and how these change over time. In-depth studies were mentioned as a way of pursuing interesting findings from the national surveys, and though these are the studies which would be most useful in terms of policy making, no discussion or elucidation of which policy questions might be answered has been forthcoming. There is no evidence that the DES produced a clear statement about which policy questions they wished the APU to address. The aim seems to have been simply to develop a national system of assessment that functioned and was acceptable with little thought as to what specific questions it might answer.

In June 1981 at an APU seminar on monitoring change over time a detailed list was put forward, for the first time, of questions they hoped to be able to answer. A modified version of this list was subsequently produced and is given in Appendix 2. When this list is analysed, however, given the way the APU programme has turned out, it is possible to provide answers to only some of these questions. Why then did the Department or the Unit not list more clearly at the outset the policy questions to which they wanted answers? Was it that the APU was intended *solely* as a monitoring exercise giving information on overall standards and nothing else? Is the story of the APU just an example of lack of forward planning? Or is it a more deliberate policy of leaving all options open in order to gain maximum co-operation from interested professional and lay people? Where do matters now stand in relation to the possible introduction of a 'core curriculum'?

The remainder of this book sets out to answer, or at least throw light on, these and related questions.

Issues and Themes

In the following chapters we deal in detail with the work of the Consultative Committee, Co-ordinating Group, Statistics Advisory Group and the monitoring teams and steering groups. We also look at underachievement and how the world of education has reacted to the APU. In these chapters and our conclusions we trace themes and identify issues which recur throughout the history of the APU. Where these are relevant to a chapter they are outlined at the start.

There are six issues relating to the history and work of the APU which featured throughout discussions of the committees, groups and teams. To set the scene we will now describe briefly each of these in turn and explain why we consider them important.

1. Areas of measurement

The areas that were chosen for monitoring are important because of their message for the curriculum. The APU attempted to develop a curriculum model to cover *all* the important parts of the curriculum, or lines of development as they were called. We shall follow the path of this curriculum model in Chapter 3 and see how successful it was.

2. The way in which chosen areas are assessed

The conceptualisation of their tasks by the monitoring teams and steering groups is crucial to the APU's impact on the curriculum. If the tests were narrowly conceived, for example limited to paper and pencil tests only, they could have a narrowing and stultifying effect. This issue will be dealt with in Chapter 5, where it will become clear that the teams have in fact conceptualised a wide task for themselves and broken new ground, particularly in practical testing.

3. Membership of APU groups and committees

It is far from clear how individuals came to be proposed for membership of the groups and committees discussed in Chapters 3, 4 and 5. It seems to have been done by a process of trawling by the HMI involved. This is important because the make-up of a group is bound to have an effect on the direction of its thinking. In some groups such as the Statistics Advisory Group, there was a heavy NFER representation while members of the science teams, for example, who were not based at the NFER, had to wait until 1981 to join this group.

4. Sampling policy

The APU made an early commitment not to overburden schools. However, with three rounds of monitoring per age group per year they have now drifted into what must be considered as fairly intensive monitoring of schools. This has had repercussions on the APU's response rate from schools which is important in terms of the generalisability of the data. It may well have long-term repercussions for future research in LEAs, if schools react to being overburdened. This issue is discussed mainly in Chapter 4.

5. The measurement of home background variables

This is an issue that features in the discussions of all the committees, groups and teams. Information on background factors is important in interpreting children's performance levels. If the APU were simply an exercise to produce a volume of educational statistics, then such interpretational data would be unnecessary. However, given the APU's brief, there is a need to make some inferences from the findings. We shall see how the Consultative Committee was against this information being collected and how, as a result, the APU has been hampered in its task.

6. Reporting

In the sphere of reporting findings the APU has exercised considerable control over the monitoring teams. First, they have insisted on regular yearly reporting, which has had a limiting effect on the research work of the monitoring teams. (They have now finally allowed the teams to hold back a report on one year's monitoring to allow further development and analysis.) Secondly, the APU has insisted that the reports should simply present facts in as neutral a way as possible and has not allowed interpretation of findings. This makes report writing a thankless task for the researchers and makes the reports themselves much less interesting to read. There is some evidence that the Unit is relaxing on this issue also.

Whereas not all these issues are relevant to every chapter, the six themes we have identified recur throughout the book. These are:

1. Planning

By this we mean forward planning and consideration of the consequences of actions. This is clearly important to the whole success of the APU enterprise and comes to the fore in examples such as the school exposure issue with its implications for school participation, the timetable for reporting and the implications of this for research development.

2. The consultation process

Regular consultation takes place both outside and inside the APU structure, and is particularly important when sensitive areas are under consideration, for example personal–social development or the assessment of West Indian children's performance. The speed and range of consultation with outsiders when the Unit is faced with a problem is of particular importance.

3. Constraints on the APU
An important consideration in the free and effective functioning of any body is the constraints upon it. For the APU these lie both within the DES (Ministers, HMI, Policy Groups) and within the framework of the Unit itself (the Consultative Committee, particularly the teacher union representatives, and the Statistics Advisory Group).

4. The APU as a research-versus-monitoring exercise
There seems to be a confusion over whether the APU is mounting a monitoring exercise or a research study. Such a rigid distinction, which views monitoring/surveying as something other than research, would not be made by researchers. This distinction seems to be maintained only by the APU, and it is important because the APU's progress is coloured by their view of their task.

5. The APU as an agent of accountability
The APU, though not set up as the result of pressure for accountability, certainly had its origins in the accountability movement. However, though the need for the educational system to be accountable via the APU has already been mentioned, particularly by the first head of the Unit, there is little explanation of how this would come about. We shall pursue the accountability theme throughout this report not only in terms of how the APU could be an agent of accountability but also how it attempted to make *itself* accountable through membership of the various groups and committees.

6. Progress of the APU's aims
We shall examine the progress made on the various aims both as stated in the White Paper and later. These are: the development of methods of assessment (Task Two), co-operation with LEAs in assessment (Task Three), the measurement of achievement related to the circumstances in which children learn, including underachievement (Task Four), and the measurement of standards and trends in performance over time.

2 Underachievement

Introduction
We consider underachievement to be a major issue in the history of the APU. Whether or not underachievement was ever intended to be a major task for the APU, the Unit was nevertheless announced in a White Paper on the educational needs of immigrant pupils who were thought to be underachieving. The identification of underachievement was in the Unit's original terms of reference, and it was the reason behind the moves to generate a study of the performance of West Indian children.

An aside is necessary at this point, for although we will continue to use the term 'underachievement' in this chapter in accordance with the APU's usage, we consider the term to be a misnomer. Without individually based knowledge of 'expected achievement' it is difficult to see how underachievement can be measured. We believe that the original intention was actually to study 'low achievement' and the use of the term 'underachievement' led to unintentional difficulties which we discuss below.

Of the themes identified in the introductory section four are of particular relevance to this chapter.

Progress of the APU's aims
Identification of underachievement is the fourth task attached to the APU's terms of reference. Though the Unit has always considered this logically to be the last task to be attempted, it *is* an aim to which they are committed. In this chapter we shall follow how the Unit attempted to make some progress on this aim by adopting a workable definition of underachievement, by suggesting in-depth studies as a way of studying underachievement and by attempting to mount a study of underachievement in West Indian children.

Consultation
The APU did consult with the Educational Disadvantage Unit (EDU)

over the problem of defining and measuring underachievement, but there was little concrete outcome. It is in their attempt to mount the study of West Indian children that the APU's consultation process can be seen at its most widespread. Whereas consultation outside the APU on technical matters (e.g. Rasch and monitoring change over time – see Chapter 4) was the result of crises of technical confidence within the APU, consultation over the West Indian study arose from the realisation that this was a highly political issue and as such had to be handled very carefully.

Constraints
The major constraint on the APU in this area was the Consultative Committee's refusal to allow measurement of home background variables in the surveys. This meant that a study looking at factors connected with, and responsible for, underachievement was not possible. Given the Consultative Committee's unchanging position on this the APU was forced to move from a general concern with underachievement to a specific study of a single group, where it seemed that this constraint might be relaxed.

Research versus monitoring
The sub-group set up to produce a proposal for assessing West Indian children's performance took its cues from the APU's existing monitoring programme. Group members quite quickly decided that their role was to mount a survey of attainment and *not* to set up a research study, a rigid distinction maintained, it would seem, by the APU alone among those working in this area. This decision had serious consequences for their final proposals and the subsequent fate of the West Indian study.

We start this chapter with a short history of the Educational Disadvantage Unit since this was born at the same time as the APU in 1974 and the plan was that these two Units would work together in identifying educational disadvantage.

The Educational Disadvantage Unit

Setting up
In August 1974 the White Paper *Educational Disadvantage and the Educational Needs of Immigrants*[50] announced the setting up of an Educational Disadvantage Unit. This Unit was to be housed within the DES and its main purpose was to influence the allocation of resources in the interests of those suffering from educational disadvantage. The way that this was to be achieved was by developing, *in conjunction with the APU*, criteria to improve the identification of such disadvantage. It was in an annexe to this White Paper that the APU's

terms of reference and tasks were first made public.

The Press Notice issued by the DES concerning the White Paper[51] gave the terms of reference of the EDU as:

to serve as a focal point for consideration of matters, at all stages of education, connected with educational disadvantage and the education of immigrants; to influence allocation of resources in the interests of immigrants and those identified, on the best currently available criteria, as suffering from educational disadvantage; to develop in association with the Assessment of Performance Unit other relevant criteria to improve this identification; to establish suitable arrangements for promoting good practice by the educational system in its treatment of the disadvantaged and of immigrants.

One of its tasks was to establish an information centre independent of the DES, to give advice on curriculum, teaching methods, etc. and it was this centre that was to disseminate good practice relevant to the education of the disadvantaged and of immigrants.

Consultation between the EDU and the APU

Though both Units (the EDU and APU) were established within the Department in 1974, there was some delay in getting members of the EDU and APU together formally;[52] at a meeting of the APU's Co-ordinating Group in July 1976, however, two members of the EDU were present and fairly detailed discussions were minuted.[53]

The EDU representatives explained that, while the APU was concerned with the performance of pupils at all levels of ability, the EDU's particular interest was in the identification of underachievement related to social, environmental or other factors which could be termed educational disadvantage. 'A measure of overlap thus existed between the two Units.'[54] Since the APU was engaged in producing instruments for assessment perhaps it could help the EDU whose needs were for instruments:

(1) to measure pupils' general performance in order to establish educational 'norms';
(2) to make comparative assessments of performance within and between such social, ethnic and other groups as may be defined;
(3) to identify changes in achievement over a period of time both within and between these groups and to expose contributory factors.

During these discussions the point was made that the information required by the EDU pointed to using a totally different sampling design to that required for the surveying techniques proposed by the APU, suggesting that the EDU would be involved in in-depth studies rather than surveys. The head of the APU proposed that they might co-operate with the EDU by identifying and appraising tests that might be suitable for the EDU's needs, and by establishing an information flow between the APU on the one hand and the EDU and its information centre on the other. (The EDU was already receiving minutes of all the APU meetings.)

In 1976/77 there were several meetings between EDU and APU representatives and at this time the plan was for the EDU to suggest ideas and projects for studying underachievement and for the APU to provide the necessary measurement technology. However, consultation between the two Units has become less formalised over time.

Education) had received no HMI advice on whether to close the Centre, *The Centre for Information and Advice on Educational Disadvantage* In 1975 the EDU set up the Centre for Information and Advice on Educational Disadvantage (CED) in Manchester. Though financed by the DES the Centre was an independent institution and its role was to act as a clearing house for information on educational disadvantage (and thus, presumably, on underachievement). The Centre was closed in 1980 when several quangos were axed. Its closure met with considerable criticism from members of the teaching profession. According to an article in *Education* in June 1980[55] there had been no advance warning about the closure; Mr Mark Carlisle (Secretary of State for Education) had received no HMI advice on whether to close the Centre, but he was of the opinion that the combined efforts of HMI and the EDU were adequate for dealing with disadvantage. In defence of his decision, Mr Carlisle said that the Centre had not produced a publication for five years and that only three LEAs had come to the defence of the CED since its closure had been announced. However, the Centre was given a brief reprieve in order to find an alternative source of funding. By the end of that September, 12 LEAs had put up £80,000 to keep it going, although the sum needed was £300,000 per year.[56] The Centre's supporters were unable to find this sum of money and it closed at the end of October 1980; thus the EDU lost its practical arm. In January 1982 the story finally came to an end when the DES announced that the Centre's library would go to the London Institute of Education.

When at the end of 1980 and the beginning of 1981 the APU was consulting with outside bodies over their proposal to mount a study of underachievement among West Indian children, both the National Union of Teachers[57] and the National Association for Multiracial Education[58] used the axeing of the CED as an example of the Government's lack of real commitment to dealing with the problems of underachievement. They claimed that collecting information on underachievement on the one hand, while on the other closing the CED which might have done something about it, illustrated this.

Current role

At present, the EDU consists of 16 individuals (four from the Inspectorate, the rest civil servants); though they have no formal relationship with the APU, the head of the APU is 'along the corridor' in the DES and there seems to be a good relationship between the Units.

Educational disadvantage is of course an extremely wide brief and the Unit's work includes advising on educational parts of the urban programme, collating information from HMI as they notice educational disadvantage in the country, and advising Ministers. Thus the scope of the EDU has widened over the years and their role *vis-à-vis* the APU now forms only a small part of their work. The original idea envisaged in the White Paper, that the EDU would propose work and the APU do it, has not come to fruition – certainly the EDU has not used any test instruments, which is what it asked for initially. Rather they function as two separate units working alongside each other under the same Deputy Secretary, and the EDU's role is more one of suggesting policy without a research base than one of conducting research to provide a base for policy.

Of the tasks originally envisaged for the EDU, then, there is little that is visible to the outsider particularly since the closure of the CED, but it is clear that this Unit sees its major role as one of advising on and suggesting policy within the DES. This internal and 'closed' procedure has resulted in the EDU having a low profile, a situation which seems not to have been intended when it was set up in 1974. Thus, the APU, which in the 1974 White Paper figured less prominently than the EDU, has come to exceed it greatly in importance.

The Definition of Underachievement

Superficially, underachievement might seem a useful and self-explanatory concept, but in educational terms its definition is problematical. In fact, the measurement of underachievement was not seriously discussed either by WGMET or Bullock and it would seem that its appearance in the APU's terms of reference was the result of a relatively late political decision, and was not subjected to such extensive debate as was monitoring. Mr Prentice, however, in his 1974 speech to the National Association of Schoolmasters' conference announcing the EDU,[59] referred to underachievement as the big challenge of the 1970s and 1980s, and underachievement went into the APU's terms of reference bearing overtones acquired from a concern with the performance of ethnic minorities.

Members of the Co-ordinating Group felt from the start that underachievement was a difficult concept both in terms of measurement and definition. At their first meeting in 1975 they argued that terms of reference based on *disadvantage* rather than *underachievement* would probably make better sense.[60] At their next meeting they discussed setting up a working group on disadvantage, but decided that this was premature and suggested instead reinforcing existing working groups with members having a particular interest in disadvantage.[61]

The APU has always taken the view that measuring underachievement should be preceded by measuring *achievement*, so that normal performance levels can be defined. This commitment was restated by the head of the APU in June 1981.[62] Apart from the issue of definition, another problem is that underachievement cannot be identified using the APU's current method of surveying with a light sample – this point was made by the chairman of the Consultative Committee as early as 1977[63] and more forcefully by the Statistics Advisory Group (see Chapter 4). If it is true, as suggested above, that measurement of underachievement was incorporated late into the APU's aims, and in particular after the early discussions on monitoring and sample size, then this weakness seems explicable.

In 1978 the APU outlined its position in a paper entitled 'Identification of the Incidence of Underachievement' which was discussed by the October 1978 meeting of the Consultative Committee.[64] This paper explained that since the Committee had decided in June 1977 that the collection of information from teachers or parents concerning pupils' social background was unacceptable, and at the same time agreed that there was a clear need for an in-depth study of the performance of pupils in ethnic minority groups, the identification of underachievement had been extensively reviewed within the DES by the APU and EDU. The APU had concluded that underachievement could not be identified via its own surveys as these did not collect enough information. The paper presented both interpretations of underachievement, i.e. an individual achieving 'less than some measure of his potential (however measured) suggests he ought to be able to achieve', and an identifiable group, e.g. pupils of one ethnic origin, performing lower than the range achieved by other pupils in otherwise similar circumstances. The Unit's view was that the implication of the fourth task was that the Unit should identify not only those circumstances associated with various levels of educational achievement, but those circumstances associated with underachievement which 'can be changed by administrative action *(including changes in the distribution of resources)* to the advantage of those who currently underachieve. The APU is convinced of the importance of this task'. (Our italics)

The paper made the point that use of the first definition was out of the question because the national surveys were not designed to collect information on individuals and 'even if an IQ test were employed for each pupil tested (and there are many doubts about these as measures of potential) the results could only be set against a very limited assessment of performance of each pupil'. The measurement of underachievement according to the second definition, however, was possible within the scope of current surveys though this would be restricted to identifying groups with descriptors such as size of school or location. Should the APU wish to identify possible *causes*, however, additional information would have to be collected. While accepting that the collection of additional social information posed problems of acceptability, the Unit felt that some way of relating performance data to 'information of this kind seems essential if we are to be able to establish any relationships between performance and resources'. The paper went on to state the case for the importance of measuring home background variables and requested the Consultative Committee to reconsider its view on the collection of some additional social information (perhaps in the form of a pilot study). Such social variables could then be 'partialled out' in order to establish the influences of other factors more directly related to resource provision. (This mention of resources is important in understanding the fate of the West Indian study). The Unit then suggested doing related in-depth studies, presumably because they were aware of the Consultative Committee's opposition to measuring home background variables in routine monitoring, which did not waver even in the light of these detailed arguments from the Unit.

The Co-ordinating Group at their earlier meeting in May 1978 had already accepted the Statistics Advisory Group's conclusions that it would not be possible to identify the incidence of underachievement from the main monitoring programme, but that it would be feasible to identify particular groups of pupils 'within which there appeared to be low performance relative to a national norm'.[65] Thus the second definition of underachievement was endorsed by the Co-ordinating Group and the Statistics Advisory Group. At the Co-ordinating Group conference in May 1979 members of the Co-ordinating Group and representatives of other APU groups again discussed underachievement.[66] It seems generally to have been accepted that, given the method of surveying currently in use, all that could be identified would be relatively poor levels of achievement for identifiable groups of pupils. This low performance could be judged either in relation to the population as a whole or in relation to one category of performance rather than another, within a curriculum area.

While there emerged a consensus by 1979 that underachievement should really be read as 'low achievement' nevertheless the method of sampling effectively ruled out even this. Indeed in 1980 the Statistics Advisory Group formally recorded its view that to study low achievement would require a larger sample than was feasible, thus apparently ruling out any progress at all on the APU's fourth task. Some might argue that underachievement can only be measured by comparing achievement test scores with intelligence test scores; having ruled out using IQ tests the APU had ruled out any possibility of measuring underachievement and therefore the terms of reference and the tasks should have been reframed. Or, as one academic has put it: 'Is there some agreed-upon level of performance in any of the areas under test against which underachievement can be measured? If there is, I have not been able to discover it. The APU's language, I suggest, is head of the measurement art.'[67]

Although Task Four had always been difficult for the APU because they have been constrained by the Consultative Committee's refusal to let them collect home background information, it is possible that this position may alter. The science team is collecting quite detailed information about school and curriculum factors to aid interpretation of their data and the maths team is following suit. The DES itself has funded a research project to find a surrogate for social class/home background measures, and at its March 1982 meeting the Consultative Committee set up a small working group to study again the issue of collecting home background variables.

In-Depth Studies

In 1976, an explanation of the role of in-depth studies was made to the Co-ordinating Group: a member of the EDU was present at the third meeting of that year and outlined the role of the EDU *vis-à-vis* the APU. In discussing sampling frames he made the point that the APU was not limited to light sampling: this technique would be appropriate to a first stage of monitoring, while a second stage, employing different sampling methods 'might investigate particular problems in depth . . .'[68]

In January 1977, the Statistics Advisory Group considered a paper[69] written by an HMI member of the group which set out the rationale for light sampling and matrix sampling, both techniques which are used by the American National Assessment of Educational Progress (this paper is discussed in detail in the chapter on the Statistics Advisory Group). At the conclusion of the first paragraph it was remarked, 'it may well be therefore that monitoring on a national basis might need to be supplemented by in-depth studies'. The Statistics Advisory Group again endorsed the use of in-depth studies in the spring of 1978[70] when discussing underachievement. The group supported the principle of mounting in-depth studies of pupils with low achievement in order to investigate all relevant factors, including the circumstances in which pupils learn.

In 1978 the Consultative Committee discussed at length the issue of collecting home background information, in view of what were described as the 'longer-term objectives'[71] of the APU, namely Task Four.

It was maintained that only by asking for far more background information could the survey data be used to study underachievement. By
then, however, the Committee had set its face firmly against the
collection of politically sensitive background information from
teachers, parents or children. Aware of this opposition, the discussion
paper[72] suggested, as an alternative method of dealing with underachievement, the 'related in-depth study'. The Committee agreed that
there was a clear need for an in-depth study of the performance of
pupils in ethnic minority groups. What the Committee never discussed
was whether an in-depth study would work without asking those same
questions that they had already found politically unacceptable and
dangerous.

In 1979, the Co-ordinating Group reacted in much the same way to a
paper from the Statistics Advisory Group[73] which reiterated that the
way for the Unit to deal with its four tasks was through monitoring
followed by in-depth studies in which many background variables were
measured. This was accepted by the Co-ordinating Group and effectively shelved the problem for them, since the actual variables need not
be considered until the in-depth studies got under way.

At the Co-ordinating Group conference in the summer of 1979, the
head of the Unit presented a discussion paper 'The Way Ahead – Some
Questions',[74] in which it was stated: 'it has always been assumed that
APU data and findings will generate some consequential in-depth
research'; suggestions for these studies might come from steering
groups, researchers in universities and other institutions, or the Department itself. Thus the APU's commitment to in-depth studies was
once again made quite clear. Indeed, at the seminar held in June 1981 to
consider measuring changes in performance over time, the current joint
head of the Unit reiterated this commitment.[75] The Unit had always
hoped to do in-depth studies and was still keen to do so. However, there
were as yet no firm plans for in-depth studies since the initial monitoring period had to be completed first. When they started, they might be
handed over to research organisations and not necessarily overseen by
the Consultative Committee, an important proviso given its attitude to
collecting background data.

The Unit still stands by its commitment to in-depth studies but the
problem is that the time needed for the first phase of monitoring was
never discussed at the outset and the APU's decision to go for five
rounds of annual monitoring means that, for the research teams, the
second phase is taking a long time to be realised. The science team, as it
happens, has managed to incorporate some of its ideas for in-depth
studies into the regular monitoring exercises, and both maths and
language teams have firm ideas about what they would like to do, given
the opportunity (see Chapter 5).

In brief, the oft-repeated references to in-depth studies and in particular the tendency to refer difficult or contentious issues to the province of in-depth studies, suggest that they came to be used as a means of avoiding difficult decisions. This is particularly well illustrated in the discussions of the Statistics Advisory Group (see Chapter 4).

The West Indian Study

Antecedents
The West Indian study arose from the longer term objectives of the APU, i.e. the identification of circumstances in which children learn, especially those circumstances about which action might be taken. Given the early concern about underachievement, educational disadvantage and the educational needs of immigrants, a study of ethnic minority groups was an obvious one.

The language monitoring group and team had started early on to discuss the assessment of children whose first language was not English and had produced a paper containing an outline proposal in 1977.[76] The group at first discussed the idea of doing a survey over the whole country picking up just the children whose first language was not English. There was some concern that this would not produce a big enough sample, and some members of the group felt that, in any case, different test materials would be needed. Discussions went on throughout 1978 and 1979 and then, with apparently little warning, the West Indian study group was set up in 1980 and the whole matter of studying ethnic minorities and children whose first language was not English was taken out of the hands of the language group.

The maths group and team had been thinking about the problems too, since the Co-ordinating Group was told in late 1977[77] that, at a meeting held within the DES, it was decided to recommend to Ministers that a question about pupils' ethnic origin should *not* be included in the first maths survey. The origin of the suggestion remains obscure but the reasons against it were given as:
– there was no accepted definition of non-indigenous pupils
– there was no accepted way to identify subgroups within broad ethnic groups.
Instead, it was thought that the performance of non-indigenous pupils should be covered in a separate in-depth study. Interestingly, the EDU was of the opinion that the ethnic groups would be happy about such a study provided it was made quite clear why it was being done, presumably a reference to the APU's task of making findings available to those concerned with the allocation of resources.

In the second half of the paper[78] on underachievement discussed by the Consultative Committee in 1978, the Unit had put forward an alternative or complementary approach – related in-depth studies – in case the Committee did not permit the collection of background data. Though this method would be more expensive than adding variables to the national monitoring surveys it might be considered more acceptable both to the Consultative Committee and to the wider educational world. It was also more likely to produce reliable information because the national monitoring samples would include relatively few children from ethnic minority groups. The APU suggested that a start could be made with a study of the educational performance of pupils of West Indian origin, because there is evidence of low relative performance of such pupils and a widespread belief that they underachieve. Given that an inquiry (the Rampton Committee) had now been proposed into the achievement of pupils from ethnic minorities, an assessment of perfor-mance within this group in conjunction with the inquiry might be desirable.

The result of this proposal was the setting up of the Ethnic Minority Working Group (later called the West Indian Study Group). The role of this group was to consider how a study of the performance of pupils of West Indian origin 'separate from, but closely related to, the APU national surveys' in maths, language and science might be carried out, and the aim was to produce reasonably detailed recommendations for consideration by the Consultative Committee and Ministers in the autumn of 1980.[79] The administrative head of the APU was to be the chairman and the group was to include West Indian junior and secondary teachers, the head of a school in a largely West Indian area, a member of the Commission for Racial Equality, a member of the EDU, an LEA adviser, a member of HMI with special responsibility for multi-racial education, a DES statistician, the professional head of the APU and a representative from the NFER. The group met for the first time in January 1980 and was asked to present proposals, in sufficient detail for them to be costed, by late summer 1980.

Changing proposals

The first discussion document on the proposed survey of West Indian pupils was put to the Consultative Committee in 1978.[80] This suggested that a sample size of 2,500 be considered, taken from areas of high immigrant concentration (though it was recognised that to limit the sampling to inner-city areas would be to lay the survey open to criticism in that it would only be assessing ethnic minority pupils from the poorest environmental, social and cultural backgrounds). The docu-ment argued that if the survey were to take a cross-section of *all* pupils from those schools with a high proportion of West Indian pupils then comparison would be possible of the performance of West Indian and indigenous pupils from similar environmental conditions. The APU recognised that, if the findings of a West Indian study were to shed light on the causes of underachievement, the data collected on home and school variables would have to go well beyond those being used in the main surveys. They thought that it would be necessary to obtain information on socio-economic factors, parental education, length of time in the UK, patterns of bilingualism and possibly the incidence of one-parent families and the extent of movement between schools.

Tentative proposals from the West Indian Study Group were communicated to the local authority and teacher associations in May 1980.[81] These suggested a survey of 5,000 West Indian pupils mounted in parallel to the main national APU surveys in maths, language and science, and using the same material as the main surveys so that the results would be directly comparable with them. Schools would be chosen from within the 17 LEAs with the highest proportion of West Indian children, according to their size, type and proportion of West Indian pupils. Each school would be asked to administer tests to all the children in the appropriate age group, as suggested in the first (1978) paper, and for the same reasons, i.e. acceptability and comparability. Teachers would be asked to identify those children of West Indian (i.e. Afro-Caribbean) origin and they would be given detailed instructions on how to do this.* Because of the relatively small size of the sample children would take tests in all three curriculum areas, although unfortunately this would take far more of their time than would be the case in a regular APU survey.

By the next month, when the APU met with the associations to discuss the proposed study, two major changes had been made as a result of advice from the Statistics Advisory Group.[82] First, in order not to get a biased sample, children were to be sampled from schools with less than 10 per cent of West Indian pupils and also from outside the 17 LEAs originally proposed. Secondly, pupils would, instead of doing three separate tests, be given a booklet of 50 questions covering maths, language and science. All children would be given the same booklet, and the exercise would therefore not be directly comparable with the other surveys.

The final proposal for the study, described in the Report of the West Indian Study Group,[83] was more in line with normal APU surveying practice than were earlier proposals. The group suggested a sample of 4–5,000 stratified by school size, type and proportion of West Indian pupils (e.g. less than 20 per cent, 20–50 per cent, more than 50 per cent), chosen from the 17 LEAs with a high proportion of West Indian pupils *and* those LEAs with fewer West Indian pupils; they rejected the

---

* This was justified by reference to the proposal to include questions on ethnic origin in the 1981 census, somewhat ironically in view of the later decision to drop these from the census.

idea of a single test booklet made up of 50 items from the three curriculum areas and suggested instead using test material as it was developed for national surveys, so that results would be directly comparable. 'Anything less than comparisons of performance based on comparable data collected in essentially the same way as in the APU national surveys would, we believe be open to grave suspicion, and we do not therefore believe it would be advisable to attempt to produce "special" test packages of any sort, however well-intentioned'.[84]

As for the problem of comparison with other pupils from the same schools, the group proposed testing the whole of an age group in schools where the proportion of West Indian pupils was over 30 per cent, and in schools with less than this to test all the West Indian children plus twice as many non-West Indian children: this would mean an overall sample size of 12–15,000 pupils per age group. They also proposed that a small subsample of children be tested in practical maths and science. As for 'reporting variables', i.e. those home and school variables mentioned in the first discussion document for the Consultative Committee in 1978, the group concluded that it would be 'undesirable to seek to collect information in respect of pupils taking part in a West Indian survey which is not collected by the APU in the course of its national surveys'.[85]

The proposed West Indian study thus became a monitoring exercise, in miniature, of the regular APU type. Any idea that it might have been the first of the promised in-depth studies was scotched by the desire of the West Indian Study Group that it be as similar to the national APU surveys as possible. If there was any doubt about whether it was an in-depth study the group confirmed that it was not, by saying that they recognised that it might be desirable for a more detailed in-depth study to be undertaken in this area, subsequently, either by the APU or others.

Thus the first of the promised in-depth studies failed to appear.

Reactions

The West Indian Study Group's tentative proposals were the subject of far wider consultation than other APU proposals for, understandably, they did not wish to test in a highly sensitive area without the acceptance of those involved. At a meeting with the teacher and local authority associations in June 1980 the nub of the problem had been recognised:[86] if the necessary co-operation was to be forthcoming, some sort of indication had to be given that if the performance of West Indian pupils was found to be in any way unsatisfactory, an attempt would be made to take remedial action. Also, it would be important for the research to identify causal factors. In the event, the APU and DES failed to commit themselves to either of these courses of action.

The Rampton Committee had picked up this second point too: it said that a survey without background data was worthless. Members of the West Indian Study Group, in response to this, stated that it was *not a research study*, merely an attempt to get nationwide data:[87] 'It was more than likely that the results of an APU West Indian survey would point towards the need for subsequent in-depth research, but it was neither possible nor desirable to convert the proposed survey into a detailed research study'. The confusion over whether the APU was a monitoring or research exercise is clearly stated here, and this refusal of the study group to propose a research study was an important factor leading to the failure of its proposals.

The final report of the study group was put to the Consultative Committee on 16 July 1980. The conclusion of the report was that the co-operation needed from LEAs, teachers, parents and pupils would be forthcoming if there was widespread and open consultation and provided that 'the West Indian population can be given reason to believe that, if significant deficiencies in performance are identified, a serious attempt will be made to do something about it'.[88] There was, as the minutes put it, 'wide-ranging discussion'[89] and the result was that the Consultative Committee decided that if widespread consultation was in favour of the proposed survey, it should be carried out, *with the proviso* that resources could be made available by central government if they were shown to be needed. Here is the key to the ultimate failure of the West Indian survey: from the start, based on early statements about the role of the EDU and APU, the impression was created that extra resources would be forthcoming if they were shown to be needed as a result of the West Indian survey. However, when faced with firm proposals, the DES assessor declined to commit the DES to provision of extra resources saying that the 'APU was unable to give a prior commitment to any particular course of action related to the findings of its surveys'. Its job was only to make information available to those concerned with resource allocation. Members of the Consultative Committee, nevertheless, went on record as saying that resources were fundamental to the whole exercise. The NUT reserved its position until its National Executive Council meeting, but given the DES's discouraging position on provision of resources it can hardly have felt encouraged to ask its members to participate.

In view of the consultation needed before the study went ahead, the extract from the West Indian Study Group report was widely circulated in December 1980 to teacher unions, LEA associations, the Commission for Racial Equality and representatives of the West Indian community, seeking views of the group's proposals.[90] Comments were invited by February 1981, since it was hoped to start monitoring in November 1981. A DES Press Notice put out in December 1980, at the time of consultation, said that the aim of the West Indian study was to ascertain the true position of the educational performance of West Indian pupils. There was an assurance of complete anonymity and that results would go to the Rampton Committee for its use.[91]

At the beginning of the next month (January 1981), both the *TES*[92] and *Education*[93] carried articles based on the DES Press Notice. *Education* reported that if consultation was in favour of the study, the APU would give the go-ahead. The *TES* went further and said that teachers were in the difficult position of having to decide whether to identify and help to test the West Indian children – thereby facing possible hostility and criticism from parents and pupils – or whether to refuse to co-operate in which case they could lose the extra resources that might be made available for the disadvantaged. There was in fact no mention in the DES Press Notice of resources being made available (hardly surprising in view of the comment of the DES assessor), merely the sentence:

Although such a survey would not in itself indicate ways in which improvements might be brought about – if pupils of West Indian origin were in fact shown to be relatively low achievers – it would undoubtedly provide a much firmer basis of fact for possible future action than anything currently available.

The *TES* reported the Consultative Committee, 'the Unit's public watchdog', as being extremely cautious over the plans and recommending neither acceptance nor rejection; similarly the teacher union and LEA association representatives were not sure 'which way to jump'. The NUT, naturally, was concerned over the teachers' role in the survey and at the same time recognised that the APU itself had no means to rectify disadvantage.

By the middle of the month both journals were reporting opposition to the plans. *Education*[94] reported opposition from community leaders on the grounds that they thought they knew what the problem was and therefore didn't need expensive research to tell them, and that the lack of prior commitment from the Government to act on the results of any survey would only create cynicism. The *TES* article[95] and editorial reported that even the Rampton Committee was not certain about the value of the proposed survey since Rampton was interested in underachievement in West Indian children and since the APU had long ago given up the attempt to identify this, because it could not measure the potential or background of the children it tested, the Rampton Committee was considering doing its own research. The editorial went so far as to accuse the DES of holding out promises on which its Unit could not deliver. In the same article, the general secretary of the National Association of Head Teachers was reported as questioning the desirability of yet another survey: given that the Rampton Committee was already looking into the question, he wondered whether it was wise to keep isolating West Indian pupils for attention. The NUT questioned the sincerity of collecting such information on the one hand while axeing the CED on the other, since it was the Centre that might have done something about any shortcomings thus identified.

By early March 1981, the time by which the APU had requested comments, *Education*[96] reported that most organisations asked by the DES to report on the proposal had rejected it. The NUT in particular had recommended to its members that they should not participate, and this would make it almost impossible to run the survey. The NUT was not opposed to the study in principle, but on grounds of methodology: because it was proposed to sample children from only those schools with more than 10 per cent West Indian pupils, the sample would be biased. The NUT felt that the only value of the survey would be if the government was prepared to guarantee extra resources for the children seen to be doing badly.

The Secondary Heads' Association expressed strong reservations about the survey[97] on the grounds of problems of definition of 'West Indian origin' and concern over the use of the data by extreme political groups; the survey should only go ahead if the West Indian community was in favour. The National Association for Multiracial Education[98] urged the DES to drop the proposed surveys on the grounds that West Indians fail for a complex of reasons and the survey would only attempt to measure the extent to which children fail and not look at what causes them to fail.

The final decision
Before making a final decision on whether to go ahead with the West Indian study, the DES waited for the interim report of the Rampton Committee, as well as feedback from the consultation process. Mr Anthony Rampton's interim report was sent to Mr Mark Carlisle, Secretary of State for Education, at the end of February 1981. At the same time the NUT announced that it would tell its members not to co-operate in the survey and at this point it seemed inevitable that the Department would decide against it.

The decision was finally made public on May 1st 1981* when in a written reply Mr Carlisle said:

I have decided that the Unit should not carry out the proposed survey. In reaching this decision I have taken into account views expressed by the local authority association, teachers' organisations and representatives of the West Indian community about the form of survey proposed.

* This was the week when Rampton 'resigned' – though it was widely accepted that he was told to resign by Mr Carlisle after criticism of weak leadership from some members of the Committee.[99]

Reporting this parliamentary reply, the APU circular[100] to the Statistics
Advisory Group and the subject steering groups also stated:

The Department is to consider alternative ways forward in this important area,
and the comments received in the course of the Unit's consultations will assist
this process. However, any further action will almost certainly be outside the
sphere of the APU's work.

Conclusions

The APU has made little progress in its fourth task. Instead, what it has
discovered is the kind of study which is *not* acceptable to the Consultative Committee, teacher unions and outside bodies. While the ramifications of the decision by the Consultative Committee not to allow
collections of home background data has spread into almost every area
of the APU's work, it is particularly evident in the APU's attempt to
make progress in its aim of identifying underachievement

What lay behind the failure of the proposed West Indian Study? The
answer seems to lie partly in bad planning: if one wanted to arouse
opposition to attempts to study underachievement one could hardly do
better than to identify a particular minority ethnic group, and make
it clear that first, only partial information would be collected and
secondly that no remedial action would be likely. Also, it was technically weak in the identification of West Indians and in the sampling.

It was the consultation process, both inside and outside the APU
committees, that finally determined the fate of the West Indian study,
but the outcome of the consultative process was inevitable given the
constraints operating on the APU. First, there was the DES which
refused to commit itself to the provision of extra resources should
the study show that West Indian children *were* underachieving.
Secondly there was the Consultative Committee which refused to allow
collection of home background information, leading the study group to
produce proposals which followed the APU's main monitoring plans.
Then the APU was hoist by its own petard when the West Indian Study
Group announced that the APU's task was to monitor rather than to do
research and so planned a survey, not an in-depth research study. A
survey of the APU type was not acceptable to those consulted by the
APU since, at best, the results of such a survey could only show *whether*
children of West Indian origin were performing at a lower level than
indigenous children and not *why* this was happening (if indeed it was).

How else could the APU have approached the study? With more
careful forward planning the situation might have been averted. The
APU could have suggested a study of several ethnic groups, rather than
isolating West Indians for study. It could also have modified the
timing, mounting a study either before the Rampton Committee

interim report or preferably afterwards when it could have based its proposals on any recommendation made in the report. Whenever it had been started, however, lengthy consultations presumably would have been necessary, and it is difficult to see that the outcome would have been very different. Instead, the Unit could have made it clear to the West Indian Study Group that what was required was an in-depth study offering some explanatory information. Given the constraints operating upon the APU it would probably have been more fruitful to have put the study out to a research agency, which could do an in-depth study using the necessary social background information. If they had really wanted to get in-depth studies off the ground, they would have been better advised to have started with a less contentious issue, established a research style, and then turned their attention to several ethnic minority groups. However, this kind of research perspective has not been visible so far within the APU.

Postscript

In 1981 the House of Commons Select Committee's response to the Rampton Committee Interim report commented on the APU's proposed survey. In regretting that the APU had not mounted a national survey it said:

This omission is the more regrettable because the Unit's terms of reference include the task of seeking 'to identify the incidence of underachievement', and the Unit itself was set up largely in response to the 1974 Government White Paper on 'Educational Disadvantage and the Educational Needs of Immigrants.' . . . Despite the problems outlined in the Study Group's report and in evidence to the Sub-Committee, we are convinced that an authoritative survey of this sort would produce useful results which could be acted on. It is therefore most regrettable that the Department should have been deflected from their proposed course of action by opposition from teacher's unions, local authority associations and some West Indian organisations. A greater determination on the part of the Department might have paid off. There are alternatives to such a survey . . . but . . . there is no viable alternative to a national survey . . . *We recommend that the Study Group be reconvened in order to find some means of producing national figures on the performance of West Indian children.*[101]

3 The Work of the Consultative Committee and the Co-ordinating Group

The main themes and issues covered in this chapter are:

Constraints We shall show how the Consultative Committee's decisions have had a constraining influence on the APU.

Accountability The Consultative Commitee has acted quite effectively as an accountability body for the APU; the Co-ordinating Group on the other hand had no such role.

Reporting We trace the origin of the Unit's non-interpretation policy, its effects and its eventual weakening.

Areas of measurement The Consultative Committee spent much time discussing the proposed assessment of personal–social development and of West Indian children. Eventually it recommended against assessing in both areas and these recommendations were accepted.

Home Background Variables This is the area where the Co-ordinating Group could have made a major contribution, preferably early on in the life of the Unit, but did not do so. The Consultative Committee's insistence on not measuring home background variables has caused considerable problems for the APU.

The Consultative Committee

Introduction
The description in Chapter 2 of difficulties over the proposed West Indian study showed that the Consultative Committee's decisions have had a constraining influence on the APU. The committee refused to allow the assessment of personal–social development and the measurement of home background variables, and refused to support the proposed West Indian study. The former decision contributed to the

disintegration of the cross-curriculum model and the latter decisions have impeded the Unit's attempts to deal with Task Four. The trade-off for the Unit, however, has been the co-operation of the LEA associations and teacher unions whose members are represented on the committee, which quickly became the Unit's main consulting body. As an attempt to be accountable to the educational and outside world the committee has succeeded: the APU has received support from teacher, LEA and other groups in exchange for a willingness to incorporate their views in its programme.

Because of the committee's firm line on reporting – that is the presentation of bare facts with little interpretation of findings – the published reports have tended to be somewhat uninteresting to read. Dissemination of reports has been poor and this recently has been of major concern to the Unit.

Origins, membership and role

Origins As the historical account of the APU (Chapter 1) showed, the Consultative Committee did not meet for the first time until mid-1976. This was six months after the Co-ordinating Group and the language working group had their first meetings, seven months after the science group first met and ten months after Kay published his seminal cross-curriculum article.[102] The committee was aware of the tardiness of its appointment, resulting from protracted negotiations over membership and the search for a suitable chairman, and in the first meeting complained that 'so much work' had been put in train before it was established.[103] At the next meeting there was a similar complaint to the effect that not enough material and information was being put to the committee to enable it to do its job properly.[104] Already the committee was flexing its muscles and giving an indication that it meant to be a force to be reckoned with.

Membership The committee began with 33 members: three academics – one of whom was the chairman – five heads and teachers, six LEA education officers at various levels, nine representatives of teacher unions and local authority associations, a representative from the National Confederation of Parent Teacher Associations, a CBI representative, one from the TUC, the editor of the *TES*, an education committee chairman, a parent, the principal of a teacher training college, the chairman of an employment agency, an educational researcher and the director of the NFER. By 1981 there were 31 members with the group's make-up remaining much the same.*

* For membership lists see Appendix 6, available separately from the Institute of Education

This comprehensive range of individuals brought with them very different ideas about the APU and the role of the committee. We interviewed nine members of the committee, past and present, and the four heads of the Unit who at one time or another had dealings with the committee. The picture we have pieced together is one of early stormy meetings controlled by a well-respected chairman who was a major influence on the committee's growth and the development of its influence. Of course, not every meeting was stormy but there were several tension points springing from the composition of the committee. There were many representatives from the teacher unions who generally wanted to restrict the amount of assessment, and there were the subject teachers who lobbied to have their own subject assessed in order to give it a high profile. There were several representatives from the NUT who formed the only definite 'faction' on the committee. The other teacher unions tended to agree with the NUT on most issues while the Chief Education Officers (CEOs) tended, if not to agree at least not to disagree with them. Thus the NUT was a powerful influence on the committee because of its number of representatives, their co-ordinated policy approach and the other two, much smaller groups, the CEOs and other teacher unions, which tended to align with them. Given the NUT's potential ability to impede the monitoring programme, should they so wish, the APU and the DES would be well aware of the need to listen to the views of the Consultative Committee as a whole. We shall see how crucial the NUT role was in preventing both the measurement of background variables and the assessment of personal and social development.

Role The minutes are not clear on the role of the committee but if it was originally intended that the Co-ordinating Group should be the top group with the Consultative Committee set to one side, it did not work out this way. Once the Consultative Committee was recruited it was clear that its members were not going to tolerate second-class status. All the members of the Consultative Committee were busy people who were not prepared to come to London and spend the whole day talking without having any influence. They refused to accept a purely talking role, so they started having votes and tabling motions. As a result they tended to acquire a power of veto if not direct executive power. Some members wanted a commitment from the APU that nothing would be done without permission from the committee. There was in fact no need to demand *de jure* censorship since they had *de facto* censorship: if enough members of the Consultative Committee were against something, the APU would never push for it. Thus the APU has not acted on any issue that the committee has voted against, and this has had important, even dramatic, consequences for the APU's ability to fulfil its brief. To this degree the committee has not been simply consultative for then the APU might well have been expected to reject its advice on some matters at least.

Having developed into a strong committee, members were not happy when the APU got on and did things without consulting them. At the last meeting of 1977 members complained about the lack of information reaching them from the working groups. Lord Alexander, a local authority association representative, went so far as to resign because he was unhappy with the way things were progressing, particularly in the areas of personal, social, physical and aesthetic development. His fear was that APU monitoring would lead to centralised control of the curriculum. Other members were worried too and complained that exploratory groups had been set up *in spite* of the committee.[105] The concern of the APU/DES over these rumblings in the Consultative Committee can be measured by the fact that at the next meeting Shirley Williams, then Secretary of State for Education, was present. Her role there was to impress on the committee the importance of the APU's task and to prevent the more powerful members from sabotaging the project. She seems to have succeeded, for after this date no serious concern was voiced about the overall direction of the APU's work. Nevertheless, the Consultative Committee had demonstrated its strength sufficiently to ensure that development plans were brought to it at an early stage.

Why did the APU consider that it was necessary to have a Consultative Committee? It seems to have been the experience of the American evaluation programme which was responsible for the decision to have such a committee. NAEP had run into some serious problems because it had no teachers participating on the planning committee. Not surprisingly, this caused considerable trouble with the teachers and NAEP had to widen its planning committee to include teachers and lay people too. The APU, therefore, decided to have a wide consultation process from the outset. While it was not obliged to have a consultative group, had it gone ahead and done everything as it had wanted to, it probably would have turned out that teachers and LEAs would not have co-operated with it. Thus it would eventually have been forced to have a consultative body. In the growing atmosphere of accountability a committee of outsiders was an obvious way for the Unit to be accountable for its programme of work.

How the Consultative Committee reacted to the major issues

The areas that were to be assessed   At the outset, in 1976, the committee expressed reservations about monitoring personal–social, physical and aesthetic development. Members were concerned that APU activity in these areas could interfere with the curriculum. On the other hand it was argued that 'the APU should not be thought to be concentrating exclusively on basic attainments to the exclusion of other important aspects of the education process.'[106] While the Co-ordinating Group was strongly in favour of assessing aesthetic and physical development, the Consultative Committee was divided.[107] In 1977 reservations were again expressed but the point was made by the APU that it ought not to abandon the attempt to do what was difficult and concentrate only on what was easy.[108] It was at the end of this year that Lord Alexander resigned over proposed monitoring in these areas, particularly personal–social development. By this stage it was also clear that the NUT, at least, was implacably opposed and in fact tried to stop all three exploratory groups in early 1978, a move which was not supported by the rest of the committee.[109]

Personal–social development From the end of 1978 there were many discussions of the assessment of personal and social development. The exploratory group asked for an extension to undertake a thorough review of research in the field. At this stage the DES assessor made the point that the APU was not limited to surveys using paper and pencil tests. The Unit was required to 'promote the development of methods of assessing and monitoring achievement' and there were a variety of ways in which this could be done.[110] This was said in relation to personal and social development indicating that testing was perhaps not the best way to approach monitoring in this area, although it could also be taken as a general comment on the direction taken by the APU.

By mid-1980 the exploratory group had produced a draft report and two members of the group presented it to the committee. As the minutes have it, 'discussion ranged widely'[111] and the two group members 'who had joined freely in the discussion' left before any decisions were reached. The Schools Council representative was outspoken in his criticism of the document, as was the NUT spokesman. The only person who was strongly in favour of supporting the proposals was the representative from the CBI.

The APU had asked the exploratory group to stress some points in the report and omit others in order to make the report more acceptable to the Consultative Committee. Some members of the group were very strongly against doing this; they did not want to play a political game. In the end they compromised and, under pressure to adapt their paper, ended up with what some thought was a rather weak document. Some members of the committee did indeed think the draft report was naïve and that it did not pay enough attention to how the measurements were to be made, and this cannot have helped the group's cause.

That the APU was keen to assess personal–social development is borne out by the fact that in 1979 it sponsored a visit to the USA by a member of the exploratory group and an HMI attached to the Unit. This represented quite a financial commitment at a time when the teacher union opposition was already apparent. The APU gave several reasons for its failure to get monitoring in this area agreed. The teacher unions, especially the NUT, had been opposed to it from the start taking the view that, unlike maths and language, personal–social development is not taught in schools and is not therefore an area for monitoring. There was an emotional swell against assessing it, symbolised by the resignation of Lord Alexander, but it was eventually floored in the committee by arguments which pointed to the sheer difficulty of assessing it, with statements such as 'beauty is in the eye of the beholder'.

There is also the possibility that the APU was maladroit in its handling of these discussions; though the Unit was keen to assess personal–social development, it failed to get it through because it was handled badly. Every time the committee met, it discussed the personal–social issue: as one member said, 'it was like picking at a scab every time' and they were never allowed to forget it, hence its sensitive nature was constantly emphasised.

Was the failure to get personal–social development monitored the result of bad management on behalf of the APU, or the result of forces in the committee beyond its control? It seems to have been a mixture of the two. Whatever the interpretation of events, at the second meeting of the committee in 1980 it was reported that the Secretary of State had decided that monitoring in personal–social development should not go ahead, nor would the document produced by the group be published.[112] The influence of the Consultative Committee on this decision was clearly crucial, and so the committee was instrumental in the demise of the APU's cross-curriculum model, since the assessment of personal–social development was crucial to this model. The exploratory group rewrote as a final report the document they first presented to the committee in 1980 and this was discussed by the committee in July 1981. The committee felt it would make a valuable in-service document and it went to the Secretary of State who approved publication, which took place in January 1982.

Other areas There was far less contention about the possibilities of monitoring in modern languages and technological development. Groups were set up to consider these in 1977 and 1979 respectively with no minuted criticism from the Consultative Committee. Of course, these are conceptually quite different areas from personal–social or physical development; they are regular school subjects, perhaps not widespread as far as design and technology are concerned but certainly definable – and therefore testable – curriculum areas. For this reason they were bound to attract less contention. Discussions about modern language concentrated on which languages to assess and at what age, and development work began in 1981. Discussions about technology were mainly concerned with whether the 'activities and competencies identified in the report in fact find a place in the school curriculum at the present time'.[113] As a result of this latter concern, the DES decided to commission a survey to identify how, when and where the competencies in design and technology identified by the group appeared in the average school curriculum. On the basis of this and the Consultative Committee's recommendation, a decision will be made on whether to go ahead with monitoring. No decision has yet been made on whether to monitor aesthetic development but it is likely that this decision will be affected by cost, regardless of whether the Consultative Committee recommends monitoring or not. It appears that monitoring of physical development will not now go ahead.[114]

Background variables In early 1977 the committee discussed the specific variables that should be built into the sampling design. These included school size, type, location, regional grouping, pupil/teacher ratio and class size. As for socio–economic background of the pupil, the variable that was to cause so much trouble, the committee agreed that it was important. The suggestion was made that some group measure might be based on the characteristics of the area or of the school.[115] The next time the committee met it made a strong recommendation that parents should not be asked to complete any kind of questionnaire; since information on socio–economic group was difficult to obtain without asking parents, this variable would have to be given further thought. The committee was told that the American monitoring programme, NAEP, had got round this problem by using parental education as a proxy measure, but the committee was not keen to follow suit. It suggested instead that some measure of local unemployment rate and deprivation be investigated.[116]

Detailed discussion of background variables did not take place again until the end of the next year (1978) when the science team brought the issue to the fore.[117] The committee and the team discussed school-related variables, home background variables and a cognitive ability indicator. The committee was happy about the first and authorised the mounting of a pilot study of school-related variables. As for home background, members were still adamant that the information should not be obtained via teachers, parents or children and suggested that the APU consider alternative ways of obtaining similar information. The cognitive ability indicator did not get very far either, since the committee was told that the Statistics Advisory Group had advised against it (see Chapter 4). At this same meeting the committee discussed a paper put up by the APU concerning attainment of the longer-term objectives of the Unit,[118] that is, identifying underachievement and looking at performance in relation to the circumstances in which children learn (Task Four). The paper stated quite baldly that this task could not be carried out by the existing surveys because they did not provide enough information. Aware of the committee's opposition to the collection of home background data, the paper suggested 'in-depth' studies. The committee agreed that there was a clear need for an in-depth study of the performance of pupils in ethnic minority gropus, and the Ethnic Minority Working Group, later superseded by the West Indian Study Group, was set up. By endorsing the notion of in-depth studies the committee no doubt felt that it had managed to avoid the home background variables issue, but as Chapter 2 showed there was no hope of an in-depth study which did not ask those same questions which had frightened the committee.

The APU was clearly aware that the Consultative Committee was forcing it to jettison a major part of its brief, for at the end of 1979 a member of the DES argued in the committee for the collection of background data.[119] The science team had come back with another request to collect data on home background, or home support, variables. The DES observer pointed out to the committee that there was a clear need in monitoring science to attempt to relate performance to the provision of facilities for teaching science in school. He went on to argue that relationships between performance and school-based variables could not be isolated unless some account could also be taken of *home-based* variables. Indeed, he thought it questionable whether there would be any point at all in attempting to collect school-based data without home-based data. It was agreed at this meeting that the Unit would prepare a detailed research specification for consideration at a future meeting. The outcome of this was that the Department funded a two-year research project at Leeds University on 'the feasibility of making social classification of schools from variables not involving a direct approach to individual pupils, teachers or parents'.[120] In other words it was an attempt to find a surrogate for home background measures but at the school, not pupil, level. So the issue was shelved again. This project is due to end in 1983, and the APU seems to be no nearer to making progress on an issue which is crucial in the fulfilment of its fourth task.

Reporting and interpretation   The Consultative Committee supported the APU line, enunciated first by the chairman of the Co-ordinating Group, that reports should present a statement of facts without interpretation of findings. As the first in the field the maths team suffered most from this dictate and their first report was heavily edited by the committee. The language team were less concerned about strictures against interpreting their findings, particularly with regard to background variables which they considered less relevant to language performance. The science team, however, fought for the inclusion of relational variables, that is school information, with the help of which it would be possible to interpret the findings. By the time the science team came to the reporting stage the Consultative Committee had relaxed the ruling and the Chelsea team were able to tell a story around their findings (see Chapters 4 and 5 for further discussion).

In the area of reporting the APU, via the Consultative Committee, was a definite constraint on the monitoring teams who would have preferred to have written reports with more 'life' to them. One result of this policy on reporting has been that reports have been little read, and the APU is very concerned about this. Dissemination has become a regular topic of discussion at Consultative Committee meetings. In mid-1981 the professional head of the Unit said that he thought 40 per cent of teachers read the summaries sent out by the APU, but that few read the actual reports. It transpired that both the APU and the HMI were considering dissemination by means other than reports. 'While the committee and the Unit were concerned to minimise the backwash effect on the curriculum of APU monitoring, the published reports contained much evidence about the processes of teaching and learning. It would be of great value to get this information to teachers'.[121] The Unit has now started to issue a regular newsletter to be distributed to schools.

Given the nature of the reports – their length, expense and the heavy even heads, read them. There is by no means widespread satisfaction in the committee over the reports. It was felt at an early stage that two reports should be produced for each survey: one very detailed and technical, which would be available to researchers and academics, and one which was easy to read and would be made available to the general public; but this second type of report has never materialised.

On the other hand the fact that the reports are low-key has probably contributed to the APU's survival. As for the policy of non-interpretation of findings, one of the reasons why the reports make dull reading, this seems to have been advocated by the HMI and particularly those on the Co-ordinating Group. Needless to say, the doctrine of 'facts only' was unpopular with researchers. However, the APU is wavering on this issue under pressure from the researchers and in the light of reports of the NAEP evaluation council,[122] one of the major findings of which is that, in order to be useful, data must be fully interpreted and contain value judgements. The Unit takes the view that, now that monitoring has been going on for some time, interpretation is safer and for the science reports more relevant particularly because of the amount of school and curriculum information that has been collected.

Conclusions

To what extent did the Consultative Committee act as a constraint on the APU? The APU was in accord with the majority of the Consultative Committee over the issue of non-interpretation of reports, but there were other important areas in which the committee blocked the APU's progress: the measurement of home background variables, the assessment of personal–social development and the assessment of West Indian children.

As far as home background variables were concerned, the teacher unions were keen to look at the effect of resource input but would not accept the APU's point that one must first measure social class in order to discount its effect. It is probably fair to say that the APU wished to measure home background variables all along, since the DES observer argued for the collection of this information in 1979 and the Unit started to renegotiate on this in 1982.[123] Members of the committee seemed aware that by refusing to allow collection of background data it had destroyed the Unit's hopes of fulfilling Task Four. It stuck to this line, however, because the teacher unions in particular were concerned about the integrity of the teacher's relationship with the child: the collection of home background information would constitute prying and would put this relationship in jeopardy as well as imposing an extra burden on teachers. These objections might have been overcome at an early stage by agreeing to minimal involvement of teachers, using home interviewers to collect the information and safeguarding confidentiality. This is, after all, a common practice in many educational studies and does not arouse particular opposition from teachers or their representatives. Such a procedure would have been costly however, and this may have been the principal reason why it was not put forward. With the measurement of personal–social development and assessment of the performance of West Indian children (see Chapter 2), the APU did wish to assess in these areas but was persuaded to drop them largely because of their politically sensitive nature. Perhaps the Unit was fortunate that, in the end, it was constrained by its Consultative Committee in only three areas.

How effective was the Consultative Committee as the APU's attempt to be accountable? It is clear that the Consultative Committee was the APU's attempt to have a public body through which they could be seen to be accountable. The decision to set up this body was influenced by the American experience where NAEP had not had a consultative body and had been forced to set one up. Once suitably prestigious and relevant individuals had been invited to join the committee and had begun to understand the nature of the APU programme, they took their task seriously and refused to accept a secondary role. They exerted their 'muscle' and they eventually rendered the Co-ordinating Group superfluous. The result was the dissolution of the Co-ordinating Group and the co-option of some of its members onto the Consultative Committee (see next section).

So the Consultative Committee has acted as an accountability panel. All major issues and decisions have been before it, and the Unit has listened to its advice and recommendations. The result has been a change in the direction of the Unit's programme, which it might not have sought, but in return it has had the tacit co-operation of the teacher unions and the LEA associations.

The Co-ordinating Group

Introduction
As its name implies, the Co-ordinating Group was set up to co-ordinate the work of the groups, teams and committees. It met for the first time in October 1975, before the Consultative Committee. By 1977/78 it was clear that the group was less powerful than the Consultative Committee and even the Statistics Advisory Group. In 1978 and 1979 dissatisfied members discussed their role without coming to any major conclusions and the group was finally disbanded by the Unit in early 1980. In what follows we shall discuss the contribution that the group made to the work of the APU and the reasons why it was eclipsed by the other two committees.

Membership and role

Membership In the beginning the group consisted of 15 people, with representatives of the educational establishment outnumbering the others. Six were HMIs of whom one was the head of the APU, one was the chairman of the group and one was from the Welsh Education Office; there were also two representatives from the DES. To balance these, there were three head teachers, one LEA representative, one college lecturer (who later became a head), one academic and the deputy director of the NFER. The lack of academic representation in contrast to the number of HMIs is noteworthy. The research teams had no direct representation, and their own attempts at co-ordination took place outside the official APU committee system.

By 1977 one HMI, the chairman, and one DES representative had left. They were replaced by two HMIs, one of whom was from the Scottish Education Office. Thus the balance remained unchanged but with the HMI contingent increased by one. In 1979 two more academics were brought into the group, and the chair passed from an HMI (Brian Kay) to Jean Dawson, administrative head of the APU. At the Co-ordinating Group conference in May 1979 there were 16 members present: six HMIs (including the Scottish and Welsh representatives), the original DES representative, a Northern Ireland representative, three head teachers, three academics, the LEA representative and the deputy director of the NFER. So by the end of the group's life the HMI and DES representatives were actually outnumbered by other members, although this change came too late to affect the course of the group's work.

It is interesting to compare the membership of this group with the membership of the Consultative Committee. That had fewer HMIs and included representatives from LEA associations, teachers' unions and non-educationists, none of whom were included in the Co-ordinating Group. The Co-ordinating Group had a powerful HMI input but it was not until 1979 that the group was chaired by an APU head, although the current head was always a member. The first chairman was an HMI and the second, also an HMI, took over only when he had relinquished leadership of the Unit.

Role The Co-ordinating Group had two basic tasks: to keep the working and steering groups on the path of the cross-curriculum model, and to look ahead and anticipate opportunities for cross-curriculum integration. The group's other role was to act as a sounding board for the Unit's ideas, and it was expected that the group would be able to offer the sort of technical and professional opinion which was not so readily available in a more 'representative' group – such as the Consultative Committee was to be.

The official view of the group's role was put to members by the APU at their second meeting. They should decide, on the various working groups' recommendations, what aspects of performance to test, the ages when assessment should take place and the sampling arrangements.[124] This was the only early reference to the Co-ordinating Group's function. As the members realised in 1979, the group would have benefited from clearer guidance on its role; we shall see that the role of the group became a more pressing concern for members as time went on and the Unit's work became more established.

In mid-1976 it was decided that in future they would meet three times a year; this was in response to some disquiet from members about how they were to fulfil their role of co-ordination in the space of two meetings a year which seem to have lasted half a day only. (In fact, there were four meetings in 1976, 1977 and 1979). It may have been at this point that some of the more dissatisfied members began to think that, in addition to having more work than could possibly be done in two meetings per year, they were being called in too late to affect the course of events.

In 1978, discussing a paper about a seminar which had been held to consider the possibility of monitoring technological development, the serious concern of group members became apparent for the first time. They felt that they should have been informed about this seminar earlier and been given the opportunity to participate. After a lengthy discussion they were assured that:

- no exploratory group would be set up as a result of the seminar without prior consultation with the group;
- the group would be consulted whenever major decisions about priorities had to be taken;
- members of the group might welcome the opportunity in future to offer advice at an early stage about membership of seminars, groups, etc.[125]

In 1979 concern over their role was again voiced by the Co-ordinating Group members. The Statistics Advisory Group and the science group had agreed about the collection of information on cognitive ability; this would be put to the group and then to the Consultative Committee. Some members were concerned that they had not been involved at an early stage when they might have influenced the outcome. 'They felt that this was often the case: proposals and new developments were so far advanced before the group was consulted that it was difficult as well as embarrassing to alter them significantly'. The chairman (and head of the Unit) sympathised and agreed that their role should be clarified.[126]

At the next meeting in 1979 the role of the group was discussed at length: the problem seemed to be that it had not been given terms of reference and therefore there was some overlap between it and the Consultative Committee. The head of the Unit felt that there had been some misunderstanding among group members about the powers of the Co-ordinating Group: no APU committee could have decision-making powers – that was the DES's role. The Consultative Committee advised the Secretary of State and therefore the Co-ordinating Group could be seen as a think tank. This was the only reference to a 'think tank' role, which might have been more useful had it been made earlier in the group's life.

At this same meeting members discussed why things had gone wrong. As the work proceeded, the steering groups had become more independent and the Co-ordinating Group's role, i.e. making sure that the groups were on the right lines, had become 'if not obsolete, quiescent'. Some members felt that circumstances had prevented them from keeping in close touch. Although there were large numbers of documents, there were not enough meetings to discuss them and 'opportunities to influence events or contribute to policy making were often lost as a result'. Unless this could be sorted out some members saw little point in continuing. Others thought that it was worth doing so, perhaps under a different name, and they could consider general problems – for example, background variables, the burden of testing on schools and ages for testing.[127] However, the APU secretariat apparently saw little point in the group's continuation: before the next meeting, at the beginning of 1980, members received a letter informing them of the Unit's intention to close the group. At this meeting, the group's last, members were informed by the chairman that the decision to scrap the Co-ordinating Group had simply been part of a general restructuring of the APU.[128]*

What the group had to say about the major issues
Before looking at what the group said, it is interesting to see how the APU's role was put to it in the early days, in the era that preceded the Consultative Committee. At its first meeting the group was told that the APU's function was 'mainly one of promoting enquiry and development through other agencies'. In replies to questions about finance and costing it turned out that there was no fixed timescale to the APU work, nor apparently a fixed budget. Although the APU could not be free of general financial constraints, the need for it had been accepted and 'the cost represented a very small part of the total education budget'; a veritable *carte blanche*.

Ages for monitoring At their third meeting, in 1976, the group discussed a fundamental issue – ages for monitoring. This discussion is interesting because it illustrates for the first time the weak position that the group was in. At this meeting it was decided that the ages should be common to each assessment area, they should be 11 and 15 and that additional ages (e.g. 9 and 13) could be covered later if desired.[129] Members agreed to return to this discussion at their next meeting, but at that meeting the chairman pointed out that the DES would have a policy view and that there was an opportunity for teachers' views to be aired at the next Consultative Committee meeting.[130] In other words, it did not matter too much if the Co-ordinating Group could not come to a firm decision about ages, since they were dispensable. This must have been a blow for those members who were concerned about making significant contributions to discussions.

---

* Four members of the group were redeployed to other parts of the APU machinery: one of the head teachers went to the maths group, one of the academics went to the Statistics Advisory Group and the two others joined the Consultative Committee.

Background variables This issue was discussed at length by the group; indeed one member considered this to be their greatest contribution. The academics on the group were not at all happy with the papers which came from the Statistics Advisory Group and made it their business to criticise them. Since there were no social scientists on the Consultative Committee these members felt that the Co-ordinating Group was more suited to deal with this subject. In 1978 the group was told that the Statistics Advisory Group had decided that social class was important and it had asked the Consultative Committee to reconsider its refusal to allow parental questioning. The group was aware of the controversy surrounding attempts to collect information on individual pupils and that indirect school-based indicators were unreliable. It asked the Statistics Advisory Group to discuss the issue further. At this same meeting the chairman tried to reduce the importance of background variables by saying that 'the intrinsic richness of the educational information would be of more value than its relationship with educational and social variables'.[131] This attitude surfaced again later in the year when the science team's ideas on relational variables were discussed. The group said that measures like cognitive ability and home background variables, if used in surveys, should only be used for analysis and not for reporting purposes,[132] a puzzling sentiment which would not be entertained by most researchers.

The group does not seem to have produced anything concrete on the background variable issue, despite what some members may have felt about their contribution. By 1979 it had become clear that part of the reason for this was that the group was not involved early enough in the discussions. Some members suggested that representatives from the group should be with the Statistics Advisory Group when background variables were discussed, so that the Statistics Advisory Group had the views of the social scientists available and also that the Co-ordinating Group would be better informed.[133] Nothing came of this suggestion, but by this time the APU had new joint heads, the streamlining process was in hand and the group's days were numbered. By this time also the Statistics Advisory Group had become clearly established in its role as the group responsible for giving general research advice.

At the group's final meeting members were told that the Consultative Committee had asked for a research proposal on the use of surrogate variables. Members of the group said that in view of the complexity of this subject there should be a proper working group set up which should include people from the Office of Population Censuses and Surveys and other social survey organisations. Had the group been fulfilling its proper function this decision is one that should have been made much earlier, particularly if anything was to have been learned from NAEP's experience in the importance of background data.

Conclusions

The group's success in actual co-ordination was very limited. There was little co-ordination among the groups and teams, and that which did take place in later years, for example between the science and maths teams, originated from the teams themselves. Nor was the group able to act as the guardian of cross-curricularity. The reason for this failure, however, was largely outside the group's control. For example, the crucial advice not to monitor in personal–social development was given by the Consultative Committee and the decision to go ahead with the monitoring of modern languages was made by the Unit. The group did have a conference on cross-curricularity in 1979, but by then the model was already eroded and there were no major outcomes from the conference.

In so far as the group articulated the doctrine of reporting facts only, it did act as a constraint on the APU. Non-interpretation has turned out to be more of a stumbling block than was imagined at first, and while it was the Consultative Committee that applied this policy to draft reports it does seem to have originated in the Co-ordinating Group. As for accountability, since the main power block on the group was made up of HMIs and other members of the educational establishment, the group was far less of an accountability body than the Consultative Committee. Though there were three or four head teachers on the group at any one time they had limited influence.

We interviewed seven of the group's members to ascertain what were the facts behind its demise. Naturally enough opinions varied, but all were agreed that as the Consultative Committee became stronger the Co-ordinating Group became weaker. One member felt that once the cross-curricular model had been eroded the group lost its *raison d'être*. An academic on the group said that it had tried, sincerely, to review what was going on in the steering groups but lost its way. It was no accident that it was disbanded soon after the APU's joint heads were appointed. Certainly one of the tasks of the joint heads of the Unit when they were appointed in mid-1979 was to streamline the committee structure, to give the groups and committees terms of reference and to give members periods of service. Indeed, one member of the Consultative Committee saw the winding up of the Co-ordinating Group as no more than a manifestation of this streamlining process.

The Unit's head who presided over the demise put it like this:

The original function of the Co-ordinating Group was to provide advice to the then head of the Unit on the assessment model to be adopted and the related committee structure. By 1980 this initial task had long been completed, while its role as an advisory body examining priorities within the APU programme and matters of interest common to a number of APU groups had quite properly passed to the Consultative Committee. (As you are probably aware, the Consultative Committee, which advises the Secretary of State, is broadly representative of education, industry, commerce and parental interests.) Members of the Co-ordinating Group recognised that they could have no co-ordinating function in a real sense of the word and were in general agreement that the group was no longer viable.[134]

In other words, the closure of the group was regarded by the Unit as a perfectly natural process in its development.

Another academic put it rather differently. The group never did act in a co-ordinating capacity, neither did it make decisions; these were made either by the head of the Unit, or by the Secretary of State on the advice of the Consultative Committee. The timing of meetings was partly to blame for this: 'it was chance whether issues came to us or went to the Statistics Advisory Group'. It was not a group giving expert advice on research since the Statistics Advisory Group fulfilled this role. Nevertheless, two of the academics who were social scientists did feel that they should be giving expert advice to the Unit since there was no social science expertise on the Consultative Committee. This illustrates the dilemma facing group members who were not part of the APU: their role was not supposed to be one of advising on issues, merely one of co-ordinating the work of the groups, and not all members were happy with this. The academics in particular, who joined the group later on in its life, pushed for more of a steering role, and it was this which partly contributed to the group's downfall. The Unit was not prepared to have a second group as powerful as the Consultative Committee. In any case the real steering role did not lie with the Co-ordinating Group but was the job of the managerial structure within the APU, comprising the chairmen of the various committees and groups together with the joint heads of the Unit.

Whatever the reasons for the group's eclipse, there is general agreement that the result has been to give more power to the Statistics Advisory Group. Some observers feel that this is the group that has had most impact on the direction of the APU. The increasing importance of the Statistics Advisory Group seems inevitable given that a large-scale monitoring programme was under way. Questions of sampling, research design and analysis were bound to dominate once the overall plan was thrashed out. As the Consultative Committee grew in strength it made the important policy recommendations while recommendations on the statistical and design features of the monitoring programme, which became so vitally important in the late 1970s and early 1980s were made by the Statistics Advisory Group. The Co-ordinating Group was never able to develop either of these roles, and so its days were numbered.

4 The Statistics Advisory Group

Introduction
This account of the Statistics Advisory Group differs in an important respect from the remainder of the report in that one of the authors was a member of the group for much of the period under review (from February 1978 to August 1981). Like other chapters, this account identifies and traces themes; it is in the judgement of which themes are important that this 'inside knowledge' has had a major effect. It has also enabled us to be rather more confident than otherwise that the APU minutes of meetings reflect fairly faithfully the outcome of the discussions held; where highly technical issues were discussed, these are usually only briefly summarised, but care was taken to ensure that the summaries were accurate. We would also alert the reader to the fact that the same author who was a member of the Statistics Advisory Group has also been associated publicly with various criticisms of some of the technical methods originally proposed for use with APU tests – the so-called Rasch model procedures. We do not feel that this invalidates our account, rather it has enabled us to focus more sharply on the interesting relationship between the objectives of the APU and the methodology proposed to achieve them.

Themes and Issues
This chapter is organised into six sections and a final overview. The sections are: a discussion of the origins and precursors of the Statistics Advisory Group; sampling; background variables, in-depth studies and research; reporting of results; discussions of draft reports; the Rasch debate and trends over time. They are based on the issues which the group discussed, and within these sections, four of the six themes identified in the Introduction to this book are apparent. The themes are as follows.

Consultation with outsiders

The Statistics Advisory Group deliberately instigated seminars (on the Rasch model and trends in performance over time) at which outsiders were invited to give advice. From time to time it also invited outsiders to meetings or sought particular technical advice from them. That it felt advice was necessary in some areas and not in others reflects both the particular composition of the group and also the lack of relevant expertise within the DES. The theme will be developed with emphasis on the way the composition of the Statistics Advisory Group influenced its own confidence to pronounce on technical matters and the trust placed in its judgements by the APU. It seems clear that the major consultations with outsiders took place largely in response to crises of confidence within the APU and were attempts to settle issues by appeals to 'experts'.

Progress of APU aims

Two of the aims of the APU were discussed repeatedly by the Statistics Advisory Group. The first, implicit, aim of identifying trends over time, appeared early on and was linked closely to the use of the Rasch model which it was assumed would provide the basis for time comparisons. The subsequent debate on Rasch occurred during a period when the discussion of change over time subsided and it was only after the 1980 seminar on Rasch, designed to resolve the controversy surrounding it, that explicit discussions of trends over time emerged again and led to the 1981 seminar on the topic.

The second aim, which greatly concerned the group, was that of measuring underachievement and the related use of in-depth studies. As is pointed out in Chapter 2, these two aims quickly coalesced into the West Indian study, in the planning and demise of which the Statistics Advisory Group played a large part. Furthermore, as will be clear in the section on sampling, decisions on sample size taken in 1977 effectively closed off a large number of options for assessing underachievement.

Forward planning

The essentially short-term perspective surrounding most of the APU planning is perhaps most evident in the way in which the early commitment to 'light sampling' which imposed a small burden on schools, was overtaken by subsequent decisions on monitoring in several areas simultaneously. Decisions about the mathematics monitoring sample size and its distribution over regions and schools were made by the Statistics Advisory Group early on without much thought for the implications of similar decisions in the areas of language, science and modern language, until the transmogrification of light sampling of schools into moderately heavy sampling had already taken place.

Research versus monitoring

The continuing tension in the APU over whether it should perform a purely 'monitoring' function or a 'research' function underlay many of the discussions in the Statistics Advisory Group. This surfaced in the repeated emphasis by the APU on 'presentation of results without interpretation' and caused disquiet within the group, becoming a source of particular concern when the group came to discuss the reports. The group debated the issue of whether 'mathematics' should be reported as a single attainment or by subcategory (e.g. geometry, statistics), it discussed the categories within which results could be presented (e.g. school size, region) and it discussed the intended audience. The Statistics Advisory Group quite quickly came to view its task as one of giving general advice on research matters.

Origins and Precursors of the Statistics Advisory Group

Origins

The original (1977) terms of reference[135] of the Statistics Advisory Group were 'to provide the Unit as a whole with expert advice on all matters concerned with statistics, sampling and item 'banking'.* As will become clear in later sections, the group never felt itself to be restricted solely to giving technical advice and we shall trace how the Statistics Advisory Group developed from a group which was intended to provide purely 'technical' advice to a group which came to have an important influence on the whole direction of APU work.

The decision to set up the Statistics Advisory Group seems to have been taken within the DES without prior discussion in the Consultative Committee or the Co-ordinating Group. It is not clear whether the setting up of the Statistics Advisory Group reflected a desire to obtain and be seen to obtain independent statistical advice from outside the monitoring teams, or simply to provide a convenient forum where NFER researchers could discuss their proposals with APU staff. A study of the initial composition of the group† suggests that both aims were present. Statistical expertise on the group was limited, however. One representative from the NFER was a research statistician, but there was only one other statistician present, from the DES Statistics Branch. As the DES statistics branch is concerned mainly with the collection and compilation of 'vital' statistics of the education system, its staff would not generally regard themselves as competent to advise

---

* In 1980 the formal terms of reference became: 'To offer professional and technical advice on statistical and related matters to the monitoring teams and to the Unit's steering groups and other committees, and to advise the heads of the Unit on statistics and related matters as required.'[136]
† A list of members is included in Appendix 7(i), available separately from the Institute of Education.

on the more complex mathematical aspects of statistical techniques. The two outside members, surprisingly, were not statisticians at all, although one had extensive expertise in testing. One might infer from this that their special brief was to pay attention to the relatively new techniques of 'item banking' for test construction purposes. It seems clear, therefore, that the APU did not anticipate any controversy of a mathematically technical nature and presumably felt that a single statistician from the NFER could provide the necessary research expertise.

Precursors of the Statistics Advisory Group

As explained in Chapter 1, there were several important discussions of monitoring issues during the early 1970s in the DES working group on measurement of educational attainment (WGMET) and the Bullock Committee, and here we have selected three issues which were to occupy much of the Statistics group's later discussions: sampling; the Rasch model and trends over time; and research and monitoring.

Sampling for monitoring   At the end of 1971, WGMET produced a lengthy report on the feasibility of monitoring, together with detailed calculations of sample sizes. Their recommendation was for a small (1600) national sample in order to gain initial acceptance, increasing steadily over time in order to bring in comparisons between regions and other groupings of the population.

The sample size calculations assumed that monitoring was at the secondary school stage. They were based on the assumption that the need was to be able to show – with a high chance of success – that a statistically significant change in, say, mean reading scores had happened between surveys. The calculations also involved assumptions about the likely 'design effect' (see later) and the likely average change in test score over time (1 per cent per term). It was recognised that these assumptions were speculative and might need to be revised, but what was not mentioned at all was the sample size needed to estimate accurately the proportions of low scorers – a key problem in the study of low achievement. The idea of light sampling was introduced in this report, and it was envisaged that each school would be tested only every ten years.

Another group concerned with monitoring was the Bullock Committee of Enquiry into Reading, which began work in 1972 and published its report in 1975.[137] Chapter 3 of the report endorsed the idea of light sampling and mentioned a figure of 5,000 children a year with termly monitoring. The monitoring subcommittee of the main committee, at its first meeting in December 1972, referred directly to the previous working group on monitoring, the chairman of the subcommittee having been a member of that group. In the course of its discussions the NFER was entrusted with the calculations of sample size, on the basis of its reading survey experience and its current experience with item banking in mathematics.

While the term 'matrix sampling' (see later) seems not have been used by these early groups, they did discuss the reduction of the burden on children by having a number of subtests, so that each child would not have to take the full test, and subsequently combining the results.

Research and monitoring　During these early discussions, it seems to have been taken for granted that the process of designing and interpreting the monitoring was a task for experienced educational researchers and in the Bullock report the NFER was mentioned explicitly. While the clear focus of these early discussions was that of 'standards' and their routine monitoring, there was little indication that this should be anything other than an extension of previous studies such as the NFER national surveys of reading.[138] Certainly there was no hint of the structure that was later to emerge as the APU.

The Rasch model and trends over time　The idea of using the Rasch model goes back at least to 1966 when the Schools Council asked the NFER to carry out a feasibility study of item banking in connection with CSE exams. This project examined the idea in some detail, and devoted a little of its report[139] to a discussion of the use of the Rasch model. The report concluded: 'Although we firmly believe that item banking is the examining system of the future, we are equally convinced that it needs further study before it can be implemented on a national scale'. The authors were aware of the assumptions required for item banking to work and how 'the gulf between what we would like to say about a pupil's performance and what the data allow' was a real one.

Briefly, the Rasch model is a mathematical equation which describes how the probability of a correct response to an item in a test is related to two characteristics: one is the so-called 'difficulty' of the item and the other is an assumed 'ability' of the person taking the test. It supposes that the difficulty of each item is unchanging so that in particular, for every child tested, the items have the same ordering of difficulty. It also assumes that an individual's response is determined by one single 'ability' or 'trait' only (i.e. is unidimensional). The principal controversy has centred on the reasonableness or otherwise of these two assumptions. The critics have argued that it would be educationally absurd to suppose that children exposed to different curricula, with different backgrounds etc, should behave according to these assumptions, when considering, say mathematics, or even a somewhat more narrowly defined topic such as arithmetic. The proponents of Rasch have tended to argue that while the model might not be a perfect description of the educational reality, it was nevertheless a useful starting point and did give simple useful summaries of test score data.*

WGMET saw item banking as an extremely exciting 'new style of educational assessment'. The group took its technical advice from the NFER and an appendix to the group's report was very positive about the potentialities of Rasch-calibrated item banks. While it did have reservations about the homogeneity of the items in the bank, it simply noted that this 'would need to be thoroughly checked'. It had no reservation, however, about the method being 'sample-free', claiming that 'a nationally representative sample would not be required in order to provide appropriate national norms for groups of peripheral questions'. The advantages of item banking were seen to be to allow a large curriculum coverage and to avoid a 'backwash' effect in schools.

The Bullock Report (in Chapter 3) took up the idea of item banking enthusiastically, using descriptions of the technique identical to those in the WGMET report. The Bullock Report goes further by linking item banking implicitly to a means of discarding 'out-of-date' items while retaining a common 'calibration' in order to allow a valid measure of change over time.

Thus, by the time the APU was set up in 1974, several guidelines had already been laid down. Light sampling was to be used in order not to place a heavy burden on schools, item banking was seen to be the answer to a number of objections concerned with 'backwash' and the Rasch calibration of item banks was the technique which, while it needed further empirical work, was to make possible the underlying aim of studying trends in standards over time.

Sampling

Sample size

The issue which was debated more than any other at the start of the Statistics Advisory Group's existence was that of sampling, and in particular the sample size which would be needed for each survey. The discussion hinged on the need to balance two opposing requirements. The one was to have as large a sample as possible so that precise statements could be made about average achievement levels, and differences in achievement between subgroups such as boys and girls. The other was the need to avoid imposing too large a burden on schools and children either by going back to a school too often or by asking children to complete too long a test. These problems were raised at the very first meeting of the group in January 1977 in a discussion paper[141] prepared by a member of the APU staff. It recommended the adoption of 'light'

---

* The interested reader is referred to articles by Choppin and Goldstein in the volume edited by Lawton and Lacey[140] for further elaboration of these issues.

sampling whereby relatively small groups of children were to be monitored frequently – in this case yearly. It was claimed that the infrequent involvement of schools would also limit any 'backwash' influence of the tests on the curriculum. The 'matrix' sampling scheme advocated in the paper meant that each child completed only a subtest, containing a few of the total number of test items being used. This not only limits the burden on the individual pupil, but by spreading the different subtests suitably over the sample obtains valid information about the whole area being tested. An initial attempt was also made in this paper to indicate the 'background' variables (sex, region, school type, school size) by which achievement could be reported, and the implications of this for sample size. Socio–economic group and ethnic origin were also included, reflecting the intention present at this time to measure these variables.

The discussion in the group was concerned mainly to 'flesh out' the paper which went through three more revisions following the first Statistics Advisory Group meeting and a meeting of the Co-ordinating Group. By the third revision, the paper emphasised the need for sufficient accuracy to 'allow detection of trends' and comparison of subgroups, and reassured its readers that the matrix sampling approach would 'avoid any possible disruption of the schools' timetable'. In this and other discussion documents in this early period, the basis for discussion seems to have been a series of tests only in the area of mathematics. Nobody is recorded as having pointed out that when all testing programmes were in operation, the assumptions about the extent of involvement of schools would no longer hold.

A further paper presented to the first meeting[142] discussed sample precision by presenting examples of the accuracy with which a sample size of 10,000 would give estimates of average performance, and also the probability with which it would allow the detection of statistically significant trends over time assuming subsequent 'monitor' sample sizes of 2,000 (the reverse of the original WGMET recommendation). It said quite clearly, however, that the number of children to be tested would depend on the choice of categories for the variables (such as school size) which were to be used for reporting. A later paper[143] updated this with estimates of 'design effects'.*

During the group's discussion, most of the paper's suggestions seem to have been adopted. The group endorsed the idea of an initial 'heavy' sample followed by 'light' monitor samples. The group asked urgently for costings based on sample sizes of 5,000 and 10,000 while at the same time agreeing that the actual degree of accuracy needed was a matter for

---

*The 'design effect' is the factor by which the sample size in a complex sampling scheme involving several stages of selection, needs to be inflated in order to achieve the same accuracy as a simple random sample of all children.

further discussion and should be determined by 'educational' considerations. By this was meant, presumably, the accuracy which 'educationists' would find acceptable. There was one reference later in the paper to the fact that the Consultative Committee had not given guidance on this issue and the matter was fully discussed again only when the first maths survey draft results appeared in 1979. Meanwhile, the figure of 10,000 was used in further discussions of the accuracy to be achieved when reporting by specific variable categories.[144] By the April 1977 meeting of the group a further comprehensive paper from the DES statistics branch, on sample size and cost, was written explicitly on the assumption of an initial sample of 10,000 and subsequent yearly samples of 1,000. It was pointed out, however, that given the matrix sampling approach, the effective sample size might be the equivalent of only 2,000–5,000 for the heavy sample, and that if the monitor samples were to be only 1,000, several years' aggregation of results would be necessary before these could be used. No doubt this point was influential in the later decision to use a 'heavy' sample for each year of monitoring.

Following the discussion on sample size in the early summer of 1977, no further detailed discussion took place until the next meeting in October, when members expressed concern that the sample size for England might fall below the established figure of 10,000 and this was referred to the APU for discussion. The sample size was effectively determined by the early summer of 1977. Despite initial caveats about the need to discuss educationally significant differences, the precision required for subgroups of the population, and the effective reduction in size as a result of matrix sampling, the very first 'example' figure of 10,000 was the one eventually adopted and came to be used for each year's monitoring, with the Statistics Advisory Group's early recommendation for subsequent 'light' samples being quietly forgotten.

One is left with the impression that once mentioned, the figure of 10,000 was regarded as reasonable, and because of lack of guidance about 'educational' considerations, somewhat inevitably it became the accepted figure.* The Statistics Advisory Group had looked for 'educational' guidance and obtained little. It no doubt began to realise that such research guidance was not readily available, and we will return to this in the next section where the research role of the Statistics Advisory Group is discussed.

The lack of 'educational' input to the sample size discussion is also illustrated in a brief note to the Consultative Committee from the

* Interestingly, there was a much later admission, in the December 1980 meeting of the group, to the effect that the maths sample size of 10,000 was 'partly a presentational/ political decision'.

NUT[145] in response to the above sample size paper whose recommendations were accepted. The NUT pointed out, for the first time in any discussion document, that even if the proposed sample size was adequate for the estimation of average (or mean) values, it would almost certainly not be adequate if one wanted to obtain accurate statements of the percentages of children at the extremes of the achievement range. Since one aim of the APU was to study 'underachievement' (which was later to be taken as 'low achievement') the failure to consider this was most surprising. Whether or not this failure was deliberate or merely an oversight it effectively destroyed the possibility of achieving this aim at an early stage, and it illustrates how the decision-making process of the APU implicitly, though inadvertently, precluded certain possibilities – even important ones enshrined in its original terms of reference. None of the reports published so far attempts to study anything other than mean scores either for the whole sample or for selected categories.

By March 1979 concern was being voiced that, at the secondary level, language testing of both reading and writing might begin to impose quite a heavy load on schools, especially in Wales and Northern Ireland. The group seemed to feel that it would be better, by using the same school for reading and writing, to increase the burden on individual schools rather than increase the number of schools used. Soon after, the Welsh Office Education Department also added its voice[146] complaining that when all three areas of monitoring were underway, an unacceptable burden would be placed on Welsh secondary schools. They proposed an 'APU day' each year when all testing would take place. A paper on future APU sample strategy[147] outlined how such a proposal would work and at its April 1979 meeting the Statistics Advisory Group generally seems to have been in favour of it. It was clear by now that, as far as schools were concerned, the APU was readily accepting the practical abandonment of the 'light sampling' aim, at least in Wales and Northern Ireland, even though in subsequent public documents it still maintained this stance. For example, in a publicity leaflet[148] in July 1980 it is stated: 'A typical APU survey involves no more than about 2 per cent *of the total age group* . . . small enough to keep inconvenience to *schools* to the minimum'. (our italics)

Concern over the burden being imposed on schools, especially those in Wales, surfaced again at the January 1980 meeting of the group. No detailed figures were presented but the general feeling seemed to be that 'light sampling' was no longer in force and some schools were beginning to complain of the testing burden. The suggestion of an 'APU day' was revived, in order to enable the APU to guarantee for each school several years free of tests. The group noted this advantage and also the possibility for comparisons between the 'lines of development' which this scheme would allow. It emphasised the administrative difficulties, however, and without coming to a firm decision, decided to ask the steering groups for their views. There was also a hint[149] that monitoring might become less than annual.* By February the NFER had supplied detailed figures of the school 'burden'.[150] These showed, for example, that in 1979 nearly a third of all maintained secondary schools had taken part in some APU work, and it was estimated that in the early 1980s in Wales, where proportionately four times as many schools would be sampled, every secondary school would be involved at least once a year.

At the June 1980 meeting of the group there was further concern expressed about the additional load the new science monitoring would impose on Welsh schools. It was reported that the idea of an APU day generally had been received with little enthusiasm and the APU was reconsidering its sampling strategy and was hoping to circulate a paper later in the year. By this time, therefore, there were obvious pressures on the APU to reduce the frequency of testing as the only acceptable solution to the school burden problem. The group continued to be concerned at this burden. In October 1980 it was informed[151] that in Wales and Northern Ireland 27 per cent and 37 per cent respectively of primary schools were to be involved in 1981 testing just for maths and language. It was becoming clear that the APU policy of not including a school two years running was becoming unworkable and would need reconsideration. Several possible avoidance strategies were discussed, including testing the whole age group within a school, lengthening the testing time and having a single sample of schools for all monitoring areas. Pending further consideration it was agreed to drop the original agreement to spare schools two years' consecutive testing, and in 1981 in England all primary schools would be considered eligible for sample inclusion irrespective of previous participation. Discussion on Wales and Northern Ireland was postponed.†

In January and February 1981 two papers[153] giving details of a multiple testing scheme were discussed. The group was most interested in the proposal for combining the testing of maths, language and science with an increase in the fraction of pupils sampled per school. Fears about administrative difficulties were aired with the representatives of the science and language teams arguing for the removal of science from the scheme. Nevertheless the group did recommend the proposal to include all three areas of testing and it was decided that the LEAs and the unions would be consulted. By March 1981 the group

---

* This paper went through two revisions in February and June 1980, a mark of the importance attached to this issue.

† The various sampling options to reduce the impact on schools were discussed by the group in December 1980.[152] There was some feeling that at least in language the sample size could be reduced with few ill effects.

was becoming so concerned that it recommended that as a matter of urgency this strategy be adopted for Wales and Northern Ireland from November 1981. In June it was reported that this had indeed been accepted and agreed. For England, too, the consultations initially had looked encouraging, but there were doubts from the teacher unions,[154] and a decision not to introduce multiple testing in England was taken in December 1981.

Non-response

Non-response, either by schools or individual children, was recognised early on as a potential problem. In October 1977 the group recorded its concern about possible biases arising from non-response, specifically pupil absenteeism, and agreed to keep the issue under review. It was not then raised again until December 1980 and at greater length in January 1981 when there were detailed discussions of sample losses, based on a paper[155] which gave detailed figures for 1978, 1979 and 1980. It is somewhat surprising that the group did not look seriously at this issue until two years after monitoring had started and well after the first results had been discussed, since in 1978 the school non-response was 12 per cent overall and 16 per cent in Northern Ireland for the secondary maths survey. By 1980 the non-response rates had gone up, for primary maths, for example, from 4 per cent to 11 per cent in 1980 in England, and was 18 per cent in 1980 in Northern Ireland. More worrying were the figures for science with a 23 per cent school non-response at 11 in 1980, rising to 34 per cent and 38 per cent for written and practical testing respectively in Northern Ireland.

Somewhat belatedly, the group made it clear that it felt that insufficient attention had been given to discussing the non-response in APU reports. In January 1981, after the non-response issue had been discussed by the science steering group, the Statistics Advisory Group had a further discussion. Members were concerned at the biases which might be introduced by high non-response rates, especially when making comparisons over time. They recognised that judging the responding sample in terms of its representatives on the background variables ignored possible biases due to other unmeasured factors, and they asked the NFER to do what it could to study the problem further. This was done in a paper[156] discussed in July 1981, which showed that at least for the 1978 and 1979 secondary maths surveys, those schools which had to be chased to participate performed noticeably worse than those which did not. The group seems simply to have noted this and agreed to keep the issue under review. In view of its earlier concern, the group seemed surprisingly complacent, and indeed, at its November 1981 meeting took the somewhat defeatist view that it would not be worthwhile, or politically acceptable, to ask the non-responding schools even to complete the questionnaire on school resources. Instead it decided to wait and see what the next set of figures on refusal rates would show. Conceivably the APU was worried not only about being seen to pester schools, but also about drawing too much attention to the high non-response rate for fear it would undermine confidence in the validity of results.

There was another curious omission from the discussion of non-response bias. In a paper from the NFER[157] which came to the group in December 1980, it was clearly shown that the children who were tested but who had to be 'chased' after the main date of testing tended to have lower average scores, especially at the secondary level, than those who responded on the day chosen; also that the date of testing was related to the values of at least some background variables. The paper concluded that serious biases would result from the exclusion of those children not tested on the appointed day. The group simply noted the paper and agreed to try and include those children. This paper, however, did not draw attention to the fact that some 4 per cent of children selected in the 1978 secondary maths survey were never tested at all, despite the fact that these would be expected to show, on average, lower scores than those tested on the appointed day. The group, likewise, seems not to have noticed this 'oversight', and did not return to the topic.

Background Variables, In-depth Studies and Research

While the issue of sample size was clearly of principal concern to the Statistics Advisory Group rather than the Consultative Committee, the choice of background variables and policy towards in-depth studies was not obviously so. Nevertheless, the Statistics Advisory Group had quite a lot to say on both these issues, and was used by the APU to prepare proposals about suitable background variables for discussion by the Consultative Committee.

After a brief mention of background variables in the first paper on sampling discussed by the Statistics Advisory Group, these were not elaborated until the paper on sample size[158] was discussed at the March 1977 meeting. Members were asked to comment on the usefulness and feasibility of measuring school, teacher and parental characteristics before the Consultative Committee or the Co-ordinating Group had debated them. This paper argued that school and teacher variables were difficult to collect and in any case not very useful. The school variables it had in mind were such things as streaming policy, syllabus and state of buildings, and the teacher variables seemed to be related to qualifications. It gave most attention to standard variables such as school size and type, information on which was available from existing DES data. It also recommended the measurement of ethnic origin and socio-economic group. The Statistics Advisory Group seems to have accepted easily the paper's recommendations to use these variables and made one of the earliest references in the APU to in-depth studies as a means of pursuing the effects of variables which were not being measured in the national monitoring.

The idea of in-depth studies seems quickly to have become one means of ensuring that the basic monitoring programme would not be held up by a wish to obtain more detailed and informative research data. For example, at the April meeting the possibility of relating different areas of performance in mathematics to each other was relegated to an in-depth study, and at its December meeting, in a discussion of the variables to be measured in the science monitoring, the chairman reminded the group that it was the first priority of the APU to produce a national picture of performance levels. It would be necessary, therefore, to investigate a number of the proposed variables within the context of in-depth studies, separate from but possibly linked to the main national monitoring.

The next paper on background variables[159] followed very quickly and was sent to the Consultative Committee and the Co-ordinating Group. It presented a slightly lengthier discussion of background variables and the reasons for including or not including them, although it hardly ventured beyond vague statements such as 'it is not considered useful' or 'the problem is probably too great for any meaningful analysis'. It specifically identified the four easily available measures (region, location, school type, school size) which were to be used to stratify the sample and recommended (at primary level) the collection of data on pupil/teacher ratio, percentage of pupils having free school meals (both of which were subsequently gathered), area-based measures of deprivation, parental occupation, parental education and child's ethnic origin (none of which have yet been gathered). At secondary level it was proposed to give a questionnaire to pupils enquiring about their ethnic origin, examination intentions etc.

The attitude of the Statistics Advisory Group to its research advisory role can be gleaned from its response to the NUT reaction[160] to the above paper. The NUT maintained that the paper was proposing a *research* study rather than the original intention of *monitoring*. It cautioned against drawing causal inferences from observational data: that is attributing a difference in performance between children say from different types of schools to the type of school *per se* rather than to concomitant but unmeasured factors such as the social composition of the catchment area. In connection with this the NUT was worried about the lack of explanation of the statistical procedures to be used to analyse such 'concomitant' variables as *might* be measured, and pointed out that some of the variables which could be used in this way (i.e. teacher and school variables) were in any case not being measured. Interestingly, the NUT did not raise at that time specific objections to ethnic group or parental occupation, although these were the focus of much subsequent debate.

In its reply[161] the Statistics Advisory Group adopted a broad view of 'research' to include test development and 'extensive data analysis' using many different variables. Somewhat tartly, it remarked that the 'NUT may rest assured that the APU and its agents are fully aware of the difference between correlation and causation'. It dealt very briefly with the other points raised by the NUT and generally adopted a somewhat dismissive attitude. The teachers' representatives continued to express their disagreement over the omission of teacher variables, resulting in a further representation to the statistics group[162] but there is no record of further discussion of this issue by the group. The disquiet over the omission of school and teacher variables did not die down and was viewed with particular concern by the science team in a document[163] presented to the group in December. This document listed a dozen variables for possible measurement. Many of them were specific to science, but the list included home background measures of parental education and occupation, which the group was clearly still in favour of gathering.

The group was having serious doubts about identifying ethnic groups however, and at the October 1977 meeting it was suggested that it might not be possible to include this as a variable in the first primary maths survey. By the December meeting of the group the DES had decided that there should be no question on ethnic group in the first maths survey and instead that the whole issue should be given over to 'in-depth' study, which was clearly becoming a useful means of postponing discussion of complex or sensitive issues.

At the April 1979 meeting the Statistics Advisory Group expressed 'concern that information on the social class of pupils was not to be obtained'. It even considered that without obtaining such information 'there was little value in obtaining information on the variables which it had been agreed would be included'. The group decided to ask the Consultative Committee and the Co-ordinating Group to think again. The Consultative Committee discussed the issue in May[164] and expressed political reservations about collecting social class data, but did ask the Statistics Advisory Group to consider the matter further. In June the group reaffirmed its earlier views and warned that if individual social factors were not taken into account 'the data from monitoring could be interpreted falsely, which would result in severe criticism on the part of other educational researchers'. At the July meeting, however, a completely different view was taken. The statistics group now felt 'excursion into the "non-educational" field of home background, social environment, etc would convert what was essentially a monitoring exercise into a major research project'. It recommended that 'the

APU should not attempt to collect data about home background within the national surveys'.

What prompted this volte-face? The April meeting minutes give some clue since at least one member expressed the view that information obtained from parents might not be very reliable and suggested a separate research project to study this – a proposal endorsed by the group at its July meeting. In fact, despite the tone of the minutes, we know that the group was never totally unanimous on this issue, and it seems that in the face of reservations expressed by the Consultative Committee and the Co-ordinating Group, those who had doubts about the collection of home background variables were able to influence the remainder of the group. This underlines the point that having to rely for our record on reported minutes is not entirely satisfactory and that, in particular, the apparent absence of dissenting voices or discussion of issues does not necessarily imply their true absence.

At its October 1978 meeting the Consultative Committee stated that the collection of home background data was unacceptable. The science group, however, was still unwilling to accept this advice and as well as stressing the importance of home background variables asked for the inclusion of a 'general cognitive ability indicator'.[165] In this paper, discussed by the Statistics Advisory Group in July, the science group considered both types of variables necessary for meaningful interpretation of results and considered the measurement of general cognitive ability essential for proper comparison of results from pupils following different science curricula. The Statistics Advisory Group was somewhat hostile to this idea claiming that there was 'no real need to assess "cognitive ability"', and expressed concern that it appeared to be similar to an IQ test and that 'public opinion was likely to be hostile' to it.

At its October meeting the Consultative Committee was under some pressure from the science group on cognitive ability and suggested that the Statistics Advisory Group and the science group should together resolve this issue. Thus was born the Statistics–Science subgroup and once more the Statistics Advisory Group was used to consider a non-statistical research issue and reach agreement on it with a monitoring group.

The Statistics–Science subgroup

The subgroup held five meetings between December 1978 and May 1979. It decided that it was just as concerned about home background as about cognitive ability and was 'even more convinced of the necessity of taking account of pupils' home background'. Now, however, because of the views of the Consultative Committee, a detailed proposal for a pilot study was put forward to see whether school-based measures could act as a surrogate for individual-based measures. The committee was sympathetic to this proposal when it discussed it in the autumn, referring it back once more for further details.

Most of the subgroup's time, however, was taken up with the 'cognitive ability' issue. The science group's principal concern was that because children were allocated to different curricula (e.g. specialised or general science) at least partly on the basis of 'general academic ability', any comparisons (at the age of 15) between the performance of children following different curricula would be 'confounded' by general ability. The statistics group representatives reiterated that the proposal would be 'politically unacceptable' and doubted whether it 'would be possible to partial out cognitive ability in a statistically meaningful way'. At the fourth meeting of the subgroup the Statistics Advisory Group representatives put forward details of an alternative proposal, namely that questions about the science curricula followed by the children be put into the maths and language questionnaires. From then on the idea of measuring a general cognitive indicator did not reappear. Instead, in a science team paper in July the maths and language questionnaire data idea was put forward together with the suggestion that teachers' estimates of 'ability' be obtained. This was approved by the science steering group. However, it encountered a further obstacle at the September 1979 meeting of the Statistics Advisory Group whose members were as much against 'subjective' estimates of cognitive ability as they were against 'objective' ones. Thus, having persuaded the science group representatives to move a long way from their original position, the Statistics Advisory Group eventually was not prepared to compromise, and felt confident enough to dig in its heels. The issue was handed back to the Consultative Committee and never came before the group again.

In September 1979 the group returned to a discussion of background variables with a paper prepared for it by the APU.[166] The paper was primarily concerned with the possibility of a 'common core' of items for all surveys. It recognised the 'research' interest in a wider range of background variables which had appeared since the original decisions on 'stratifying' variables taken in 1977, and it suggested a new list of these. Although the paper itself did not seriously address the issue of the APU as a research versus monitoring exercise the Statistics Advisory Group pointed out that the current programme was definitely a monitoring one which was attempting to establish a 'baseline', and wished for clarification about the precise function of the APU before giving further thought to the matter. The paper itself, despite the considerable discussion of the issue during the previous two years, displayed a certain amount of confusion over the purpose and likely effects of including extra background variables. For example, it stated that 'unless we remove from our analyses the variability in the survey data which can be attributed to social background, any variability which may be associated with other background factors will be obscured'. This statement in fact is almost the opposite of the reasons usually advanced for taking account of social background, namely that failure to do so may encourage one to *overemphasise* the real effects of other variables! This vagueness (by the APU rather than the group) over the substance of this issue may well have contributed to the inability of the APU, over a period of several years, to resolve the issue one way or another.

At its February 1980 meeting, the group voted to keep the current stratifying variables, to which had been added 'locality' (metropolitan, non-metropolitan), placing the onus on the monitoring teams to make out a detailed case for any additional variables to be included. The group declared that the current variables 'did provide a means of identifying areas of interest in which in-depth studies might be carried out'. The group was then informed that the maths team wished to collect information about the catchment areas of the schools, a possibility first discussed by the Statistics Advisory Group in March 1978, as a surrogate for home background information. They expressed scepticism, and suggested instead that a pilot study on the use of census data for this purpose might be set up. The issue was discussed again at the June meeting when the group re-emphasised its lack of enthusiasm.

A new idea which arose in this period, coupled with the discussion of background variables, was the idea of composite tests incorporating more than one of the areas tested. An interest had developed in relating the three current lines of development, as we have already seen in the discussion of background variables and the 'APU day' idea. At its January 1980 meeting the group discussed a paper[167] which outlined a scheme for administering tests containing items from science, maths and language. Although this idea arose out of the 'APU day' discussions which were aimed at reducing the burden on schools, its justification quickly became that it would allow a study of interrelationships between the three lines of development. It became clear, however, that its operation would be expensive and there was a distinctly lukewarm reaction from the heads of the language and maths teams. The paper also raised difficult problems of sampling and administration and the group was clearly unenthusiastic. It suggested the proposal be deferred until the question of future sampling strategy had been resolved (although the adoption of the scheme would presumably influence the sampling strategy) and, as a final expression of apathy, recommended that at that stage the APU might consider an in-depth study.

Underachievement

At its April 1978 meeting the Statistics Advisory Group had an interesting discussion of the fourth of the APU's tasks 'to identify underachievement'. The group agreed that 'underachievement had necessarily to be related to a pupil's potential'. It not being possible either to define or to measure potential, 'it was concluded that the only course for the APU was to concern itself with the incidence of relatively low achievement'. This somewhat belated acceptance of the obvious by the statistics group, and indeed the APU, nevertheless failed to penetrate very far in the published material. For example, the first primary language report published in 1981 referred to underachievement as one of the APU's tasks.

From this time on, underachievement as such was barely referred to by the Statistics Advisory Group until a reference at the December 1980 meeting. This noted that to study low achievement it would be necessary to look at the extremes of the ability range which would require a larger sample than was 'feasible'. 'It was therefore agreed that the test basis should not be changed in the short term'. With that sentence it would seem that, within the group, the formal burial took place of the fourth APU objective.

The West Indian Study

In March 1978 a detailed paper[168] discussed the problems of carrying out APU studies of minority groups. It was at pains to point out the difficulties of such studies, particularly the definitional ones and the problems of finding suitable sampling frames. In particular, the paper presented a detailed case against including simple ethnic origin questions in the main surveys but did argue for parallel surveys so that results could be compared. In November it was reported that the Consultative Committee had agreed to a planning study to look into the possibility of monitoring underachievement in West Indian children, a proposal which was also billed as being an 'in-depth' study.

The Statistics Advisory Group was presented with the draft West Indian Study Group report[169] in June 1980. This study group, which included two members of the statistics group, had been asked to make recommendations for a study of West Indian children. Briefly, it recommended that a sample of about 5,000 'Afro–Caribbean' pupils should take the main APU test material. Only schools with more than 10 per cent of such children were to be included, and these only in the 17 LEAs which were estimated to contain 75 per cent of all West Indian children. Teachers were to be asked to identify the pupils by such factors as 'appearance', 'names' and 'dress' and from knowledge of family background. For comparison purposes non West Indian children in the same schools were to be tested. The Statistics Advisory

Group was critical of the sample size, the decision to use existing APU tests rather than specially designed tests and the use of LEAs and schools with the highest concentration of West Indians. It never again discussed the West Indian survey, simply being informed in January that its comments had been incorporated in a revised draft. In fact this draft[170] more or less accepted the points about sampling, but rejected the notion of using specially constructed tests. Whether in any ensuing discussions on this latter point the view of the Statistics Advisory Group would have prevailed we shall unfortunately never know, since four months later it was formally announced by the DES that the West Indian survey had been dropped (see Chapter 2).

Reporting of APU Results

Interpretation

By September 1979 the Statistics Advisory Group was voicing concern at the determination of the APU to restrict interpretation of results and to make only a 'neutral statement of performance'.[171] The group was reminded that the extent of interpretation was not a question for the statistics group to answer. At its November meeting, during a discussion of the draft report of the first secondary mathematics survey, it was suggested that 'the report should provide a guide to the educational significance of the survey results', and once more the group was told explicitly that the maths teams 'had been instructed by the Consultative Committee not to offer any comments or judgements and had accordingly not done so. Interpretation of the results should come from elsewhere'.

The point was made again in January 1980. Some members of the Statistics Advisory Group took the opportunity to criticise the attitude which 'deprived monitoring teams of the opportunity to relate their findings to existing research and this tended to make reports appear bland and insular'. The monitoring teams were clearly becoming concerned at this policy and it was suggested that 'the academic standing of the members of the monitoring teams might suffer'. On this issue the non DES members of the group seem to have been united. Nevertheless, the chairman, despite noting 'the dissatisfaction expressed by the group' had to remind members 'that the APU had not been set up to carry out traditional "academic" research but to produce a profile of pupils' performance'. Moreover 'APU reports were not aimed at the same audience as most research reports and that the inclusion of details of other studies would be a deterrent to teachers and parents'. In the face of such dogma, it is not surprising that the group was worried that the reports would appear 'insular'.

The group continued to express disquiet over the lack of commentary and interpretation in the reports. During discussions of the second secondary maths survey in March 1981 the NFER regretted 'the constraints placed on their researchers by the APU's policy of non-interpretation of results'. A glimmer of hope however, was expressed by the chairman of the group who said that 'it was possible that there would be a change in the Unit's stance on the interpretation of results'. This statement seems to have referred particularly to what was happening with the science monitoring.

Release of items
At the February 1978 meeting of the Statistics Advisory Group, Professor Cronbach, who had had experience of the American NAEP programme, described how it reported results at the individual item level and recommended that at least some APU reporting should be done in this way, a proposal which has been partly met by the release of some individual item results in the maths, language and science reports. This release of individual items, however, is not as informative as it might seem.

To begin with, in mathematics, only 10 per cent of the items and their responses are reproduced in the reports and these are chosen to illustrate points rather than be representative of all items. At its November 1978 meeting a majority of the statistics group felt that for a representative set of items to be useful it would need to comprise a much larger percentage than that currently used and this could lead to schools 'teaching to the test'. The teams appeared to accept the policy of limited release and in February 1981 were still opposing a wider release on the grounds that they wished to re-use items and were concerned that item difficulties would decrease if they were publicly available. At the end of 1978 it was still assumed, and reiterated in a paper from the NFER on LEASIB in December 1978, that LEA access to APU tests would be via this NFER item bank, a position stated at the third meeting of the Co-ordinating Group in 1977. Thus the policy on release of items was ultimately dependent on the validity of LEASIB which itself was dependent on the validity of the Rasch model.*

Reporting level
An early paper[172] discussed the level of reporting of APU results. It suggested that results should be presented only at the national level, and possibly separately for boys and girls, but it left open the possibility of reporting by school size and region. These suggestions were made

---

* It was proposed that the test items in the item bank would be calibrated using the Rasch model. Since the bank contained some APU items the remaining items would have difficulty values directly comparable with the APU test items. Thus tests based on LEASIB would be directly comparable with the APU tests.

before the detailed discussions on background variables took place, at which stage it seems to have been assumed that reporting would be in terms of the background variables that were measured.

A related aspect of reporting was whether to report, for mathematics, at the so-called 'subcategory' level or whether to produce a single overall score. At its June 1978 meeting it was noted that the Consultative Committee, among others, regretted the absence of a single overall mathematics score which would be understood by most readers. The statistics group was aware of the difficulties of deciding how the subcategories were to be 'weighted' in any aggregation, but nevertheless felt that the pressure to produce an overall score could not be resisted and accordingly agreed to draft a paragraph for the first primary maths report promising a 'global' score in the future. To date, after the publication of three primary and three secondary reports, this has still not occurred. The Statistics Advisory Group implicitly accepted the reporting of subcategories and indeed expressed surprise in July 1980 that 'reading' was considered as a single measure rather than being reported in separate categories, whereas both science and mathematics were reported in subcategories. There is no recorded response to this and it remains to be seen whether these procedures are continued in later reports.

Discussions of Draft Reports

The draft reports of the first primary and secondary maths surveys became available in 1979 and were discussed by the Statistics Advisory Group in January and November respectively. In its discussion of the first draft, despite an instruction to concentrate on the statistical aspects of the report, the group appeared to spend as much time discussing presentation and reporting as on statistical issues. For example, the separate reporting of independent schools' results featured in their discussions. The group made many references to the usefulness of particular analyses. For example, they were worried 'about the rather simplistic reporting of (background) variables one at a time, believing that all the variables were very closely interrelated'. The discussion of the draft report of the secondary survey later in the year followed similar lines.

From June 1980 until August 1981 the most important and time-consuming activity for the Statistics Advisory Group was the discussion of draft reports, eight in all. There were no further exhortations to the group to keep strictly to 'statistical' comments and discussion ranged over a wide area. In fact, apart from the Consultative Committee, the Statistics Advisory Group was the only group which saw all the reports, so that it could, and did, play a useful role in highlighting problems of compatibility between them.

On the mathematics reports, the group commented several times on the need to distinguish carefully between 'educational' and 'statistical' significance. It continued to recommend more interpretation, going so far as to 'recommend that they (regional differences) should either be omitted or their interpretation expanded'. When looking at reports from the language survey the group seemed to spend a great deal of time commenting on non-statistical issues. For example, discussing the first primary survey in July 1980 'members discussed the difficulty in defining literacy'. In science, the group had quite a lot to say about presentation of results for both primary and secondary reports, emphasising good graphical presentation, no doubt drawing upon their experience of the maths and language reports.

The group's comments on the interpretations in the science reports are interesting. Rather than emphasising the need for more interpretation the members seemed to feel that the science team had over-interpreted their results! 'The team needed to be wary of stating that no differences in performance existed or of making speculations at this early stage; instead they should concentrate on reporting what pupils had done'. Several times the team were accused of being 'too speculative' and it seems that the Statistics Advisory Group was as much concerned with the educational interpretations as pointing out, for example, that the numbers involved were too small to make confident statements about the meaning of differences found.

The Rasch Debate and Trends Over Time

Although not actually in the APU's terms of reference it is clear, both from the discussions about monitoring in the early 1970s and from the Statistics Advisory Group's early meetings, that statements about trends in performance over time were very much part of the agenda. At the March 1977 meeting, for example, it was stated that 'the purpose of the APU was to monitor trends in performance over a period of time'. This was a reference to the issue raised in the Bullock Report which recognised the difficulty of retaining the same test over a long period of time because some of the items became 'outdated' so that comparisons based upon them would not present a fair assessment of trends in achievement. Nevertheless, both Bullock and at this stage the APU were keen to make statements about 'absolute' changes over time, for example, that average attainment in mathematics has changed by a certain amount, rather as one might discuss changes in children's height. The first discussion paper from the group[173] discussed how trends over time could be measured, and linked this clearly with a 'Rasch-scaled' item bank. Although not mentioning Rasch by name it talked of indexing items according to their difficulty and hence identifying trends; 'even though the actual items may change over a period of time'. The feasibility of matrix sampling was also assumed to depend on the existence of a working item bank, and another early document[174] went into some detail in describing the Rasch model.

The group clearly was interested in understanding the Rasch model and requested a paper which was discussed at its April meeting.[175] This paper was largely concerned with the 'exposure' problem whereby children who had not been exposed to a particular area of, say, maths could not be expected to do as well on the relevant test items as those who had been. This would lead to items with unequal relative difficulties for different groups of children which would thus not be suitable for Rasch scaling. A number of methods for dealing with this problem were discussed and the paper seemed to favour the one which involved limiting monitoring to a 'core' subset of all items to which every child could be assumed to have been exposed.

In a further discussion in June the chairman appeared to be supporting the 'core information' approach favoured by the paper. In July it was reported that 'a number of people both inside and outside the Unit were uncertain of the appropriateness of Rasch for APU monitoring purposes', and one outcome was a proposal for a seminar, involving outsiders, which took place in December. In the meantime, a paper from the NFER[176] was put to the Statistics Advisory Group in September in support of the use of Rasch for the NFER monitoring work. It stated that Rasch would be used with the first mathematics survey, principally to determine whether a single mathematics 'trait' was sufficient to describe the data or whether more were needed. It had already been decided that 13 content categories were to be used, but the paper clearly envisaged that the analysis might well result in a regrouping of items from these. The use of the Rasch model to give 'a stable measurement instrument' was emphasised and the paper stated that 'it must be appreciated that monitoring cannot proceed without such a step'.

The Statistics Advisory Group seems to have been happy with the general philosophy of the paper, but asked that 'conventional methods' of analysis should also be tried, and that, even if some items did not 'fit' the model, they should be retained in the bank 'for strong political or educational reasons'. Nevertheless, it was pointed out on behalf of the NFER that the timetable implied that a single method of analysis would be used. This would be based on Rasch.

The 1977 Rasch seminar
The APU Rasch seminar was held on 5 December 1977 and involved 33 participants, including 10 from outside the APU and NFER. Four

papers were presented to the seminar.* Two of the papers (by Choppin and Willmott) outlined the work of the NFER on Rasch and justified its use on the grounds of its suitability for maintaining a large flexible item bank and achieving comparability over time. One paper (Elliott *et al*) described other work using the Rasch model. The final paper (Goldstein and Blinkhorn) was critical of the attempt to use Rasch in APU work on the grounds that its assumptions were educationally unrealistic. As in many of the later discussions about Rasch, the major obstacle to a resolution of much of the debate lay in the technical nature of the arguments used. As the report of the meeting notes,[177] 'the results of the Rasch model are difficult to explain to non-technical people, since their derivation is too complicated to be readily understood'.

The aim of the seminar was to inform members of the APU about the model and to establish common ground between its proponents and its critics. The first of these aims seemed to have had some success in the sense that some of the educational consequences of the model were discussed and appeared in the report of the seminar, and a little common ground on these seemed to have been established. Beyond this, however, there appeared a large area of disagreement over how well the model represented, or could represent educational desiderata. Since the resolution of such disagreements had to be based largely on technical arguments and analyses, it was fairly clear that the seminar did not greatly assist the APU in coming to any definite decision about its attitude towards Rasch. In the report itself there is an explicit statement that the NFER considered that the use of Rasch was 'experimental for time being'. The seminar established clearly that there were at least two opposing views about the philosophy and use of Rasch which the APU needed to recognise, even if the issues themselves were not properly understood in their full complexity. The working out of this conflict was one of the most persistent themes of the group's discussions during the following two and a half years.

Increasing doubts about Rasch

With the appointment of Goldstein to the group in February 1978, the debate over Rasch became a constant feature of Statistics Advisory Group meetings. The group returned to the subject of Rasch at its June meeting where the NFER's deputy director expressed some caution, claiming that 'the NFER was, in fact, taking a very neutral stance on methods of analysis in advance of data being available'. Nevertheless,

---

* For lists of participants and papers presented, see Appendix 7(ii), available separately from the Institute of Education.

others suggested that if the APU wished to measure absolute trends over time 'it would be necessary to use some form of latent trait (Rasch) modelling'. In response to this, it was suggested that 'the Unit might have to face the possibility that comparability over time was not possible'. By this time many of the arguments over Rasch were simply being reiterated, with little resolution.

The debate, however, had reached a wider audience. Following an article in the *Times Educational Supplement*[178] quoting the criticisms made by Goldstein and Blinkhorn, letters from Willmott, Goldstein and Blinkhorn, Leonard, and Wood provided a public discussion of the issues being debated within the Statistics Advisory Group. The APU was clearly unhappy with this and the chairman of the statistics group 'hoped it would be possible to continue the debate in private rather than in public'. At the July meeting, a further lengthy discussion of Rasch took place, going rather deeper than before into technical detail, but again without any clear resolution of differences.

At the next meeting in September, Nuttall produced a paper[179] in which he pointed to the logical inconsistency involved in assuming both that items may change in their relevance over time (hence the need for item banks) and that item difficulty remains constant as assumed by Rasch. He recommended the possible adoption of methods used by public examination boards to attempt to ensure year-to-year comparability of standards. In the discussion it is recorded that while there was some scepticism about monitoring 'absolute' trends over time, 'relative' trends were possible and useful. Little more seems to have been said on trends over time until the seminar on this issue which was eventually held in 1981. Enough had been said, however, to indicate that the possibility of making absolute comparisons over time, a basic aim of the APU, was indeed predicated on the validity of the use of Rasch.

At the end of 1978 a project to study the relationship between test item scores and 'exposure' was funded, and reported during 1982. Since the question of exposure was central to the arguments over Rasch, the decision to fund this project could be seen as an attempt to establish a basis for postponing again the need for a decision on the use of Rasch, presumably while allowing it to continue to be used for reporting results.

While the Statistics Advisory Group had no further serious discussion of Rasch until mid-1979, the Rasch debate did continue in academic circles outside the APU. In October 1978 the Schools Council held a one-day seminar, the papers from which have now been published[180] and in 1979 Dobby and Duckworth at the NFER published a booklet advocating the use of Rasch for public exams[181] which drew a highly critical response from Nuttall.[182] By 1979, therefore, a public debate over Rasch was in progress. However, it is clear that members of the APU were themselves hardly nearer a decision on the issues than they were at the end of 1977.

The 1980 Rasch seminar

In January 1980 Goldstein sent the chairman of the Statistics Advisory Group a technical paper on Rasch[183],[184] which claimed to have found certain statistical weaknesses in the model. This was discussed briefly at the February meeting, where it was announced that a full-day seminar on technical aspects of Rasch was to be held in June.

The seminar was held on 23 June and the participants included a number of academics familiar with testing techniques; the chair was taken by Professor Wrigley, an academic who had been involved with DES monitoring proposals since at least 1970. In reply to Goldstein's paper the NFER technical committee had prepared a paper[185] and, in addition, there was an NFER paper which presented some results of applying Rasch to the analysis of maths and language tests.*

The Statistics Branch of the DES prepared a full account of the seminar[186] and the presence of a deputy secretary and head of the DES Schools Branch III as well as the APU staff testified to the importance attached to the outcome. In fact, neither of these senior DES representatives nor the APU staff were technically competent to evaluate the argument. Rather, they seemed to be present to observe the duel in order to try to decide which side appeared the most competent. Despite the fact that the debate over the educational validity of Rasch had been thoroughly aired during the previous three years, the APU and the DES seemed, by June 1980, to be no more able to evaluate the issues than they were in September 1977. It must have been clear to them, however, that whilst there would always be room for a difference of opinion about educational relevance, when it came to possible mathematical flaws in the model there was the distinct possibility of an objective resolution of the debate which could find the model inadequate.

If the APU had hoped for a clear-cut verdict it was disappointed. Nevertheless, several interesting things did emerge which at the very least must have raised strong suspicions that all was not well. The NFER appeared to have retreated from its previous position of claiming that the Rasch model, as applied to an item bank, could be used to measure absolute trends in performance over time. It also appears that this time the NFER found itself almost alone in arguing the case in favour of Rasch, whilst the academics present were critical. No immediate decisions seem to have been made following this seminar.

---

* See Appendix 7(iii), available separately from the Institute of Education.

Nevertheless, it can be seen as a watershed; the NFER was seen as unable to respond adequately to all the technical criticisms and this led rapidly to a series of major changes.

In October 1980 the NFER told the Statistics Advisory Group that it intended to publish a description and justification of its Rasch analyses along with APU reports. The group discussed ideas for such a publication, including a free technical document to go with each report. In January 1981 the NFER produced a draft technical report[187] which gave details of how design effects were calculated and subgroups compared, together with a justification of the Rasch model and an analysis of some results from fitting it to 1978 and 1979 maths data. Following various comments a revised draft was submitted to the March meeting. There were several objections to the section on Rasch, and it was decided to delete all references to results derived from using the Rasch model and to invite the NFER and Goldstein together to produce an agreed revision which finally appeared in June.

By the March meeting, however, another series of events had effectively upstaged the statistics group's debates on Rasch. At the end of February the *Times Educational Supplement*[188] under a front page headline 'Pupil Testing may be Unsound', quoted the DES official report of the June 1980 seminar, and claimed that it 'lends weight to the claims made in the past by outsiders that the statistical method (Rasch) the Unit plans to use is at least questionable and may be completely misguided'. While the APU was still strying to make up its mind on the use of Rasch and indeed was actively considering asking independent statisticians for their views, the directorate of the NFER had finally decided that it was no longer prepared to stand or fall by Rasch. A point made by the official report of the seminar and quoted in the TES article was that the NFER was becoming increasingly worried by the apparent inability of its own statisticians to respond adequately to the objections to Rasch.

During the first half of March 1981 an agreement was reached between the director and deputy director of the NFER and Goldstein, by which the latter was to become statistical consultant to the NFER with a major brief to advise on alternative methods to the use of the Rasch model. Thus, by the time of the March meeting of the Statistics Advisory Group, the two main protagonists in the debate had joined forces. Instead of welcoming the apparent resolution of the prolonged conflict, however, the APU was not prepared to abandon Rasch, and in fact pursued the idea of calling in outside statisticians whose names were finally announced to the group in November 1981. The reasons for this unwillingness to abandon Rasch presumably came from the original reason for choosing that method, namely that of all the techniques available, it was the only one which claimed to be able to provide absolute comparisons over time.*

Generalisability theory

During 1979 the Statistics Advisory Group had begun to think about 'generalisability theory', a technique advocated by the science monitoring team as providing one method of answering questions about trends over time. Briefly, the technique involves the creation of a 'universe' of items, many more than would be used on any one test occasion, and then randomly sampling test items from this universe.† One of the aims of this technique is to study how the variation in test score is determined by the conditions of testing, marking, question format, etc. Under certain assumptions (see below) analogous to some of those used in the Rasch model, it could also be used to study trends over time, where different random samples of test items are sampled at each testing occasion.

In practice, there are several difficulties with this technique, notably that of creating a large enough 'universe'. This issue was discussed by the Statistics Advisory Group in April 1979 when members expressed their doubts about the validity of the technique when the universe of items was not very much larger than the tests selected.‡ Unlike the debate over Rasch, there was little disagreement but also little enthusiasm among the members of the group about generalisability theory. The issue tended to be discussed only when members of the science team were present.

Trends over time

Turning now to the explicit debate on trends over time, this surfaced during the period of discussion of draft reports and culminated in the June 1981 seminar. In the discussion of the second primary maths report, the Statistics Advisory Group wondered whether it would not be better to aggregate 1978 and 1979 data. However, since the two tests were almost identical it was accepted that 'carefully presented and low-key comparisons should be used'. At its next meeting in October 1980, the group became distinctly lukewarm towards these comparisons recommending 'deleting that part which referred to changes over time'. A compromise was announced at the December meeting. 'The Department had decided to retain some reference to trends over time, but with caveats as to their interpretation'. The conflicting advice must have created both difficulties and frustrations within the maths team,

---

* At the time of writing, May 1981, these statisticians had given a preliminary report to the APU but the APU's attitude towards Rasch seems still to be unclear.
† A recent review of generalisability theory is given by Shavelson and Webb.[189]
‡ The initial size of the universe was about three times as large as a test used in any one year.

particularly since at their March 1981 meeting, discussing the second secondary maths survey, the Statistics Advisory Group suggested that the 1978 and 1979 results should be aggregated. Once more however the APU decided that the results should not be aggregated, and announced at the June meeting that this time the solution was simply to delete all references to the 1978 results!

This continuing indecision once again shows the inability of the APU to plan effectively. In view of the fundamental importance of comparisons over time, and quite apart from the debate over Rasch, there was a need to formulate a clear view on the issue of aggregation long before the 1979 reports appeared. Naturally the uncertainty over the future of Rasch did not help matters and to some extent the APU may simply have been making *ad hoc* decisions deliberately, pending what they hoped would be a clear direction to emerge from the June 1981 seminar.

The decision to hold a seminar on trends in performance over time was announced at the January 1981 meeting. It was made clear that the seminar would not deal with Rasch but with alternative approaches. A wide spectrum of participants including academics and examination board researchers was invited as well as members of the monitoring teams and APU staff.* At the seminar, following an introductory paper from the APU, the three monitoring teams presented papers which described their current approach to measurement over time. The science team discussed their use of generalisability theory but had little to say explicitly about trends over time. The mathematics team's paper explained their eclectic approach, where they were looking at item clusterings, error types and studying changes in responses to items which were common from year to year. The paper from the language team simply explained their use of Rasch.

The three papers which followed these all made the same basic point that absolute measurements over time were not possible, arguing that once it was admitted that test items became more or less 'relevant' over time then their 'difficulties' would change, so that they could never form part of a common reference scale. This argument could be applied to generalisability theory as well as to the Rasch model, leaving the possibility of absolute measurement of change only for the set of items whose relevance remained constant – a restricted set of items which would be only of marginal interest to the APU. This viewpoint seems generally to have been accepted by those at the seminar. There was a discussion of the methods used by the GCE boards to achieve comparability over time using subject matter specialists, and the notion that *relative* changes (for example changes in the difference in mean score

* See Appendix 7(iv), available separately from the Institute of Education.

between Wales and England) could be measured. A further idea was that schools be used as the unit of analysis on which to base longitudinal comparisons across time, but this did not seem to find much favour, partly because it implied a deliberate sampling of schools on a rotating basis.

A representative from NAEP described some of the work of that project, and emphasised the pragmatic nature of their analyses in terms of grouping items together and looking at various possibilities for studying their changing characteristics over time. A sympathetic chord was struck in the meeting when he described the openness of the NAEP project to outside researchers and there were pleas for the APU to do likewise.

At the end of the day a clear message seemed to emerge: namely that measurement of absolute changes over time was not possible although relative changes were worth looking at. The implication of this was that, quite apart from the validity of educational and statistical arguments over Rasch, it could not provide measures of absolute change over time – one of the principal reasons for its advocacy several years earlier in the Bullock Report.

Conclusions

One of the most striking features of the Statistics Advisory Group is the way in which it came to assume the key research advisory role. Starting from a group intended to advise on 'statistics, sampling and item banking' it was eventually looked to, both by the APU and the teams, for wide-ranging comments on draft research reports and even for its views on 'political' acceptability. The APU, as early as 1977, was using the group to refine ideas and the Statistics Advisory Group at this time clearly saw itself in a research role, as is evident in its response to the NUT's criticisms. Much of the detailed discussion about background variables took place within the group, as well as the methods of reporting results. To a large extent, the role of the Statistics Advisory Group was determined by the absence of a specific 'research advisory' group but also by the personal interests of members of the group. What seems so surprising about this composition is the initial absence of research statisticians, save for one NFER member.

Why did the composition of the Statistics Advisory Group largely exclude expert research statisticians? Even allowing that suitable people might not exist within the DES, that Department's wide sponsorship of research as well as the numerous professional links of its statisticians would have allowed outside research statisticians to be identified and approached. This seems not to have been done, and one can only speculate on the reasons. Perhaps the APU felt that a single NFER statistician could provide all the necessary expertise. If this is true, as we are inclined to believe, then one might suppose that the additional non-statisticians were invited to join the group in order to give it a general research role from the outset. It may have been felt also that these numerate researchers would be able to translate technical considerations into terms intelligible to members of the APU and vice versa. A better name for the group therefore would have been 'Research and Statistics Group' for this is what effectively it became. Nevertheless, in spite of this *de facto* role, especially important after the demise of the Co-ordinating Group at the beginning of 1980, it remained primarily focused on statistical methodology and tended to approach a number of fundamental questions, such as those raised in the 'cognitive ability' debate, without the benefit of advice of members of other disciplines.

The relative absence of statistical competence in the Statistics Advisory Group may explain partly its somewhat surprising failure to give serious thought at an early stage to such obvious technical problems as large design effects and possible response biases, and to deal properly with the difficulty of obtaining accurate estimates of the proportions of low achievers. This happened despite the fact that quite a lot of time was spent discussing sample design.

The reliance of the DES and the APU on the NFER for technical advice is a feature which extends back to the very earliest discussions on monitoring in 1970. It is a little surprising, then, that on certain aspects of sampling there were important deficiencies. This is an area where the NFER seems to have had adequate expertise and yet, both on the question of sufficient numbers for studying low achievement and the possibility of non-response bias, the problems became acute before any proper discussion was initiated.

While we can only speculate on the precise reasons for these failures, they can be viewed as one casualty of the strict bureaucratic control of research exercised by the APU. The rigid timetable, determined it would seem largely by political considerations, the sensitivity to the issue of overburdening schools, and the fear of being criticised for biased 'interpretations' of the results; all these contributed to a short-term unwillingness to take difficult decisions for the sake of ensuring the long-term validity of the monitoring. Thus, even in 1981 when there was good evidence of high non-response rates, the Statistics Advisory Group preferred to wait several months for the next set of figures, rather than advise immediate action to approach non-responding schools. Above all, perhaps, the failure could be attributed to a lack of research expertise among the APU staff who chaired and serviced the group. Without an appreciation of research problems the APU staff were unable to initiate discussion of likely problems, instead having to rely on the monitoring teams themselves or the independent members of the Statistics Advisory Group. Given the pressures on the teams and the part-time involvement of the independent members, it is perhaps not surprising after all that some important issues were overlooked.

Finally, the Statistics Advisory Group's role in the debate over Rasch was crucial. It had been clear before 1977 that the monitoring of trends over time was closely linked to the use of Rasch, and any threat to the validity of the latter was therefore seen as a threat to a major aim of the APU itself. Perhaps more than any other issue this one exposed the inherent weakness of the APU. Having relied largely on the NFER for advice, it was unable to evaluate any criticism of this; it kept its fingers crossed and hoped either that the criticism would die down or could be resolved amicably within the APU structure. This did not happen, however, and the increasing public and academic discussion of Rasch posed a threat to the credibility of the APU. Moreover, by the time of the 1980 seminar the initiative in the debate had clearly shifted from the supporters of Rasch to its critics, with the former displaying signs of insecurity. The attempt by the APU apparently to postpone a decision by funding, for example, the 'exposure' project simply meant that the critics of Rasch were able to develop their arguments within the research community until the pressure of these was great enough to persuade the NFER itself to accede to them, thus leaving the APU holding the unwanted baby.

It is still too early to be certain how the APU will react to the debate about trends over time, although the results of a six-month NFER project (from January 1982) studying trends over time may help to move the APU in the direction suggested by the seminar.

Despite the critical tone of some of the above comments, the history of the Statistics Advisory Group is not solely one of missed opportunities and indecision. Towards the end of the period we describe, the group was flexing its muscles on several issues, it felt able to judge the political suitability of using a general cognitive ability measure and it ignored exhortations from the head of the APU to limit its comments on draft reports solely to 'technical' issues and instead, for example, commented on the teams' interpretations of their results. Moreover, it is clear that the monitoring teams took these comments seriously. In fact, the Statistics Advisory Group seems to have been the only forum where general and detailed research issues affecting all the teams were discussed and in this way it performed a useful role in bringing its expertise to bear to cross-fertilise discussions. Among other things the Statistics Advisory Group began to formulate its own view of what was educationally significant, having failed to obtain any guidance from elsewhere. It persistently criticised the APU on a number of issues concerned with the reporting and interpretation of results. The group also asked a number of pertinent questions, such as those about the definition of educational significance, often without getting adequate replies, and it had fruitful discussions about background variables and helped to clarify the notion of underachievement. It also held together remarkably well; despite the bitter dissensions over the use of Rasch, it was usually united on general research issues, its concern for research validity, and its sympathy for the difficulties of the researchers. Even if it was not successful in achieving all it wished, the Statistics Advisory Group did at least place a number of important ideas on the APU agenda, some of which may be bearing good fruit.

5 The Work of the Steering Groups and Monitoring Teams

Introduction

For each of the subject areas being monitored* the APU originally set up a working group to begin planning a monitoring programme. Once the monitoring teams were appointed, the groups assumed a steering role; for simplicity we shall refer to these in the text simply as 'groups'.

The maths team and the language team are based at the NFER, while the science team is based at the University of Leeds (assessment of 15-year-olds, data analysis and question banking) and at Chelsea College, London (assessment of 11- and 13-year-olds). The science team's position is different in several respects from the other two. First it is not at the NFER, secondly it monitors at three ages and not two, and thirdly it has had no forerunners to its work in the way that the maths and language teams have had. The team had to approach the monitoring *de novo* and they spent much of their time discussing the basic issues involved.

We deal with each of the subject areas separately but the material is arranged in the same order. First we look at membership of the groups and their early work; secondly we look at the monitoring teams and their approach to assessment; finally we look at how the groups and teams dealt with the major monitoring issues.

Of the themes outlined in Chapter 1, five are relevant to this chapter. These are:

Progress on the APU's aims

The creation of new instruments is the aim most obviously relevant to the work of the teams. All the teams have made significant progress in this area and have broken new ground, particularly in the area of practical testing. In addition, the science team, rather more than the

---

* Monitoring in first foreign language starts in 1983 and is not covered here. Critiques of the published reports by specialists in the field appear in Appendix 8, available separately from the Institute of Education.

others, has made some progress towards looking at performance in relation to the circumstances in which children learn. The teams have also done considerable work on measuring attitudes. The maths and language teams have used questionnaires with 10 per cent of the pupils tested asking about attitudes to maths and reading, while the science team and, since 1980, the maths team have looked at attitude-linked behaviour in the practical testing sessions.

Forward planning
The science team and group tried hard to make the APU look to the future, for example on the issues of interpretation of data and the possible effects on the curriculum, albeit with limited impact on the APU which seems to have been unable to engage in forward planning.

Consultation
The science team had the most consultation both within and outside the APU committee structure. Internally, it had many discussions, notably with the Statistics Advisory Group, but also with the Co-ordinating Group and the Consultative Committee. Many of the discussions in the Consultative Committee and Statistics Advisory Group about sampling and reporting were held in relation to the maths monitoring, however, because maths was the first programme in the field. For the language team, consultation within the APU was not difficult or laboured, largely because the team did not wish to pursue many contentious issues. As for consultation outside the APU, again the science team's activities were the most widespread. They consulted regularly with advisers and teachers to negotiate their view of the science curriculum, to validate items and for public relations purposes. The language and maths teams set up teacher liaison groups, often with the help of advisers, which gave important help with item development.

Constraints
All the groups and teams undoubtedly were constrained by both the Statistics Advisory Group and the Consultative Committee. This constraint was perhaps most crucial in the area of relational or background variables, although in this case the teams were eventually able to make some progress. The maths team was particularly constrained by the APU's initial refusal to allow interpretation of findings, which now shows signs of easing up. The language team were the least constrained by the APU committees because they wished to deviate least from the path laid down for them.

Research versus monitoring
The reason for many of the science team's attempts to negotiate with

the APU was their interpretation of their role as one of carrying out an innovatory reseach programme, rather than simply a monitoring exercise. This mismatch between the perceptions of the team and the commissioning body was greater for the science team than for either of the teams based at the NFER and seems, at least in part, to be due to the team's placement in Universities and to being given a task, i.e. science testing below CSE and GCE level, without a significant research and development history.

Science

Membership of the group

The science group met for the first time in September 1975. In the beginning, the group had six members,* two from Universities, two HMIs, including Brian Kay the first chairman, one teacher and one LEA officer. Although the minutes of the second meeting[190] state that 'The composition of the Working Group was intended to represent a microcosm of the world of science teaching', the group was short of teachers and in fact three teachers were co-opted a year later. They included, interestingly, a historian 'whose contribution to the Working Group would be mainly on scientific development in a discipline outside the traditional science subjects'.[191] Another of the teachers was appointed to represent informally the views of the Association for Science Education (ASE).

By 1981 the group numbered 12: there were two HMIs including the chairman; Professor Black from Chelsea and Professor Layton from Leeds represented the teams; there was a Polytechnic teacher, three teachers, two LEA advisers, a field officer from the Schools Council and an HMI from Wales.

The group's early work

At the first meeting of the group in 1975 the chairman and head of the Unit outlined the group's role:

It was expected not just to discuss the objectives of science in schools but also to make concrete recommendations about the efficacy of existing tests of attainment, and, where inadequacies in these were identified, to investigate and suggest alternative approaches. Within this general remit, the Group would have the widest freedom within which to operate. The Group was not expected to concentrate its efforts on underachievement but to look at the assessment of science across the whole spectrum of age and ability.[192]

Lengthy discussions on the nature of the assessment, what and how to monitor occupied most of 1976. A major problem inherent in science

* For a list, see Appendix 6, available separately from the Institute of Education.

monitoring which makes it different from monitoring in maths and language is that science at secondary level is an optional subject. Thus not all pupils have covered the same ground in science, so the group argued that they should try for 'content-free' assessment, i.e. one in which pupils' scientific development would be measured regardless of their exposure to science teaching. This meant that scientific processes rather than taught content would have to be assessed, but there was some uncertainty about whether such content-free assessment was possible.

Group members were clear that a major element of the assessment should involve practical work complemented by pencil-and-paper tests. Thus there was an early need to test the feasibility of appropriate observation techniques. It would be important, the group thought, to secure the active collaboration of teachers in developing assessment techniques and consultation with teachers and advisers has been a regular part of the science team's work.

The group was never happy about testing only at 11 and 15, the ages adopted for maths and language, and was always keen on testing at 13, the year beyond which science becomes optional. In late 1976, the group agreed[193] that monitoring should take place at 11, 13 and 15 'on the assumption that ages 11 and 15 were being imposed'. If age 13 was omitted, the situation would be different and the group would wish to reconsider the basis for assessment. The group did, in fact, agree that there was some point in testing at age 11, even though there would be difficulties in defining suitable content. 'Monitoring should take place in the primary phase because of the "cross-curricular" nature of science at this stage.'

The monitoring team
At the first meeting of 1977 the group was told that it was now time that it considered possible locations in which a future research and development team might operate. Funds had been allocated within the Unit's budget for a team to start work in September 1977. It was tacitly understood, according to the minutes of that meeting,[194] that the science team would not be at the NFER* (maths and language were already there) but the team would need to work closely with the Foundation. By the next meeting the group had received several applications, but 'enquiries from other sources had indicated that the Unit should open the field as widely as possible but because it would have been impractical to advertise or write to every research organisation, members had been asked to stimulate enquiries from other organisations thought to be suitable'.[195]

* Indeed, the NFER did not bid for the Science monitoring since they felt that they had no previous experience in this area.

Further proposals were forthcoming, and on 22 April an interview panel saw representatives from each of the seven research organisations interested in housing the project. The panel decided that it was not practical to locate the whole project within any one of these institutions. They recommended that the Unit explore the feasibility of dividing the work between the Centre for Studies in Science Education, Leeds and the Centre for Science Education, Chelsea,[196] and this is what happened. Why it was considered impractical to advertise is not clear, and since calls to tender for the most recent APU project – Modern Language Monitoring – were advertised in the national press, there clearly has been a change of heart on this issue.

The effect of placing the science monitoring outside the NFER
The main feature of the science team* – which will become evident – is their constant questioning of issues related to the APU's programme of work. For example, questions about the incompatibility of surveying and the identification of underachievement related to the circumstances in which children learn, was first raised in this group.[197] The science team did not embrace the contentious Rasch model, something which a team within the NFER would have found very difficult. Also, it was the only one to consider, in written form, the curricular impact likely to result from monitoring, on the grounds that this was inevitable and it was better to manage it than to ignore it. Professor Layton's 1978 paper[198] (which will be discussed in detail later in this section) on the interpretability and utility of the results of monitoring, was an early warning to the APU about its lack of forward planning; unless certain background information was collected, the results would be difficult to interpret and hence have limited usefulness. This was the trap into which NAEP had fallen and the APU should be careful not to follow suit. For this reason, the science team have persistently argued for 'relational variables', that is measures of school curriculum and organisation, home background and cognitive ability which they consider to be particularly important in science monitoring in order to interpret the findings. Indeed, partly because of their persistent lobbying and partly because of the position of science in the curriculum as an optional subject the science team have gone further down the route of interpretation than the other teams in the published reports.

The team's recorded attitudes towards APU decision-making stem partly from their university base. Research staff at a university are used to being given a brief by the funding body and being left to make research decisions. The NFER, on the other hand, is more used to

* The science teams will be referred to in the singular as in APU minutes and papers. This is for convenience and, although the two teams might differ in some respects, they are in accord on the major issues.

having a dialogue with the DES over what and how research is to be done. This is not to question the NFER's independence and integrity as a research body, merely to point out that it is a contract research body which is largely dependent on outside research funding and consequently will have a different attitude to funding bodies. Nor do we wish to imply that, as researchers, the teams at the NFER adopt different criteria to university researchers. Rather that they will realise their aims by different routes.

In practical terms there are some difficulties associated with having the science monitoring operating from three places: 11- and 13-year-old test development at Chelsea, 15-year-old test development and all data analysis at Leeds, and school liaison at the NFER. Those difficulties have not actually interfered with successful maintenance of the monitoring schedule, but it cannot always have been a happy arrangement.

Test development

The time allowed before monitoring got under way was much longer for the science team than the maths team. The science group first met in 1975 and surveying began in 1980, the maths group on the other hand first met in 1976 and surveying began in 1978. The science group and team had five years' development time compared with four years for language and two for maths. The science team, of course, had no forerunner in the guise of TAMS as did the maths team, or well-established reading tests as did the language team. However, even with their extra lead-in time, in the end they abandoned plans to pilot the assessment framework in the year prior to the first surveys. Instead, on the advice of the Statistics Advisory Group, the first year's monitoring was treated as a pilot for the framework.

The way in which science was to be assessed

The group and the team spent a great deal of time discussing what science is and what should be assessed. By the end of 1977 they accepted that it could not be assumed that science processes existed independently of the scientific concepts with which they were developed and it was not possible to assess scientific processes, or science activity categories as the team came to describe them, in isolation from the context in which they were taught. The team's view, which is implicit in their model of monitoring, is that science is to be viewed as a rational approach to problem solving in addition to a body of knowledge, though emphasis on the former is greater at the lower ages.

The team's case for assessing processes was made at a conference on assessment in Nottingham in March 1980. Reasons for this emphasis on processes were:

(a) the original curriculum model which was the basis for the APU policy, according to which the monitoring should relate to 'scientific development' from wherever it may spring and not be confined to what is taught in science lessons;

(b) the declared intention of the APU not to influence what is taught;

(c) the persuasions of the members of the Steering Group and the monitoring teams.

This emphasis has been criticised by those who consider that the science monitoring will not reflect what is taught: 'processes are not usually seen by science teachers as of central importance and they are not of central importance in most existing public examinations in science at 16+' is a typical expression of this point.

Whatever the rights or wrongs of focusing on process or content, the problem raised is that in a system with no central syllabus or core curriculum it is almost impossible for national monitoring to reflect what is taught.[199]

The decision about whether science monitoring should consider processes or content to be paramount was a vital one on the part of the science team with ramifications for the world of science teaching. Though it was decided that the monitoring should concentrate on the assessment of processes, nevertheless, the team argued, these do not exist in a vacuum and a field of content had to be defined.

According to an academic observer the difficulty in maintaining a clear distinction between processes and content was inevitable.

The formal properties of thinking in any area are so intimately bound up with the matter thought about that it is not at all clear how the one can be assessed without the other . . . in the sense that the content enters into the very conception of the processes themselves.[200]

In order to deal with the content issue, the team went through all published curriculum schemes and asked schools which of the areas listed in the schemes they covered.[201] The most commonly covered areas were included (after consultation with the steering group) in the team's list of science concepts and knowledge for ages 11, 13 and 15.

Thus the assessment framework is designed to explore understanding of scientific processes as well as concepts in various contexts, but the emphasis on processes is greater than has been the case in science testing previously. According to one of the head teachers on the group, science teachers are a bit sceptical about formalised assessment because it tends to concentrate on knowledge of content, and recently there have been moves to involve understanding of scientific processes more. This is what the APU team have aimed at.

Based on criteria for testing taken from the HMI secondary survey, a framework suitable for assessment was developed (see below). These criteria formed the six science activity categories which are used in the framework for the writing and reporting of questions. This was developed during the first 18 months of the team's life and was validated by 'eminent science educators'.[202] Validation of individual items is done by the same group of science educators who are sent items as they are written and then have to place them into categories. These items themselves are mostly written by the team and outside writers. Items are reviewed or 'shredded' by groups of teachers and team members, then given small-scale and national trials.

From the start the team developed practical items together with paper-and-pencil ones. Practical testing – which involves providing kits of materials and training teachers to supervise the testing – is expensive. At the first steering group meeting of 1979 the team reported that they were inadequately funded and, in order to undertake practical testing at the level proposed, they would need further funding. Team members reluctantly recognised that they would probably have to cut back on practical testing but hoped that there would be no further reductions. In fact the team was in luck; the APU had apparently realised all along that more money would be needed for the practical testing and an extra grant was duly made. This was a sound decision by the APU since in many respects the most interesting aspect of the monitoring is the practical testing – in maths as well as science.

The next decision the team and group had to make was whether to develop specialist tests (i.e. of physics, chemistry, biology, etc) for the 15+ group. At the start of their development work, the team decided to concentrate on general or common tests and to devise specialist tests a year or two later. The group were only happy with this as an interim measure but had to bow to the pressure of time on the team.[203] A year and a half later, however, (1980) the group seemed less keen on specialist tests, which in any case could not be included in the programme before 1982. The concern, apparently, was that specialist tests would help to entrench specialism when what was needed was a more balanced science curriculum.[204] The APU decided that extension questions would better serve the purpose of providing more information about the performance of children taking specialist science courses, and the team were asked to use more of these questions in 1981 and 1982. When it was discovered that the existing questions discriminated sufficiently well among 15-year-olds the need for specialist tests was effectively removed.

The assessment framework[205]
The monitoring teams have been concerned to develop test questions for the assessment of each of the categories. It was clear from an early stage that processes should not be viewed in isolation. The group envisaged the description of test questions in terms of three character-

istics: scientific processes, science concept and context. For each of the three monitoring ages, therefore, test questions could be located on a three-dimensional grid as shown in Diagram II. The six process categories are shown on the vertical axis, and concept areas and contexts on the two horizontal axes.

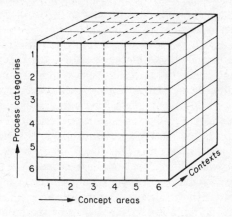

Diagram II   Three-dimensional Grid for Location of Test Questions

Process List (Science activity categories)   The list of processes sets out categories of scientific activity which are designed to be recognisable by, and have validity for, those involved in science education. It attempts to define the main aspects of school science teaching, so that a variety of audiences can benefit from the reporting of results in terms of its categories which are:
(1) using symbolic representations
(2) using apparatus and measuring instruments
(3) observation tasks
(4) interpretation and application
(5) design of investigations
(6) performing investigations

Concepts   The axis labelled 'concept areas' refers to a list that is constructed to illustrate the extent and variation of concepts likely to be covered by questions in the tests. The function of the list is to ensure that a proper balance is achieved in the setting of questions over the major areas of science.

Contexts   The context of a question is the setting in which ideas and processes are used and is represented on the oblique horizontal axis of the grid. From the many possible types of contexts three broad areas have been chosen: contexts of science teaching, contexts of teaching in other subjects, contexts of everyday or out-of-school situations. Thus, a question which involves the concept of keeping things hot or cold by insulation could be asked in the context of home insulation (an everyday context), of studying the conductivity of different substances (a science lesson context) or of ways people used to keep food cool in pre-refrigerator days (a non-science lesson context).

Monitoring scientific performance 'across the curriculum' The combination of concepts and contexts gives rise to two possible interpretations of scientific performance 'across the curriculum'. The first is the combination of science processes with science concepts in non-science contexts. The second interpretation of scientific thinking in other areas of the curriculum could be use of science processes with non-science concepts in both science and other contexts. The group felt that questions involving non-scientific concepts do not appear to have validity for monitoring scientific performance. There was also the danger that ways of thinking which are other than scientific could be wrongly ignored in marking these questions. Moreover, to carry out such a task would involve the identification of the range of non-science concepts from which those included in the monitoring could be taken and this would involve the description of all the concepts taught in school.

It was therefore decided that the most feasible and useful way of interpreting the monitoring of science performance 'across the curriculum' would be by setting questions which involve science processes and the use of science knowledge and concepts in contexts which go across the curriculum.

Attitudes The steering group is still exploring the possibility of assessing attitudes which are a part of scientific development. Two meanings of attitude in this context have been distinguished: attitudes towards science such as willingness to regard science lessons and the activities of scientists in a favourable light, and scientific attitudes which are more a part of carrying out science activities and using evidence in particular ways.

How the team dealt with the issues

Underachievement and in-depth studies We have already indicated in the introduction to this chapter that the science team took a more overtly questioning attitude to the monitoring programme than did the other teams. As mentioned earlier it was questioned in the steering group whether national monitoring and the identification of under-achievement relative to the circumstances in which children learn

(Task Four) were compatible.[206] There was 'a potential conflict within the Unit's terms of reference and tasks'. Since this early comment, the team have not attempted to deal with underachievement. No doubt, like the other teams, they are waiting for in-depth studies.

At the end of 1978 the team produced a discussion paper on in-depth studies[207] which began:

In-depth studies are frequently mentioned in our discussions – so frequently that they are coming to be regarded as an essential complement to the main tasks.

Two main types of in-depth study were identified:
(1) those which would provide information in order to improve methods of assessment and which would facilitate the main monitoring programme;
(2) those which would involve a more concentrated study of pupils in order to investigate specific factors such as aspects of low performance.

None of the other teams or groups had discussed what an in-depth study might be. This is thus another example of a characteristic of this team (and group): their concern to keep contentious issues open for inspection. This team, like the others, have been unable to advance from monitoring to the promised in-depth studies, something which has disappointed them. They have, however, managed to assimilate some of their ideas for in-depth studies into the regular monitoring exercise (see below).

Sampling   The sample size of 10,000 chosen for all three teams was not necessarily the one the science team would have chosen; it was the 'given' figure. According to science team members, the question of optimal sample size, and indeed the whole question of educational *vis-à-vis* statistical significance, has never been openly discussed in the group. Generally speaking there had been a lack of appreciation, particularly in the APU itself, of the parameters which should determine sample size. Only when monitoring was under way were the teams at the stage of knowing their instruments well enough to gauge how many questions they required to detect a certain effect. While the Statistics Advisory Group discussed this question early on, the science group was never involved in those discussions.

Related to the sample size issue was the school refusal rate. The science team found that there were more schools refusing to take part in the monitoring programme than they would have liked. They considered that they were suffering from 'impact build-up', being the third team to enter into the field.[208] The team requested that the Consultative Committee consider giving feedback to schools involved and in 1982 the APU started producing a newsletter for schools. Feedback of results is reasonably easy in small-scale research projects but is a much bigger and more expensive undertaking – some might say prohibitively expensive – for a national monitoring survey. There is evidence,[209] however, that schools are disappointed to receive no feedback from the NFER.

Analysis   The science team have used a different technique from the other teams in their analysis. They rejected the Rasch model for two main reasons:
(1) the variation of curriculum exposure and the effect of this on the difficulty of items.
(2) the apparent inability of the Rasch model to cope with non-dichotomous (i.e. not yes/no) items.
The technique used by the science team, generalisability theory, is discussed in Chapter 4 on the Statistics Advisory Group, and the reader is referred to that for further explanation.

Background variables   The measurement of relational or background variables is the issue to which the team devoted most time. The team's position was that one must have information on home and ability variables in order to say anything about the school factors that are related to performance. They considered three kinds of relational variable: home background variables, school variables, and individual 'ability' variables.

School-based variables were felt to be absolutely essential, above all at age 11, because at that age there is the possibility of little or no science teaching. Also, it is necessary to have an estimate of the resources available, physical and human, for the teaching of science in primary schools. At age 13, it is vital to collect information about the organisation of the teaching of science: whether it is taught separately or as an integrated subject, and the amount of time spent on it relative to other subjects. At age 15, there is the added problem of diversification into the various specialist groups and they felt strongly a need to describe these teaching groups in terms of some sort of ability measure so that the data could be properly qualified. It was argued that, since there is an interaction between ability and the curriculum followed, it is not possible otherwise to make sense of findings; for example, a group of children may do well on a physics test either because they are taught well, or because they are bright children.

The first tussle over background variables took place at the end of 1977 when the group and team considered the Statistics Advisory Group's paper[210] on the identification of variables in APU monitoring samples.* Members were unhappy with the small number of variables to be measured because it meant that information on the 'circumstances in which children learn' would be limited. Ideas were put forward for variables which ought to be included. The chairman suggested that a small subgroup should consider whether different variables might more profitably be used in science monitoring exercises.

At the first meeting in 1978 a member of this subgroup introduced a draft paper.[211] It was explained that science was at an early stage and had had more time than maths and language in which to identify variables and measure them. The main points were these:

(1) Members appreciated that without information on a number of variables it would not be possible to make corrections for their effect on performance and it would thus be difficult to interpret data from the monitoring exercise.

(2) The recommendation by the Consultative Committee that parents should not be approached for information would cause major difficulty in collecting information on some of the variables.

(3) The chairman suggested that many of the variables would be more suitably the subject of in-depth studies undertaken after areas of concern had been identified during the main monitoring programmes.

(4) However, 'It was recognised that the Unit could be open to criticism if it were not able to make some comment on the important factors affecting children's learning'.

This paper was discussed by the Statistics Advisory Group which threw out a number of variables the team wished to measure. The group was not too satisfied with the statisticians' response which was reported to them at their next meeting, and one of the HMIs suggested that a subgroup be established to investigate the possibilities of finding acceptable methods of obtaining information on variables such as pupils' home backgrounds without approaching parents.

At the same meeting in early 1978, Professor Layton tabled an important paper from the team on the interpretability and utility of the results of monitoring programmes.[212] This paper is a landmark in the story of the APU's inability to act upon criticisms of their programme design and planning, even when offered in a positive way by 'insiders'. Briefly, the paper's argument was this: the American NAEP project ran into criticism because, due to lack of forward planning, the results were of limited use to educational decision-makers and practitioners. While realising that the APU was in a number of ways quite different from

* It should be noted that the science group were not members of the Statistics Advisory Group which by this time had already assumed a general research advisory role. There were at least three NFER members of this group so that a consensus between the Statistics Advisory Group and the NFER teams was always more likely.

NAEP, the APU, including the teams, should be wary of falling into the same trap. In particular the paper made the point that the science team needed to seek reassurance that 'the variables included are ones which relate to possible remedial action for "underachievement".' Nowhere else in the minutes of any of the other APU groups and committees is the underachievement task mentioned in this way, that is as though it were real and actionable. Layton also wanted to make clear the responsibility of the teams in relation to the 'usability' of monitoring results. This responsibility should be agreed with the steering group 'so that at a later date *the teams* cannot be criticised for failing to "deliver" (as in the NAEP case).'

Certainly the science team could not be criticised for failing to attempt to produce results which could be related to the APU's aims and tasks. It is the APU itself, and the Consultative Committee, which has acted as a constraint on the teams in limiting measurement of information which could be used to interpret data. The paper did not arouse much interest within the science group and Layton was told by the chairman that 'only a limited amount of information can be collected during a monitoring programme'. This must be put alongside the view from the Statistics Advisory Group which was that some members thought that the approach being adopted by the science group was more appropriate to later in-depth studies than to national monitoring. Perhaps Layton's paper got a poor reception because it was ahead of its time: now that the team has some data members find themselves emphasising Layton's points more and more.

The subgroup that had been deputed to explore variables that could be considered unique to the science monitoring programme reported to the rest of the steering group in the middle of 1978. The paper, a crucial one,[213] recommended that several variables be employed. These fell into two categories:

(1) those which were essential to minimum data interpretation: general cognitive ability and home background.
(2) those affecting the utility of results: school-based variables.

Specimen home background and school questionnaires were offered as supporting documents, along with a specimen test held to be suitable as a general cognitive indicator. The group thought the paper 'a suitable basis for the investigation of variables, if this proved possible within the constraints of the APU as a whole'.[214] The paper was referred to the Statistics Advisory Group for comment.

As it turned out, the Statistics Advisory Group supported only the measurement of school-based variables and suggested that there be a small pilot exercise involving the school questionnaire. The science group was not very happy with this reply; it expressed itself still strongly in favour of using a general cognitive indicator and urged that the pilot exercises favoured by the Statistics Advisory Group be mounted as soon as possible. In the ensuing discussion, it became apparent that the group might have a different outlook and expectations from other groups. The chairman told the group that a number of members of other committees within the APU took a different view of monitoring and were less optimistic about how much detail it could be expected to reveal. In what had become a stock APU line, largely because of the Consultative Committee's decisions, the chairman reminded those present that even limited information was better than none.[215] Just how that sentiment was received is not recorded.

Unbowed, the team came back at the next meeting with a revised version of the subgroup's paper on relational variables. Again they talked of variables 'affecting the utility of results'.[216] The upshot was that the group recommended pilot trials of three instruments:

(1) a measure of cognitive ability (in defiance of the Statistics Advisory Group).
(2) a home background questionnaire.
(3) a school questionnaire.

Would the Consultative Committee and the Co-ordinating Group agree to small-scale pilot trials being undertaken? The answer from the Consultative Committee came at the next meeting: they could go ahead with pilot questions on the school-based variables; they could not proceed with the social background pilot and a decision on the general cognitive indicator was deferred pending a meeting between the science group and the Statistics Advisory Group to reconcile their differences. They could not proceed with the social background pilot because questions about home circumstances should not be asked of children, parents or teachers. The Consultative Committee thought that perhaps some information about social background could be collected at school level, and from existing statistical sources.

How did the group and team take this rebuff? A reply from Layton criticised the Consultative Committee's decision (and implicitly that of the Statistics Advisory Group on the general cognitive indicator), maintaining that the Committee had chosen to disregard the considerable expertise, care and effort which went into the preparation of the three instruments. He reiterated the science team's view that without information on relational variables the ability to interpret the science test results would be seriously weakened, perhaps even to an extent that called into question the overall value of the science-monitoring exercise.[217]

Eventually, the Statistics–Science subgroup agreed that, in place of the proposed general cognitive indicator, an ability 'composite', based on the results of maths and language monitoring, should be constructed. By asking pupils in the language and maths samples about the science curriculum they follow it should be possible to construct *group* measures of ability, which, in theory, could be used to 'adjust' differences in science performance, or at least help to explain them where they appear. A more detailed account of the discussion over the cognitive ability indicator is given in Chapter 4.

Did this 'composite' prove acceptable to the science group as a general ability measure? It was obvious that the science group was not happy with what the Statistics Advisory Group had pressed on it, mainly because the 'composite' would only provide *group* scores when what they wanted were individual scores. By the end of 1981 advances had been made on the ability 'composite' measure: for all children given maths and language tests at age 15 science curriculum information would be collected. Thus, information will be available on language and maths scores for children in different science curriculum groups.

The school questionnaire is in regular use, and a similar questionnaire will eventually be used by the maths and language teams too. According to members of the science team, however, more information on school-based variables is still needed and for some variables the information being collected is not fine enough.

Curriculum impact   We have already mentioned that specialist testing was dropped because of the adverse effect it might have on the curriculum. In fact, characteristically for this team, they were concerned about curriculum impact throughout the period of test development. Professor Black of Chelsea produced a paper in 1980 in which he stated that curriculum impact was inevitable and that the best thing was to 'manage' it.* The ways in which Black suggested science monitoring could affect the curriculum were: through *what* they were testing, through the test instruments themselves or through considerations of the results of monitoring.

. . . it is essential to arrive at implications in the knowledge that the monitoring relates only to some and not to all aims of teaching. There are other aims, not covered in the monitoring, and teachers will have to have regard to these also and to adjust the emphasis they place on various aims according to the needs of their pupils.

However, the monitoring does emphasise and report upon important aims of science education for all pupils, for otherwise the expense and trouble of the APU exercise could not be justified. To this extent we cannot avoid or evade the fact that we shall influence the curriculum and we shall feel more easy about this fact the better the job that we do.[219]

According to team members, it was the contact with teachers in the early days that made them realise that there would be an effect on the

---

* Interestingly, the current evaluation of NAEP adopts a similar line.[218]

curriculum and they have tried to make the DES aware of this. It is likely that the monitoring will have differential effects at ages 11, 13 and 15. At the primary level, teachers may be inclined to latch onto the list of science concepts – which indeed some people call a curriculum document – because of their great need for help and guidance in the teaching of science. For example, heads of primary schools might think that they should *start* doing something about science. Members of the group seem to be concerned that the list of science concepts is being called a document for a core curriculum, when they feel that schools should design their own curriculum. However, given that there is little guidance about teaching science at primary level (and few teachers trained to do so) one could say that they were being naïve in *not* expecting primary teachers to clutch at this straw. At a steering group meeting in July 1980, the team reported that there had been some discussion with primary science advisers over the list of concepts and, as a result, the team wanted to make minor alterations to it. The group, however, was very much against altering the concept list at this stage. The team also wanted more communication with primary teachers to explain that the concept list was not a list of what teachers should teach. The group suggested holding a conference of science advisers to put this point across and to clarify the status of the concept list. It was hoped that the advisers would bring the monitoring to the attention of teachers. This conference was duly held.

At the secondary level, there is more consensus about likely effects. The feeling is that the control of the examination boards over the curriculum far outweighs any impact that the APU could have. The team feel that at this level the test instruments themselves might be useful rather than the concepts, in other words, a rather different situation from that at 11. As yet, though, they detect no great eagerness among secondary school science teachers to adopt the assessment framework.

One member of the group felt that the team's emphasis on processes might have a positive effect in encouraging teachers to be more adventurous. In any case there have been recent moves towards basing teaching on processes rather than content. The science monitoring would accentuate that trend: 'Once you start assessing things like that then teachers will start to spend time on it'. Another group member thought the effects would be insidious, that is in terms of making teachers think about science teaching or think about teaching science. Within the group there is a fair range of opinion about the likely effect of monitoring on the curriculum, and it is an issue that the group and the team return to regularly.

Consultation   A theme running throughout this section has been the consultation that the science team have had with others: the steering group, the Statistics Advisory Group, teachers and advisers.

As early as 1977 the team produced a consultative document 'The Assessment of Scientific Development'. Several thousand copies of this were circulated and a summary was presented at the 1978 conference of the Association for Science Education. The team were seeking feedback, which they received – and, as a result, modified their process list[220] – and to inform the world of science educators, in which they also succeeded. As well as the presentation at the 1978 conference, the team did a display for the ASE annual meetings in 1979, 1980 and 1981 and intended to make a major contribution to the 1982 meeting. Conferences for science educators were held in 1978 and 1979, and in addition, a two-day conference of science advisers was organised for April 1981. The reason why the team and group have had a lot of contact with advisers was once explained in the minutes. 'Members agreed that advisers formed a useful link between the APU and teachers in the field.'[221] As with the maths team, there was also a direct line to individual teachers through their training as practical testers.

At later stages in the development programme, the team's aim was dissemination whereas at the earlier stages they were concerned with validation. Teachers were involved with both item writing and validation.[222] The team also carried out a consultation exercise asking advisers and teachers to write in and give examples of their curriculum, though only 40–50 people did so. Members of the team and group also had individual meetings with advisers because they were well aware of the possible impact on the curriculum and therefore of the importance of consultation and feedback. The consultation process and the public relations work seem to have resulted in the high level of acceptance of the monitoring.

Reporting   The other monitoring teams have been bedevilled by the APU's doctrine of facts-only reporting. For the science team, however, there has been some relaxation of this rule, and this will carry over into the future maths and language reports. When it came to writing the first report[223] there seems to have been little pressure for interpretation from the science team. The draft first report on 11-year-olds was written along broad APU/Consultative Committee lines, but made readers aware of the interpretative dimension by raising issues though not answering them. The team was then invited by the group chairman to 'write a story' about the findings. This invitation was accepted with alacrity and an extra chapter was added to the report.

Why should the APU have relented on its facts-only reporting policy? There are probably two answers: first the science team is last to report and it might have become clear to the Consultative Committee that the researchers were increasingly dissatisfied with the bald style required. Secondly, because of the background information collected by this team more interesting interpretation is possible and, indeed, because there is a system of options within the science curriculum, important. The science team have also gone beyond the others in the number of items they have released in their published reports: 20 per cent in the first 11-year-old report and almost 30 per cent in the first 13-year-old report.

To sum up, the science team and group have been seen to take issue with the APU and its committees in many areas: they first pointed out the contradiction between monitoring and Task Four; they negotiated on sample size; they were allowed to test an an additional age; they tried to get a dialogue going on in-depth studies; they declined to adopt the Rasch technique; and they have been allowed to use a questionnaire collecting information about the school and the curriculum followed by pupils. In all of these cases, the different style of the science group and team can be partly related to their 'outsider' role. They had no direct representation on the Statistics Advisory Group (until 1981), Co-ordinating Group or Consultative Committee and were not involved in the pre-APU discussions on monitoring. This, and the fact that they, more than the other teams, were breaking new ground are the two major factors which seem to have resulted in the different approach of the science group to the APU monitoring programme.

Mathematics

The mathematics group was set up in the Autumn of 1976 in the early days of the APU. As with all APU committees an HMI was selected as the chairman. Unlike other committees there was no change of chairman until Autumn 1980 when he was replaced by another HMI. In addition to the chairman, the group contained two HMIs, two academics, four teachers, one LEA adviser and two representatives from the NFER. By 1978 there were 17 members. Following publication of the first report the group was reduced slightly and by Autumn 1981 consisted of 11 members.*

One of the academics on the group was connected with the Tests of Attainment in Mathematics (TAMS) project and its extension. He actually developed tests for the extension project and was thus a link between TAMS and the APU in the way that one of the HMIs on the language group was a link between the APU and the Bullock Committee. As we said in Chapter 1 the APU maths project was seen as a continuation of TAMS; indeed, the TAMS project will be referred to several times in the following pages as we look at the work of the team.

Throughout the history of the group there were one or two dissenting

* For membership list, see Appendix 6, available separately from the Institute of Education.

voices to be heard. We shall outline these intra-group disagreements where they are important.

Tests of Attainment in Mathematics: the forerunner to the work of the group
The mathematics monitoring programme was a follow-up to the Tests of Attainment in Mathematics in Schools (TAMS) project, which was commissioned by the DES at the NFER in 1972. The APU's decision to monitor in maths was made in 1975 but the establishment of the working group was deferred until 1976 to await the completion of the TAMS extension project. The members of the group were fully aware of the expectation that they would use TAMS as their basis. At the first meeting of the group in 1976 the head of the APU informed them that 'the three years of research work already completed by TAMS meant that the job of formulating tests by the maths group was different from that of other groups which, with no pre-organised material available, were having to specify their own performance areas and commission research'.[224]

The TAMS research work covered not only the development of paper-and-pencil test items for use in primary and secondary schools but also the development of practical tests – a new area. In addition the TAMS project made a start on the design of instruments which 'could assess pupils' powers of generalisation and proof, their capacity for investigation and creative thought and their attitudes towards and about mathematics'.[225] There is no doubt that TAMS was useful as a source of items although, given the wider brief of the APU team, many items had to be revised. The group however seem to have been in doubt as to whether TAMS provided a suitable model on which to build a national assessment programme. In 1976 one of the academics in the working group drew attention to the conflict between the mainly content-based TAMS material and the Unit's intention to monitor ability and attitudes across the curriculum.[226] Although it was agreed that the two conflicting purposes could be combined, it was felt necessary to set up during 1978 a working group to 'look at the underlying philosophy of the Group's work, in particular whether TAMS still provided an adequate foundation'.[227]

The early work of the group
At the group's first meeting the head of the APU was there to brief the group. They were told that the assessment of mathematics (and language) was being given a high priority by the Department and the aim was to begin a national survey of mathematics by 1978. While he appreciated that the time-scale was short he hoped that, given the stimulus of the TAMS material, this would not be too impracticable. Members complained immediately that the time-scale would not per-

mit the production of high quality test material. This feeling of being rushed was a foretaste of what was to come since pressure of time has been a constant issue for this group.

Members were told at this meeting how to set about the monitoring exercise: the Co-ordinating Group and the Consultative Committee thought that assessment should take place at the end of the primary and secondary phases.[228] There was no serious discussion of testing at ages other than 11 and 15. On sampling policy the group was told at its second meeting in 1977 that a large initial sample of about 10,000 should be used to give a general stagement of performance and to provide general 'correlations'.[229]

The group was united in wanting to go beyond paper-and-pencil tests. They felt that practical testing was a priority even for the first survey and the head of the APU replied that it was accepted APU policy that non-paper-and-pencil tests could be employed, if desired. But at the second meeting in 1976 the chairman of the group stressed that their main task was to advise on the development of the final tests which would be mainly paper-and-pencil in the first instance. Other forms of testing would be explored, plus a wider range of mathematical ideas. For the present, however, it was necessary to make short-term compromises in order to meet accepted deadlines.[230] The chairman's directive notwithstanding, at the third meeting in 1976 the group resolved that the following four modes of assessment should be employed:

(1) paper-and-pencil tests
(2) assessment of practical maths
(3) observation
(4) coursework assessment.[231]

The group was successful in resisting pressure to concentrate on paper-and-pencil tests because practical testing began in 1978 at the same time as paper-and-pencil tests and an attitude questionnaire. Of observation and coursework assessment (modes 3 and 4), neither of which was investigated in the TAMS studies, little more has been heard.

The monitoring team and the assessment model
There was no question of the maths monitoring being done outside the National Foundation for Educational Research; since it was an offshoot of the NFER's TAMS project it was to be based there, and the research did not go to tender.

Members of the team first met with the group in mid-1977. Much of 1977 was taken up with reviewing TAMS items and considering the model of mathematics underlying the assessment. A particular issue was the number of content categories to be assessed and reported on separately. A curriculum framework was drawn up in which the assessment items were classified into five main categories of mathematics content (geometry, measurement, number, algebra, probability and statistics) and these were then further divided into subcategories. Towards the end of 1977 the leader of the team reported to the group that '13 traits or categories would be looked for in the analysis of the data'.[232] This concern over the number of categories was in response to an idea that was being put around at this time, that a single global score might be required for reporting purposes, that is for public consumption. The group agreed with the team leader and put on record that they were in favour of identifying 12 or 13 measurement traits.

For the written tests, the team at first concentrated on developing items assessing concepts and skills and analysing them in traditional ways, although there is now interest in 'error analyses', that is looking at the types of error made by different groups, for example high and low achievers.

Work on the practical tests, which got under way when the team started, was based originally on the TAMS extension project, although the team also produced a considerable amount of new material. Since 1978 the team have been developing items in a new area, problem solving. Work at first concentrated on practical items and since 1980 the practical tests have been made up largely of problem solving items. Written tests of problem solving were then piloted in 1980 and have been used in the surveys from 1981.

The assessment framework in 1981[233]

Problem-solving strategies   The main features of the current assessment framework (Table 1) are the same as those described in the first report of the secondary maths survey,[234] although it is continually reviewed. In 1979 categories of context were added to the framework in order to place more stress on the cross-curriculum aspect of monitoring. In 1980, the column in the framework labelled 'investigations and problem solving strategies' contained the initial assessment categories that were proposed during the development work in progress since 1979. In the 1980 practical survey three topics were related solely to problems in mathematical and everyday contexts. In addition, several of the more standard topics contained smaller-scale problem situations. Written tests of problem solving strategies were also administered that year to a subsample of the pupils who took the survey written tests of concepts and skills. These were revised for inclusion in the 1981 survey. Both practical and written modes present the problems in a structured form with questions on various aspects of the situation, leading the pupil progressively through familiarisation with materials and task to the

Outcome* Content**	Concepts and Skills	Problem-solving Strategies	Attitudes
Number	Concepts Skills Applications of number	Investigations/creativity: to be developed Processing information Formulating problems Strategies and methods of solution Generalising solutions Proving Evaluating results	Attitudes to practical mathematics; willingness to handle apparatus; confidence; anxiety about success; verbal fluency; persistence
Measures	Unit Rate and ratio Mensuration		Enjoyment, utility and difficulty of specific mathematical topics in the curriculum
Algebra	General algebra Traditional algebra Modern algebra Graphical algebra		Liking, difficulty and utility of mathematics as a subject
Geometry	Descriptive geometry Modern geometry Trigonometry		
Probability and Statistics	Probability Statistics		

* *Mode of Assessment* Outcomes can be assessed in written or practical test forms.
** *Context* The content can be set in Mathematical, Everyday or Other subject contexts.

main ideas which are involved. The possibility of including exploratory investigations to provide pupils with opportunities for more creative work is currently under consideration.

Attitudes   Pupils taking the practical tests in 1980 were rated by the testers on scales relating to their willingness to handle apparatus, and their confidence, anxiety about success, verbal fluency and persistence. These scales have been added to the diagram of the framework.

Concepts and skills   The main dimensions of the framework are content and learning outcome. It was recognised that the categories of learning outcome are not clearly differentiated and also that the classification of an item must depend in part on the way in which a pupil tackles it. The implication is that an item cannot be regarded as testing purely a concept or a skill, although it may focus more on one of these than on the other.

Mean scores are computed for each of the subcategories of content. For this purpose each item testing concepts and skills is assigned to one subcategory only – that one in which its content is considered to be most adequately represented. However, since mathematical ideas are highly interrelated, the boundaries between subcategories are not seen as impermeable. Consequently, in addition to subcategory mean scores the results of individual items are reported within groups or clusters of items of related content which may come from more than one subcategory.

'Concept' refers to mathematical entities such as 'parallel', 'angle', 'prime number', 'square root', 'equation', 'average', 'number', 'proof'. Clearly these examples are not all at the same level of generality: the structure of mathematical knowledge is viewed by the team as a network of linked concepts some of which are subordinate to others. Even the simplest concept has a large number of aspects, and a particular item may test only one of them. For example, concepts may be represented verbally, in a diagram or in symbols; several items may be required to assess each of these aspects. Additional items may be needed to assess pupils' knowledge of a concept's attributes (classifying and identifying mathematical entities or noting similarities and differences between them) and their understanding of its relationship to other linked concepts.

The main types of concept are:

(1) class concepts such as 'triangle', 'factors of 12', 'prime numbers', consisting of individual entities which can be sorted into groups labelled with the concept name;

(2) relations, which link two or more objects, e.g. 'is parallel to', 'is longer than';

(3) operations like 'multiplication', 'squaring', 'intersection', and 'enlarging', which are rules for changing the state of a mathematical entity; and

(4) notational concepts: the means by which mathematical relationships and ideas are represented. Notational concepts include 'place value', 'index', and ways of representing variables.

Since the understanding of mathematical concepts is viewed as a matter of the way in which learners organise knowledge so that it is readily and flexibly available for use in appropriate situations, that availability cannot be properly demonstrated without involving skills. 'Skills' are defined as learned routines such as measuring with a ruler, using a subtraction algorithm, drawing a circle with compasses. However, just as the availability of concepts cannot be demonstrated without exercising skills, it is argued that many skills or practised routines are dependent for their success on an understanding of underlying concepts. Moreover, as learning proceeds, the range of situations in which a practised skill can be used is widened and the range of procedures which become practised skills is also increased. Skills can be related to the five main categories of content but it is not supposed that each of the skills would be confined to items in the related main category (for example, that calculating skills will only be relevant to the Number subcategories or visualising to the Geometry subcategories). Concepts and skills are assessed in both of the modes used in the surveys, written and practical.

Requests for a break in monitoring

All the way through the history of the group runs a thread of members' concern that things were too rushed. The group had hoped, for example, that they could have had three pilot surveys, when in fact there was only time for one.

At the fourth meeting in 1978 it was accepted that the first round of monitoring would have many unsatisfactory features and it was proposed that the second round be delayed one year in order to study fully the outcomes of year one, although one member did think it was preferable to complete the first two years before pausing. No delays were to be brooked however – 'such delays in the programme would hamper the APU's function of detecting trends in performance'.[235]

A further paper in 1978 showed that in terms of workload the team was engaged on different phases of four different surveys (1978 primary and secondary and 1979 primary and secondary) simultaneously. 'These facts lead inevitably to the conclusion that the scale of the 1979 surveys would have to be reduced as compared to the first round'.[236] There was not only a danger of the 1979 survey being reduced but that the results of the first survey would not influence the second survey.

Part of the problem lay with turnover of staff on the team, and the resulting shortage of personnel. The language team had similar problems and in both cases it resulted in the team leader holding a reduced team together and struggling to keep to the timetable.

Later in 1978 a member of the group involved in educational research submitted a paper, 'The need for a one year break in the Mathematics Monitoring Programme'.[237] In this it was pointed out that the maths team was at a disadvantage compared with the science and language teams because of the speed at which they had to start monitoring.

A break of one year in the testing schedule would, we feel, allow the team the opportunity to undertake the sort of work which other teams have been able to carry out prior to their initial surveys, in particular the correction of the shortcomings which have become obvious in the first round of testing together with a considerable extension of the range of monitoring instruments available.

It would not be surprising, the paper concluded, if the quality of the maths programme was lower than the other two. A one-year break would enable the maths team to 'catch up', that is to do the thinking which the others had been able to do. These sentiments were echoed by the leader of the team, who said that they were having to concentrate on administration rather than research tasks; more time for development was required, however it was obtained. In spite of the comments, the chairman of the group warned that a break in the programme was unlikely to be acceptable before at least three rounds had been completed, 'because the Department believed that this would be needed in order to identify trends'.[238] The group endorsed the call made in the 'one-year break' paper but asked that it be redrafted, sent to the head of the APU, and also to the Statistics Advisory Group for its views.

The redrafted paper appeared early in 1979 with the revised title, 'A Consideration of Factors Affecting the APU Monitoring Programme in Mathematics'.[239] It went to the APU and Statistics Advisory Group as requested. The chairman of the steering group reported back to the next meeting that discussions held within the Department and the Unit had resulted in the decision that a year's break in the monitoring would not be permitted at present.[240] However, the group won a partial victory in the end. In 1980 the team was finally given notice of a year's grace: they were to test for each of the five years but no report was required on the fourth round of monitoring. What the team had really hoped for however was a break in monitoring, as well as in reporting, so that they could concentrate on the development of problem-solving items. Indeed it was not until 1980 that the team was informed that there were to be five years of annual monitoring; had the decision been made earlier, the team could have made more efficient use of the five surveys – another example of poor forward planning.

Consultation between the group and the team

Generally, the relationship between the group and the team was good but at the second meeting of 1978 the team leader, who felt that a lot of time had been spent in meetings on reviewing items, argued that he was not convinced that the group either could or should be the sole body responsible for the review of items. He thought that the steering group might spend less time looking at items and more on policy issues. Though the group's response to this suggestion was not recorded, at the next meeting it was resolved that at least one or two members of the group should stay close to item development and reviewing.[241] Since the work of the team has got under way the group as a whole has become more distant from the team. This tends to be the case with all the steering groups, and is no doubt one reason why the APU prunes the steering groups on publication of each team's first report. Now that the early planning phase is over, the ideas come from the team rather than the group.

Outside consultation

In order to provide more consultation to help the team in its monitoring programme it was agreed that four group members would explore the possibility of establishing small groups of teachers in their own areas. It was suggested that contact be made with two polytechnics and a teacher training college. Tasks allocated to these groups would be the production and review of items and the generation of ideas for extending the scope of the programme, both in terms of content and assessment techniques.[242] The idea of these teacher groups was eventually dropped because, as the team leader put it, 1978 was an extremely rushed year and they could not afford to have a timetable which depended on outsiders. This was an unfortunate side effect of the rushed programme of the maths team because it meant that apart from the four teachers on the group there was little early consultation with teachers.

Once the team began work on the development of problem-solving items, however, more consultation with teachers took place. The team held a conference on problem-solving in 1979 to which maths educators, teachers and academics came. After this they established teacher groups in Sheffield and Northern Ireland which discussed the team's framework for items. The groups were useful to the team both in making suggestions about the framework and in providing ideas for items.

There was also consultation with teachers via the practical testing. At each survey some LEAs were asked to provide a teacher who could be trained as a practical tester; the testers were then asked for comments on test development. Also, teachers who have been trained as practical testers in the past are sent new items as they are written, for comments and for piloting. Within LEAs there has been a ripple effect from training the practical testers, because more teachers get to know about the tests and are interested in them. The team now has videotapes available for training testers and hopes that this will form a useful part of in-service training.

How the team dealt with the issues

Underachievement An issue which the maths team have considered regularly is the directive in the APU terms of reference to 'seek to identify differences of achievement related to the circumstances in which children learn including the incidence of underachievement'.

This subject was raised by the chairman at the third meeting of the group in 1978.[243] He said that the Unit was becoming increasingly aware of the need to explain what was meant by underachievement in the context of APU national monitoring. There was not a great deal of debate within the group but two minuted points are worth noting: first that underachievement is difficult to define and, since it presumably relates to a pupil's potential, impossible to measure; secondly, under-achievement is not always low achievement since there could be underachievement within the higher ability range.

In 1980 the issue was brought up again. The discussion was insti-gated by a paper[244] that highlighted the concern of some of the members of the group that the APU's terms of reference were not being fulfilled. Though members appreciated the difficulties involved in measuring underachievement, they considered that there were three questions that should be investigated:

(1) Were children performing at their true ability level?
(2) How could the distinction be made between pupils of low ability and pupils who had been inadequately taught?
(3) Was it the same group of pupils who were underachieving in each area of mathematics?

The discussion of a further paper[245] on underachievement showed how uncertain the group was about the concept of underachievement. Most of the group thought that it must be related to the somewhat obscure notion of potential and saw that there was little point in attempting any absolute definition of underachievement. Instead most members agreed with the team leader that it would be useful to concentrate on low performance as one possible definition of underachievement, the definition now favoured by the APU (see Chapter 2).

The outcome was that in 1981 the group and team approached the APU with a request to carry out a study looking at profiles of per-formance of low and high achievers, and how these changed over time. It is not yet clear whether these studies will be funded in time for the retrospective report but it seems unlikely since one of the heads of the APU informed the group that the first priority for funds is for methods of analysing changes in performance over time. A six-month project on this started at the NFER in January 1982,[246] and reported in July 1982.

Background variables The other big issue to surface in group discussions was the measurement of background variables. Consideration of this issue was first minuted in 1977 when the group discussed the paper on variables produced by the Statistics Advisory Group.[247] Members thought the list far from complete: they wanted information collected about streaming, maths teaching and about the head of the school's maths department, for instance. The group was told that variables such as these had been discussed by the Statistics Advisory Group which found that they were impossible to define for the APU's purpose. They also argued that the inclusion of more variables would mean that the sample size would need to be increased. Members of the group did concede that a number of variables had to be ruled out but felt that some were very important and should form the basis for subsequent in-depth studies.

The findings of the first primary survey produced data on pupil/teacher ratio which was difficult to interpret as it showed that the higher the ratio the higher the performance. As a result in 1979 the team introduced into the surveys a question about the size of the teaching group, and data is now collected on this as well as on pupil/teacher ratio. Despite the Statistics Advisory Group's comments above, the team have also introduced questions about the qualifications of the maths teachers involved. From 1980 they have collected information on setting and streaming in the primary school. However, performance is not yet reported in relation to these variables as the team considers that these are still at the piloting stage.

In 1980 one of the group members produced a 'think-piece' paper[248] in which he pointed out that the variables against which performance was reported – area of the country, metropolitan/non-metropolitan LEA, size of school, type of school and number of free school meals – hardly related to the circumstances in which children learn. It was imperative to decide upon, and measure, the factors which influenced the effectiveness of the teaching/learning process. Possible factors were: length of service of teachers, initial and in-service training, style of teaching employed, use of text books and materials, aims of the scheme of work followed, and whether there was a post-holder for mathematics in the school. In addition, he said, there ought to be an extended enquiry into social variables which could replace the free school meals indicator which would cease to be a reliable measure of social need after 1981, because of recent legislation about LEA's responsibilities in this area.

At the first meeting of 1981 when a draft of the secondary survey report was being discussed the same LEA adviser argued that the pupil/teacher ratio variable was of no value and should be omitted.[249] The rest of the group, while agreeing that it was of little use, felt that it was up to the team to decide whether or not to report by any particular variable. This dissenting group member then suggested, as he had in his 1980 paper, that the team should investigate more relevant variables which would be of use to LEAs, for example those relating to the actual circumstances in which children learn. The team leader replied that they were analysing the location of schools using a categorisation developed by the HMI based on metropolitan/non-metropolitan area. The team did introduce this variable and the APU has subsequently asked the other teams to include it. A categorisation of schemes of work followed and the use of apparatus in schools will be included in the 1982 survey. The only variable which the team wished to measure and which has been turned down by the APU committees is home background.

The team's attitude to background variables, in general, is that many of these are difficult to define and members are not happy about including variables in the surveys which might be difficult to interpret. They have also delayed reporting performance in relation to some of the variables measured until they are convinced that these are measured accurately. They feel that their item cluster analyses are likely to provide more data for interpretation than information from poorly developed background variables. They suspect that variables which would be of value to them, i.e. those that affect maths performance, would be too 'slippery' to measure reliably, and believe that this sort of research is best done via in-depth studies.

Reporting   An issue over which the team most definitely felt constrained by the APU was that of interpretation in reports. In 1979 the draft of the first primary report was discussed and some members expressed a desire for the report to include more interpretative material, that is discussion of findings in relation to those background variables that were measured. They also wanted the reports to draw out points which they considered would be of interest to teachers. The response from the APU was that it was not the job of the team to interpret the data.[250] The group then asked whether its own commentary on the first primary report might be included as an appendix. The group was told that this might be possible[251] but they would have to produce a draft quickly in order to meet publishing deadlines. A member of the group did just that and produced a draft within a month. This draft argued that LEAs were intensely interested in information on school structure and facilities which promoted good learning environments, and that the report failed to provide this sort of information.[252] Not surprisingly, the draft was not considered suitable for publication as an appendix: the APU would hardly have wanted a dissenting voice such as this in their first published report.[253].

The group and team, whatever their views about the first report, were soon to get some feedback about its impact on teachers. First, they were told, very few teachers had seen it and even fewer had read it carefully. The group was very concerned about the lack of interest shown by teachers and wished to find some way of focusing their attention on the main issues. Secondly, comments from advisers had been mixed: many had criticised the analysis of subcategory scores by background variables as meaningless and unhelpful, while others recognised that the report could have valuable implications for in-service training.[254]

At the end of 1980, the same concerns were also expressed within the group: APU material, including report summaries, were not reaching classroom teachers. They wanted to know whether survey reports were useful to teachers and whether enough information was included to enable teachers to reach valid conclusions.[255] By the time the draft of the second secondary report[256] was discussed in early 1981 the situation had changed. The team was congratulated for producing a very readable document which contained much of interest for teachers. More specifically, on background variables, members welcomed the exposition of interrelations between variables which had been analysed in greater depth than hitherto.[257]

It seems that in this area, more than any other, the maths team has suffered through being a guinea pig. In producing a bland first report they were acting under instructions from the Consultative Committee which went to great lengths to remove words like 'only' from the drafts in sentences such as '80 per cent could draw the image of a simple figure in a vertical mirror but only 15 per cent could do so when the mirror was placed diagonally'. Naturally, this experience affected the way the maths team wrote their next report but neither they nor the other teams were pressed to the same extent again on style of reporting. In 1981 the maths team was asked by the APU to follow the style of the science team's report and this involved increasing the amount of interpretation of data.

Effect on the curriculum   The team leader's view on curriculum impact has always been that release of items could not possibly narrow the curriculum and he wrote a paper[258] in 1978 outlining this view. But APU policy was not to release items, save for the ones included in the reports. One of the group members, a teacher, was unhappy with this policy and in 1980 he presented a paper detailing some personal concerns. On 'washback' he asked a most pertinent question:

Are the NFER (and the APU) so worried about releasing material, that the few items they do release are actually more *harmful* in terms of the 'derision' they might attract or the over-narrow approach to teaching they could induce? If more and richer material were to be released, would not the dangers of harmful washback be reduced? [259]

This obviously set the group thinking along these lines, for when the new problem-solving tests were discussed divergent views about curriculum backwash emerged. The argument of those with fears was this: there is very little problem-solving done in schools as a rule, to do too much testing of it would affect teaching practice. Other members took the opposite view: since problem-solving is important any backwash would be positive and beneficial. [260]

The team's position on the backwash issue was this: they never believed that there would be teaching to the test except by the most thoughtless of teachers. If there were approximately 1,000 items per age group, how could teachers possibly train their children on this much material? The leader would be happy to see all the items released and, in any case, as reports are published the released material becomes richer and richer. In particular with regard to the practical testing and problem-solving items what the team had to ask themselves was whether they should deny themselves the chance of having positive backwash.

To summarise, this is a team which concentrated on test development. They produced (on time and despite staffing problems) tests containing a mixture of conventional items to assess the basic skills, and more adventurous material to assess newer curriculum areas. They were in the unfortunate position of being the first team off the mark and because of this they suffered in two respects. First they had a rushed timetable and secondly they were guinea pigs for one of the APU's least successful ideas, that reports should contain bland descriptions of only the baldest facts. Nevertheless, they were not slow to move away from these early constraints when it became possible to do so, and it seems reasonable to suppose that their experience and opposition to these constraints were important in making it easier for other teams to move away from them also.

Language

Membership of the group
At its first meeting in 1975 the language group consisted of two HMIs (one of them the head of the APU and chairman of the group), three teachers, one adviser and two academics. All of these original members,

with the exception of the chairman, were still in attendance at the beginning of 1980. The group members did a considerable amount of work in these five years. By 1980 there were two more academics on the group together with an HMI from the Welsh Office, an observer from Northern Ireland, an ILEA adviser with special skills in ethnic minorities, the deputy director of the NFER and the leader of the monitoring team.

The group was changed extensively in 1981; membership was reduced, but the group retained the same number of HMIs and the Northern Ireland observer, three academics, one adviser, two teachers and the leader of the monitoring team.* One of the HMIs has been the secretary to the Bullock Committee and thus provided a direct link between the Bullock Report and the APU language monitoring.

There is no evidence on how the group members were selected, though no doubt the time-honoured DES 'trawling' technique was employed. Nevertheless, members of the group are agreed that for the large part they shared certain basic assumptions, for example that testing reading through sentence completion tests was undesirable. This commonality undoubtedly make their task easier, though there was disagreement over one aspect of the monitoring programme – the assessment of oracy – as we shall see.

The post-war history of language testing

Of the three areas first chosen by the APU for assessment, science, maths and language, the last had the most precedent since there had been regular reading surveys since the last war.

The first of these surveys took place in 1948. It was run by the NFER and provided the basis against which subsequent results were measured. In the *Progress in Reading 1948–1964*[261] prepared for the DES it was claimed that over this period there had been an advance of 17 months in reading age for 11-year-olds and 20–30 months for 15-year-olds. However, it was thought by some educationists that the 1948 scores were depressed as a natural result of the war and therefore presented an artificially low baseline which would flatter subsequent test results. The first test used, the Watts–Vernon (WV), was a silent reading test of the incomplete sentence type. It had 35 items and took 10 minutes. Later the National Survey Six Test (NS6) was added (it was developed in 1954). This was similar but had 60 items and took 20 minutes.

The Watts–Vernon tests were used in 1952, 1956, 1961 and 1964; the NS6 in 1955 and 1960. In 1970/71 the NFER, at the request of the

---

* For membership lists see Appendix 6, available separately from the Institute of Education.

DES, undertook another national survey using the two tests with equal numbers of children. The NFER published a report on this survey called *The Trend of Reading Standards*.[262] This reported that mean scores for 11-year-olds had fallen slightly between 1964 and 1970. However, as the report showed the survey was beset with problems: there was a high refusal rate from the schools; it was conducted at the time of a postal strike which resulted in even fewer replies being returned; and some tests were destroyed in error. Also there was a ceiling effect on the tests, that is, they did not allow the older, more able children to show their full ability.

Largely as a result of the publicity surrounding the apparent fall in standards shown in the 1970/71 reading survey the Secretary of State for Education established the Bullock Committee to enquire into all aspects of the teaching of English. The terms of reference included considering the extent to which arrangements for monitoring the general level of attainment in language skills could be introduced or improved. The Bullock Committee examined the NFER reading surveys and said of the tests used that they did 'not regard the tests as adequate measures of reading ability. What they measure is a narrow aspect of silent reading comprehension'.[263] The Bullock Report went on to argue that these tests were also unsuitable because they had aged, for example, they used such words as 'mannequin' and 'wheelwright' which had become outdated by 1970 and therefore it was difficult to make valid comparisons of performance over time. The Bullock Report also commented on the need for a rolling system of testing, rather than four yearly bursts, but more importantly it expressed the belief that a 'monitoring system . . . must present a comprehensive picture of the various skills that constitute literacy'.[264] The role of the Bullock Committee as a precursor of the APU is discussed in more detail in Chapters 1 and 4.

The early work of the group

At the first meeting of the language group in October 1975 the chairman outlined the work of the language group as he saw it, namely to see how far they could carry out the recommendations of the Bullock Report, *A Language for Life*. He stressed that they were not to be constrained by testing at the ages of 11 and 15 which had been used in previous reading surveys.[265] The group spent the next four meetings discussing their task and planning how the assessment could fit into these guidelines. By the third meeting of 1976 papers had been written on the assessment of reading and writing. It was decided that the working group should decide as fully as possible the criteria for assessment of writing in order to give guidance to the test constructors for example, on spelling, punctuation, vocabulary and usage.

The group decided that there were several roles for the monitoring team besides carrying out surveys. They should react to feedback both from the tests and from the public reaction to the publicity material. What prompted members to say this is not clear, but it is one of the few times when accountability cropped up in discussions. They were also required to extend their work to explore oracy. The final role of the group and team was to pay due attention to the possible positive and negative effects of tests on teaching practice and the degree to which the quality of the learning process could be evaluated as well as the end product.[266] At their first meeting the group endorsed the cross-curricular model.[267] However, though there has been some contact between the monitoring teams, and, in particular, discussions on the use of language in maths and science assessment, there has been little progress in this area because of the practical pressures of surveying.

Given their link with the Bullock Committee, the team could not fail to be influenced by the recommendations of the Bullock Report. In assessing the tests used in previous surveys (Watts–Vernon and NS6), the language group agreed with Bullock that 'Tests limited to only one facet of a complex intermingling of skills cannot supply information of the right quality'.[268] It was decided that the APU surveys would try to test a wider variety of skills than those assessed in simple word recognition tests. Thus from the outset the group was committed to the assessment of writing and a wide-ranging assessment of reading. Another problem that Bullock and the language group were aware of, and keen to avoid, was that of the 'ceiling effect'. The tests used in earlier surveys did not do justice to the abilities of the more skilled 15-year-olds; even the hardest items in the tests were well within the bounds of the more able pupils. The group hoped that by keeping the items for testing 'open-ended' they could avoid that problem. The rest of this section will chart the tempering of the group's ideals with the practicalities of testing.

A further acknowledgement of the group's links with Bullock and the NFER reading surveys was the decision to give a subsample of approximately 1500 11-year-olds the NS6 test as well as the APU test in the initial 1979 survey, 'in order to relate results obtained in the 1979 survey with those of national surveys of reading carried out since 1955'.[269] The first primary report stated that there was no statistically significant difference between the scores on the NS6 and those found by the HMI using the same test as in 1976.[270] There is, however, little discussion of this point.*

---

* This issue is dealt with in the critique of the Language Report in Appendix 8, available separately from the Institute of Education.

The monitoring team

By mid-1976 the development of assessment techniques was a high priority; the chairman proposed that a team should be established at the NFER. There does not seem to have been any prior discussion or consultation – certainly none minuted – at the steering group meetings over who might do the monitoring and, like maths, the proposal did not go to tender. In October 1976, just over a year after it was convened, the group consulted with the Deputy Director of the NFER. She announced herself impressed by the range and richness of the tasks suggested by the group in two discussion documents.[271] She made the point, however, that the first priority was to decide upon the information needed and the type of report envisaged before detailed work could begin on test development – a rare example of a forward planning approach in the APU's work.

It was decided that the appointment of a team leader should be made in December of that year and the person chosen should start in April 1977. The post was not advertised; as the Deputy Director of the NFER explained, they had not obtained clearance on the terms of the contract until November 11, and in order that the new candidate might have time to resign his present position he must be selected before the end of December, and this had precluded advertising.[272] A team leader was duly appointed, whose previous experience had been mainly in the USA and Africa,[273] which was thought to be an advantage in that he would not be seen to be associated with any particular school of thought on language.

Though the team were based at the NFER, it was in agreement with the group that the old type of NFER reading test was unsatisfactory. The team have questioned very little of the APU's programme, in contrast to the science team, and saw their task as the straightforward one of monitoring, the research aspect being test development. They seem not to have been concerned very much with background variables, in-depth studies or underachievement and as a result led a much quieter life in terms of consultation with the APU than did the science team, or the maths team.

Test development and the relationship between the group and the team

At the first meeting the team leader attended he referred to the importance of consultation between the team and the group. The chairman replied by confirming that their proposals were guidelines, not directives, and that 'the aim of the group was to achieve a consensus of views including those of the project team'.[274] Thus the working relationship between the group and the team was clarified at the outset. It was not until 1980 that the joint heads of the APU provided terms of reference for the steering groups giving official recognition to what had

been worked out informally. These were:
(1) to provide professional advice and guidance to the monitoring team;
(2) To steer the monitoring team's programme of work according to the specifications already prepared;
(3) to advise the heads of the APU as appropriate.[275]
It was the role of the language group to produce a description of what they wanted to assess, and why.

It was then the role of the team to implement a testing programme, deciding, in agreement with the APU, which wishes of Bullock, the teaching fraternity, the politicians and academics were technically possible. This was a process of practical compromise between what was considered desirable and what was feasible. It was not a destructive process but inevitably entailed some dissension between the group and team.

The first real disagreement was in 1978 when the group discussed a paper on the progress the research team had made towards piloting the reading and writing tests.[276] This was the first time that material was presented to the group for discussion. Some members expressed reservations about the lack of open-ended writing questions and that the projected tests did not follow the guidelines originally laid down. Eventually the group accepted that the cost of marking and the difficulty of development prevented such questions from being used at this stage of the project. On reading, the group felt that there had been a marked shift towards closer control by the tester: 'The reading categories selected were open to amendment, realignment and involved the use of value judgement'.[277] In reply the team leader maintained that they had not excluded the group's original suggestions but had added to them. What the group was looking at was only a framework for pilot testing. He said that it was impossible at this stage to experiment on as wide a front as they had hoped. There was then general agreement that 'whatever happened in the pilot testing, the main survey package should be balanced'.[278] This is the only occasion that disagreement was recorded over the actual test material and was perhaps inevitable when the group was faced for the first time with tests which they had thought about with such care, but had handed over to someone else to produce.

Members of the steering group have commented on the constructive nature of the consultation between the group and the team. This is due to the fact that, partly because of the way they had been selected, and partly because of the general acceptance of Bullock guidelines, members of the steering group shared certain basic assumptions about the importance of viewing language assessment in the context of communication. Extended discussions in the team's first year enabled the group and team to come to shared viewpoints over basic issues so there was no danger of a real rift between them.

Teacher liaison groups were formed by the language team in 1977. It was hoped that these would be a means of getting teachers to help in item writing, but this was not completely satisfactory. They are primarily used now as a means of vetting material once it has been written, and in this their role is seen as very valuable to the team. Two groups have been involved specifically in investigating the feasibility of sampling written work produced under classroom conditions.

During 1978 the research team were busy with pilot surveys. The steering group were pleased with this work and commended them on their open approach and the 'exploratory way in which all possibilities were being considered'.[279] The team were also congratulated for their ingenuity in devising test booklets and keeping to schedule. Although the team kept up with their schedule, there were several changes in personnel. The result was that in 1979 the team was below strength and it was necessary in the first secondary survey to use some tests which had not been piloted, although the team felt that this should not cause problems, and that the APU might be open to more criticism if the survey timetable was not adhered to.[280] Although some work suffered, the leader, like his maths counterpart, seemed able to hold the project together well in spite of the shortage of experienced staff. The feasibility study on the sampling of written work produced under classroom conditions was concluded with the decision by the group and the APU that it should form a part of the monitoring programme.

1980 was a year of consolidation for the group and the team. The team worked to evaluate the results of the two surveys carried out in 1979. With more researchers on the team they were better able to assess the problems of monitoring. It also marked a developing interest in the feasibility of assessing listening and speaking skills. In March 1980 the NFER and APU organised a seminar on oracy. This was the year when the whole issue of assessing oracy was finally decided and pilot work for the survey of speaking and listening skills was begun.

The assessment of oracy

From the outset the Consultative Committee had always wanted to extend the work of the language group to assessing listening and speaking skills. At their second meeting in 1976 the committee stressed that the assessment of oral aspects of language should not be overlooked, even if there were difficulties.[281] At the third meeting of 1978 the language group urged the testing of oracy yet again, even at the expense of another language project. This followed the concern expressed in 1977 by many group members 'about the desirability and practicability of assessing in this area, but it was agreed that it should be examined and the Consultative Committee advised accordingly'.[282] However, the group had mixed feelings about whether oracy should be assessed. Though they agreed that the assessment of oracy was sound in principle because of 'the message you are giving to the public and teachers if you can't assess it', they also pointed out that the HMI secondary survey showed that in classrooms 'children are first listeners, second writers, third readers and last of all talkers'. It might be invalid, and possibly even hypocritical, to test something that was not a regular part of classroom activity. There is an interesting contrast here with the argument from the maths and science groups that it was beneficial to test something which might be done more in schools. There were also problems and questions about the practicability of testing oracy. The only previous model of oracy testing had been 'those dreadful CSE oral exams which are nothing to do with oracy but are spoken writing'. Fears were expressed over the role of the tester since it is difficult to test dialogue without the tester being in a superior position. There were added doubts about the problems of making valid comparisons over time.

Despite the doubts of the group, the team were enthusiastic about attempting the assessment of oracy in order to make the testing of language complete. The team leader produced two papers on oracy[283] and felt that a feasibility study could start in July 1979. The steering group agreed eventually that one member of the team should spend 50 per cent of his/her time on oracy. Following this decision three members of the Consultative Committee were present at the second meeting of the language group in 1979 in order to discuss the problems of assessing listening and speaking skills. They decided that because the previous oracy tests, which had been mostly at secondary level, were so inappropriate the APU work should start from scratch.[284]

It had been hoped that the piloting of oracy tests would start in November 1980 but it did not start until October 1981, due to the continued shortage of personnel. Thus it does seem that, although early progress was slow, the assessment model will eventually encompass a wide range of skills and tasks, as the group had always planned.

The assessment model

As we have already made clear, there was assent among members of the steering group and team that it was necessary to make the APU surveys different from the previous national reading surveys carried out between 1948 and 1971. They decided that the tests had to assess not just the ability to identify words but also to monitor reference and interpretive skills. The team leader has stressed that the previous tests used only 'completion of incomplete and uncontextualised sentences',[285] and thus the results from these tests provided no direct information about the ability of pupils to carry out the practical reading tasks with which they were faced at school or outside.

Reading[286]   In the first primary survey, and probably in the majority of subsequent surveys, pupils are asked to complete one of ten different reading tests. Each reading test yields evidence relating to pupils' responses with respect to between 20 and 50 questions. The tests take different forms. A number take the form of a short booklet containing a number of thematically linked expository materials with a page of contents and an index. Other tests comprise works of literature, such as poems or short stories which are included in their entirety. A further set of tests include materials that pupils would encounter outside school, for example, in a newspaper or holiday brochure.

In the majority of cases questions require open-ended responses. The guiding principle used in devising questions is that they ought to reflect 'those that an experienced reader would be likely to address to a text if it was encountered in a realistic social context.'

Writing   In assessing writing, the team has devised a range of writing tasks at both age levels intended to allow pupils to display their mastery of language in writing produced for particular purposes and a variety of readers. In the 1980 primary survey, for example, pupils were asked to complete one of ten writing booklets, each of which entailed the completion of four tasks: a short writing task common to all booklets, one of ten diffcrent longer writing tasks, a text-based exercise such as editing or note-making, and a final section comprising several short questions relating to pupils' attitudes to writing.

After each writing survey all the scripts written by the pupils are marked impressionistically by a panel of 40 teachers. A subsample of the scripts are marked analytically by a second panel of assessors. A third group of assessors mark the editing tasks and tasks that can be marked with reference to a checklist.

Activities involving listening and speaking   From May 1982 the language surveys will include tests and procedures designed to assess pupils' performance in tasks involving listening and speaking. The starting point is an attempt to differentiate between the different purposes for which pupils use sustained and purposeful talk in the classroom and outside it. For example, in the initial survey pupils are asked to describe a scene or process, explain a point of view, expound and defend a viewpoint and engage in discussion both for purposes of argument and collaboration. In a further set of tasks pupils are asked to listen to and interpret a variety of spoken discourses including stories and more anecdotal accounts and sets of instructions relating, for example, to a game the pupils play or a model that they assemble. The majority of such tasks involve pairs or groups of children working in collaboration with one another and with the assessor.

Writing tasks employed in the 1980 primary survey
Pupils were asked to produce writing relating to three of the following activities, one of which was common to all ten writing booklets.

*General purpose of writing**Written outcome or product*

1. To describe
    a) Faithful description based on similarities and differences between two pictures.
    b) Description based on personal knowledge.

2. To narrate
    a) An autobiographical anecdote.
    b) Original end to a story selected by the pupil.

3. To plan   An account of an activity to be undertaken.

4. To report   An account of something learned.

5. To request   Letter to a person in a public institution.

6. To change the readers' mind/to persuade   Dramatised argument from a particular viewpoint.

7. To explain   Explanation and justification of a personal choice.

8. To express feelings   Response to a given poem.

9. To record   Autobiographical account of recent experience.

Text-based work

10. To edit   Editing a written account.

11. To annotate
    a) Captions to diagrams.
    b) Structured note taken from text.

12. To announce   Devising a posted based on notes.

In all of these tasks, variation in *readership* and in the writer's control over *form* was evisaged.

While this brief outline has referred to the different areas of language assessment it should be noted that a number of the exercises devised are composite tasks which involve, for example, reading and writing or listening and speaking, or all of these.

How the team dealt with the issues

Effect on the curriculum   The impact of language monitoring on the curriculum was an issue that cropped up occasionally. In the autumn of 1976, a member of the group was concerned that one stated aim of the research team was to 'extend and modify the test material to make it suitable for the use of LEAs'.[287] He thought this would increase the danger of backwash, notwithstanding the reduced danger of this if the APU used light sampling. The chairman replied that they knew LEAs were undertaking assessment programmes 'using generally unsatisfactory methods'. 'A subsidiary role of the APU was to improve the quality of assessment techniques'.[288] The ensuing discussion, however, outlined the relationship between the APU and the NFER's LEASIB, rather than dealing with curriculum effects. After this, the only significant reference made by the team to the possibility of curriculum impact was in their consultative document 'Language Performance' which was published in mid-1978.[289] In this they said:

while the whole APU monitoring exercise has been deliberately designed to minimise any 'backwash' on the curriculum, it must be accepted that assessment procedures may transmit messages to teachers about curricular priorities. Accordingly it is essential for the APU to produce national forms of assessment that do justice to the intuitive model of writing acted on by most teachers. (p.2)

In proposing that pupil performance should be monitored through a response to a wide range of reading and writing tasks, we have sought to emphasise the functional nature of language, which is reflected in the varieties of language met with in the school curriculum. In this way, we hope that the monitoring process will not be something divorced from the learning process, but rather a contribution to it. (p.6)

The group and team, as it happens, have never really expanded on this issue, unlike the science group and team which have devoted considerable time to it.

Nevertheless, shortly after this document was produced, the chairman of the APU received a letter from an adviser and a co-ordinator of an LEA English Centre who were both members of a liaison group of teachers set up by the monitoring team. They criticised the model of language used and its effect on teaching practice, the effect on the curriculum of not testing certain aspects of language, for example oracy, and also some of the writing tasks.[290] In response the leader of the language team said at the next group meeting that these queries were characteristic of teachers with a background in English literature and secondary school teaching. These were not in general the views of teachers at the level of the particular reading test booklet which was criticised. Also, they were not the views of other teachers on this liaison group.[291] Yet again, there was no serious discussion of curricular impact or a reconsideration of the model used.

Once the primary language report was leaked in 1980, however, discussions were brought out into the open. A junior school head who had been involved in one of the writing surveys wrote to the *Times Educational Supplement* complaining that one of the techniques used in the writing tests – that of basing written work on passages read rather than on direct experience – encouraged bad practice in teaching.[292] This drew a reply from the group member who had first raised the issue of backwash in 1976. He pointed out that he and other group members were concerned about curriculum effects and for this reason had tried to make sure that the APU tests did not too much misrepresent the nature of reading and writing. Though he agreed that the writing tasks could be improved, he felt that the group was aware of the need to minimise the harmful effects.[293] The team has, however, received far more comments commending the departure from the conventional methods of assessing reading and writing than it has had complaints. Indeed the Senior Chief Inspector, in an address to the NFER conference,[294] said that the impact of the tests in schools was likely to be a beneficial one.

Background variables An issue which did not generate much steam in this group was that of background variables. Towards the end of 1977 they were told that they would be 'informed' of the variables to be included when these were decided for the maths monitoring. There was no further discussion of this until early 1978 when the group expressed disappointment that the Consultative Committee had decided that no additional variables were required for the monitoring of language. They felt that as a result it would not be possible to make decisions about resource allocation and mentioned that the Statistics Advisory Group had recently reached the opposite view, that is that a measure of social background was essential for meaningful analysis.* The team leader asked about putting in a 'discreet enquiry' about the language of the home into the pilot survey of the language tests.[295] The group approved, and the Consultative Committee was approached. Later in the same year it was reported that the committee was content for the development of a 'home language' variable to proceed, provided that it did not arouse controversy. This was a typical comment from the Consultative Committee but one wonders why they were happy to allow it at all, in view of their extremely reticent attitude towards other home variables.

Why were the group and team apparently uninterested in background variables, apart from the first language of the pupils, when these caused such concern elsewhere? According to the team leader, at the beginning their main concern was with developing instruments

* They subsequently changed their minds (see Chapter 4).

which would work. By 1981 their instruments were 'highly refined' and they were then in the position of wanting to get more information. However, this would be information related to schools and not to the social background of the family. This point was enlarged upon by a member of the group; it was no bad thing not to be measuring social background since these effects are well known and there seems to be very little one can do about it. More to the point would be measures of the organisational structure of the school which could be compared with children's performance, for example, whether children were withdrawn from classes for remedial teaching. Other members of the group agreed that measures of social background in language performance were not very helpful; it was more important to know how the school intervened between social class and reading performance. However, one area which the team investigated is that of children's exposure to reading and writing activities inside and outside school and this information was related to language performance.

Reporting   The team had no tussles with the Consultative Committee over their style of reporting. There seem to have been two reasons for this. First, when the language team wrote their first report it was still the case that the APU was in favour of the straight reporting of results and against interpretation and team members must have been aware of this. Secondly, it is possible that the Consultative Committee had a different expectation for the language group than for the maths group because language assessment is seen to be a more value-laden activity. Members of the group, however, admitted that they found not having value judgements in the reports, 'an APU house rule', very difficult at first. One view was that it would have been useful, for example, to say what proportion of the population was 'illiterate' since this is the sort of easy figure that those outside the world of education appreciated. Also there was little in the reports for anyone's real comfort or fear, so that if people were to ask 'What is the situation?' (re literacy) or 'What is the point?' (of the testing), it would be hard to answer either question. Another member was more optimistic about the impact that reports would have on teachers: those with an interest in language would find them useful and the reports would form a large part of in-service training.

As for the pressure to report annually, the team had longer to produce their first report than did the maths team. They did, however, find it difficult to write the second report before getting any feedback from the first report. Like the other teams, they welcomed the respite from annual reporting which the APU allowed them and chose not to report on the third of the five years' surveys (1981). They chose this year rather than the fourth year because 1982 was the first year when all areas (i.e. including oracy and the sampling of written work) were to be tested, and a report then would be important.

Underachievement In the early days particularly, the team considered underachievement to be part of their brief. As the piloting of reading and writing tests got under way, the team grew increasingly aware of the problem of assessing children for whom English was a second language. Given that one of the Unit's tasks was to investigate underachievement, this seemed a valid issue to pursue. How this assessment might be made was a frequent topic of discussion during 1977, but it was difficult to reconcile the need to study the language problems of ethnic minorities with the related problems of underachievement and the difficulties that such a form of assessment would bring. It became clear that the team would not be able to take this on without extra manpower and funds. The problem was eventually taken out of the hands of the language group when the West Indian Study Group was set up (see Chapter 2). After this, though the team reported on the performance of children whose first language was not English, it did not again broach any ideas for looking at underachievement or doing in-depth studies; presumably members felt that they had wasted enough time already and had their hands full with the assessment of oracy. Rather like the maths team, given time they would like to investigate differences in performance between the sexes and to investigate other characteristics of low and high achievers by analysing their types of error.

To summarise, this is a team which concentrated on developing assessment materials. As they were breaking new ground in the assessment of writing and oracy, this was no mean task. As for their larger role within the APU monitoring programme, the team seems to have concerned themselves with this hardly at all; they were given a task and concentrated on that. The team had the advantage of following on from the maths team, who were the guinea pigs, so that issues like reporting style were already being thrashed out. In common with the other teams however, they were under considerable pressure to stick to a 'rigid' timetable, and were largely successful in doing this.

Conclusions

How far has the work of the groups and teams contributed to progress in the APU's aims?

As the preceding pages have made clear, the teams have been assiduous in their task of test development and the carrying out of regular national surveys. Though there may be some criticism of the test material there seems to be a widespread feeling that it is on the whole good, perhaps better than many people expected.* There can be

---

* No formal evaluation of the tests is possible because the item banks are closed.

little argument that they have broken new ground, in particular in the areas of practical testing in maths and science. Indeed, the tests are to date clearly the most important outcome of the APU's work, and this is not surprising because test development is the only task that has been dealt with seriously. Monitoring change over time has come to nothing so far because, although the maths team is nearing the end of its five-year cycle and data over time is available, it is still not clear how this will be analysed. Likewise, no progress has been made on under-achievement though not for lack of trying on the part of some members of the groups and teams.

It is becoming clear that the reports are not getting through to teachers because of either their cost, their style or teachers' general unwillingness to read research reports. This is in spite of Kay's early insistence that APU findings should be of 'interest and concern to the teacher'.[296] Whatever the reasons, it does seem a fair assumption to make that if the reports were different in style and/or content they would at least be more accessible to teachers.

Practitioners at the HMI and advisory level may well find parts of the material useful for in-service training, for example, the maths concepts and science categories and the lessons to be learned from practical testing. There is evidence that HMIs would like to expand their role in exploiting the APU material in this way and this could be valuable (see Chapter 6). As for policy makers, the results as they are presented in the reports are of no value, because the background variables used are too gross, and as far as policy decisions are concerned, useless. It is of little practical value simply to know that more 11-year-olds in the South can do simple fractions than in the North. The APU has fallen – with its eyes wide open – into the NAEP trap. Though warned by the first head of the Unit that the American national monitoring results were of little use to policy makers at either local or national level, the APU and the DES have failed to avoid this situation themselves.

Why did the APU and DES not plan ahead more thoroughly so that this could have been avoided? They had, after all, plenty of prodding from members of the science team and the maths group. The answer to this lies partly in the Unit's insistence that monitoring was the business of the day. For the APU, monitoring and research are not the same thing (though few researchers would want to make such a distinction). Monitoring must come first (and that has meant, in practice, with as few background variables as possible); research may come later. All the teams are disappointed that the promised in-depth studies have not yet materialised and indeed do not seem to be on the agenda for the immediate future. The 'monitoring as opposed to research' stance may have had its repercussions on the staffing of the monitoring teams: all three teams have had problems with turnover of junior staff. The constant pressure of work combined with lack of opportunity to 'side-track' into interesting research issues have taken their toll. Though all the teams have kept up with their timetables this is hardly a satisfactory state of affairs.

In summary, the major achievement has been in test development; the reports have been disappointing at both teacher and policy maker level. If the dynamic members of the teams and groups had not been constrained by the APU and the Consultative Committee, the type of information collected and its presentation in the reports *could* have been more valuable. One must conclude, however, that it was the role of the APU, not the groups and teams, to aim for reports that were useful. In this task, then, the APU has not succeeded.

6 The APU and the World of Education

Introduction

In this chapter we examine the APU's relationship with other bodies and the reactions of various parts of the education world to the APU. In analysing the APU's relationships with others we have been conscious that the Unit's influence may be propagated in several ways. There exist in many cases direct links on a personal level through the APU's consultation process where individuals and representatives of various bodies, such as the teacher unions, sit on the APU's committees. The surveys themselves may be expected to have an influence directly on the schools and teachers involved in the testing and, because some practical testing is carried out by teachers who are specifically trained for the task, these testers may themselves disseminate information about the APU's work. This level of dissemination has sometimes been organised by LEAs which use the skills acquired for in-service courses for other teachers. Also the APU itself has provided courses and regional conferences to inform LEA advisers and others about the Unit's work. Finally, there is the effect of the APU's publicity material and the published reports and here the style of reporting is important. The reports often result in media coverage which is the means by which most people obtain information about the APU.

First, we look at reactions to the APU voiced by LEAs who responded to our questionnaire and interview survey carried out in the spring of 1980.* We then look at reactions, largely from press reports, of other educational bodies to the APU's work. Finally we look at the APU's relationship with the bodies that were most significant to it: the DES, the HMI, the NUT, the exam boards and the NFER. Of the themes and issues outlined at the beginning of the report two are of particular relevance to this chapter: consultation and reporting.

---

* The teacher survey which took place in the Autumn of 1981 will be reported separately in: *Testing Children*, Heinemann, forthcoming.

Reactions of LEAs

In April 1980 a questionnaire was sent to all 104 LEAs in England and Wales asking them about their testing activities and about their contact with the APU.[297] Information was provided by 84 per cent of the LEAs. The findings from the questionnaire survey are reported in section 1 below. We subsequently visited a sample of 30 LEAs across the country and interviewed senior staff about the same issues in more depth. What they said to us then is described in section 2.

1. The survey of LEAs

Number of schools involved in APU testing   Only 64 per cent (56) of the LEAs sampled supplied figures of the number of schools in their area involved in APU testing in the 1980 surveys. The rest either left a blank or said that these numbers were not available. Because of the limited information supplied it was not possible to look in detail at the percentages of schools sampled in different LEAs. It was apparent nonetheless that the percentage of schools sampled in the Welsh LEAs was considerably higher than in the English LEAs. This confirms the known higher sampling rate in Wales documented in Chapter 4.

Light sampling   Of the LEAs that responded, 37 per cent said that the APU's commitment to light sampling had not influenced their own thinking about intensity of testing. A further 18 per cent said that light sampling was not relevant to them, because their testing programmes were for screening or record-keeping purposes when information was needed on all children. Only 14 per cent (12 LEAs) reported that the APU's light sampling policy had had some effect on them, in addition to 50 per cent who thought they might use light sampling in the future. This does not meant that these 12 LEAs used light sampling; two of them did not even have testing programmes, and two stated that though LEA officers were convinced of the value of light sampling they had yet to persuade Education Committee members. In all, 12 per cent of LEAs used light sampling and, of these, three reported that this policy had been decided independently of the APU. All in all, the DES 1978 Report on Education[298] warning of the dangers of blanket testing and recommending that monitoring be carried out using light sampling like that of the APU, would not appear to have had much effect. We do not have to look far for the reasons. First, most LEAs are not testing for monitoring purposes and so light sampling is not suited to their needs. Secondly, if an LEA does have a testing policy, then head teachers prefer to have information on all the children rather than just a sample. As one LEA reported, rather dolefully, they use light sampling because of the APU but heads want blanket testing, and this comment was repeated several times in the interviews with LEAs. One metropolitan borough said that the APU's light sampling policy had 'highlighted the (unnecessary?) intensity' of their own programme. But this has certainly not been the country-wide response.

APU impact As for any other influence on their existing testing programmes that the APU might have had, 22 per cent of LEAs said that it had had none; 14 per cent reported that they were interested in the NFER's Local Authorities and Schools Item Bank (LEASIB) and 11 per cent had noticed an increase in general interest and discussion about testing and assessment as a result of the APU. Four LEAs thought the practical testing useful and were developing it. Only three thought APU testing might have a dangerous effect on the curriculum. No clear picture emerges of its effect on LEA testing; one LEA reported that it had eased the introduction of LEA testing, one that it had lessened the demand for testing, and one that it encouraged blanket testing requests from politicians.

The biggest group, however, almost a third (30 per cent), made no response to this question or gave an answer which was irrelevant. This, together with the high proportion which said the APU had no effect, suggests that perhaps half the LEAs in the sample had not really taken much note of the APU, as though it was something that was going on elsewhere which did not affect them.

Nevertheless, some LEAs were well informed about the APU programme. In all, six LEAs commented with some care on how the APU programme had underlined the importance of clarifying the objectives of testing. For example, it had:

drawn attention to the need to define objectives in testing and to use questions which seek information about a specific aspect;

underlined the importance of clarity of purpose in introducing assessment schemes;

helped convince Education Committee members of the complexities and dangers, as well as the benefits, of testing and assessment procedures;

reinforced the view that testing should only be carried out when the results it yields are of real value;

confirmed the opinion that a great deal of thought and co-operation is required in defining what is worth testing, so that if it influences teaching, as it invariably does, then worthwhile things are taught and proper approaches and concepts encouraged;

and according to at least one outright sceptic had resulted in:

An increased awareness of the limitations of assessment technology, also a regret that a considerable 'act of faith' is required of the educationalist in accepting the validity of statistical processes.

In-service training In reply to a question about whether the APU had led to any in-service work with officers, advisers, heads or teachers it appeared that here the APU had had some impact. Almost half the LEAs (47 per cent) reported in-service work of some sort, though this varied from a one-day course a year previously to much more extensive programmes. A further nine LEAs said that discussions had been limited to advisers. Clearly the advisers would not keep the outcome of these discussions to themselves but would have passed information on to heads and teachers, and indeed advisers are an important link between the APU and teachers. A third of LEAs (34 per cent), however, reported no in-service training on the APU at all, a figure which the Unit itself might well find unsatisfactory. Though the Unit is aware that few teachers are well-informed about its work, if LEAs are not providing in-service training then there is little chance for teachers to become well-informed.

The response from one of the London boroughs perhaps sums up the situation:

The APU has made little impact on schools. Although the process which the APU teams have used to 'describe' their particular areas of learning should be useful in assisting teachers to reflect upon their schemes of work, the information has not been digested widely.

2. *Interviews in selected LEAs*

Thirty LEAs were chosen from the original 87 and detailed interviews carried out in the Autumn term of 1980. These LEAs were selected to provide further insight into testing procedures and motives on a case-study basis rather than to establish precise estimates for the whole country or to make comparisons, for example between metropolitan and county authorities. Essentially they all had testing programmes which were being operated for a wide range of reasons. Twenty-three LEAs commented on the impact of the APU in their area. Interviews were conducted with senior advisory, administrative and psychological service staff and what we will be reporting here reflects their views and not necessarily those of the LEA as a whole.* The LEAs split evenly into those which reported that the APU had had little impact in their areas and those which thought there had been some effect.

---

* We refer to 'LEAs' however for ease of reporting.

Low impact LEAs Of those 11 LEAs which felt there had been little APU impact, one had deliberately not asked schools for feedback about the actual testing because they thought of it as a confidential exercise. The inspectors interviewed here thought that the press had had a fairly major role to play; though teachers had not read the information sent out by the APU they had picked up quite a lot from the press. Parents, too, were becoming more informed about, for example, standards in maths because of articles about the maths reports. In an LEA close to one of the monitoring teams the authority had held meetings about the maths report and generally tried to keep schools abreast of what was going on. They confessed that, despite all their efforts, the APU was very little known, even less understood, and there was little interest in it. Another LEA which had left all the schools involved in the testing well alone had actually organised a conference for teachers on the APU. Even so, the APU had a fairly low profile, 'but that's typical of *x*, there's no sweeping desire for change'.

One LEA reported that, although they had run courses and had had APU people up to give talks, the APU testing had had little impact; it was something that schools did and then sent off. In one LEA where they felt that the impact of the APU was negligible locally they speculated that the impact would be negligible nationwide. A metropolitan LEA which had given their heads and teachers ample opportunity to hear people talking about the APU felt that, even so, many teachers did not know much about it. This was for three reasons: first that communication within a school was often poor, secondly that the acutal testing programme was not particularly relevant to the busy classroom teacher, and thirdly that the reports did not draw conclusions. An insight into teachers' reactions was recorded in an LEA which said that when an HMI connected with the APU came to talk about the maths reports he was 'slated'. The response of the teachers was: 'why tell us *what* we know, why not tell us *why*?' Sometimes the actual test materials were seen to be more useful than the reports themselves.

These comments reinforce what has been said elsewhere in this report, namely that the APU exercise might have more impact if its reporting style were different, i.e. if the reports had more in them to interest the teacher by way of interpretation of results.

LEAs reporting some impact Ten LEAs had done something positive about the APU which they felt had some effect, though again, impact of the APU testing in schools was small. An LEA close to one of the monitoring teams had, through their advisers, a lot of contact with that team. Teachers had been involved in evaluating items and the area had been used as a 'test bed'. This had resulted in a lot of spin-off within the authority which they felt was beneficial: 'the APU provides an agenda about which one can talk'.

As for the effect on the curriculum and teaching practice generally, in-service training via advisers seems to be the main way in which the APU is having some impact. One of the metropolitan LEAs had made a point of incorporating the list of concepts and categories in maths and science into their in-service training. This was the first time that there had been such national guidelines in maths and science and they intended to make use of them. Another metropolitan area had put a lot of emphasis on the APU monitoring programme in their in-service training. As a result, they felt their teachers were better informed than many, a sentiment that was confirmed by their experiences in interviewing teachers from other LEAs for Head and Deputy Head posts. Their maths guidelines, while having a parallel philosophy to the APU were not, they said, based upon it. On the other hand the APU's list of science concepts and categories had formed the basis of a two day in-service course that they had run. Far from being afraid that this would control the curriculum they said they would be pleased if primary teachers *did* teach to this list because it would mean that they were at least beginning to teach science.

Three LEAs felt that the APU's work would widen the curriculum and they welcomed this. One mentioned the maths tests particularly, another mentioned both maths and language tests. These had had a sobering effect in their schools because many of the children had never seen some of the material that they were supposed to deal with in the tests. The effect was to widen teachers' ideas and, as far as they were concerned, this was the APU's most important contribution. The third LEA was looking to the APU to widen the curriculum, that is to make other areas of the curriculum seem as important as reading and maths. If the APU could show, for instance, that science could be tested at different ages this would be very influential as far as their Education Committee members were concerned. In trying to widen the curriculum this authority had produced guidelines in history, geography and science as well as maths. What they felt they needed now were testing programmes to complement these guidelines. Testing programmes developed within the authority would not be acceptable to their Education Committee, hence the need for tests from a national agency. This LEA clearly had high expectations of the APU. Yet another LEA had produced maths guidelines because of the APU. However instead of using the APU maths categories, which were thought to be in danger of defining the curriculum too rigidly, it had developed its own guidelines which covered all the APU topics and more.

Practical maths testing was mentioned several times as a useful exercise and this was no doubt because teachers were involved directly in it. Not only did teachers who were trained as practical testers benefit directly, but they usually became involved in in-service training and helped to spread interest in practical maths and problem solving. One adviser did think, however, that as the seconding of teachers for practical testing was an expensive exercise it might be better to sink the money straight into in-service training. Maths was mentioned most often by the LEAs because this was the only subject which had been reported on by the time we carried out the interviews. Comments ranged from the detailed ones described above to more general ones, for example that the value of the maths reports lay in their impetus on teachers' thinking about teaching maths 'rather than just doing it'.

Negative impact in LEAs   The other two LEAs (out of the 23) made negative comments on the APU. One said that the HMI primary survey had had far greater impact; they were particularly critical of the first reports maintaining that it was virtually impossible to use them constructively. The other had pinned great hopes on the APU but felt that the testing programme produced by the APU would not add constructively to the evaluation process.

Overall, we found little evidence that the APU was seen as a danger to the curriculum. On the contrary, some saw it as a tool for curriculum development and improvement. Throughout the interviews a recurring theme was the hope that the APU would provide LEAs with new testing material which they could use locally. They would then be able to compare their figures with the national ones obtained by the APU. However, we encountered few LEAs which had a clear idea of what LEASIB was and how it would operate although they were aware that this was the vehicle for their link with the APU. They were simply waiting for it and when they were told it was operational they would use it. (For a history of LEASIB see the end of this chapter). As we described in Chapter 4, the LEASIB project will not now provide tests linked directly to APU tests. It seems likely that LEAs eventually will have access to the APU items themselves, but this is not a simple operation to organise and will take some time to effect. If it were to happen that APU test items were used on a large scale in LEA testing programmes it would be very difficult to avoid the criticism that the APU was helping to dictate the curriculum; we shall return to this topic in the final chapter.

Press Reports of Reactions from Other Bodies
In this section we study the *public* reaction to the APU. A search of the Press from 1974 to 1981 shows a fair amount of coverage for the APU in educational papers such as *The Times Educational Supplement*, *Education*, *The Teacher*, etc., and comment on the published reports in

most of the national daily papers.* It is also interesting to look at the comments made in the media by those closest to the APU's work, that is members of the teaching profession, advisers and academics.

The National Union of Teachers has been a regular commentator. In 1977 the Vice-Chairman of the NUT's Education Committee explained the Union's attitude to the work of the APU. The Union was not opposed to the suitable monitoring of educational progress, but was committed to resisting the imposition of an externally determined curriculum and of universal testing at particular stages of education, either at LEA level or nationally. The Union had several reservations about the APU. Would the information given by a set of tests have more influence in resource allocation than the local knowledge and expertise of teachers, advisers and LEA officials? Even if it were possible to assess personal–social development to what use would these findings be put? Indeed, for what party political purposes might the results of the overall monitoring programme be used?[299] In the same year quite different concerns were voiced by a member of the NUT Executive who was a member of the APU's Consultative Committee. The very existence of centrally administered tests, he argued, can have a powerful influence on the curriculum for there is a strong temptation for schools to place greater emphasis on those areas of the curriculum which may be the subject of tests. The other danger as he saw it was that 'once given their heads, the professional test merchants may not know where to stop'. This enthusiasm had already manifested itself in the APU's proposal to monitor political and environmental awareness (later called personal–social development).[300] By 1978 the first-mentioned NUT commentator was suggesting that, particularly at the primary level, if information on national standards was needed it would be better obtained by bringing together groups of teachers to compare their work and the standards they achieved. In this way teachers could form judgements in the light of their knowledge of the pupil's background, resources available and comparability of syllabuses. This sort of exercise could involve conventional standardised tests of basic numeracy and literary but would be a more human process than that proposed by the APU.[301] He did not, however, expand on whether or how this approach would satisfy the public or the politicians. The Union's concern over the monitoring of personal–social development was voiced much more strongly in 1979. The Chairman of the NUT's Education Committee said that though the Union agreed that the Unit had a job to do, and was happy with the amount of consultation taking place, (indeed, as we have discussed in Chapter 3, the APU has,

---

* For a full list see the Chronology in Appendix 9, available separately from the Institute of Education.

through its consultation process, carried the NUT with it), it disagreed with the Unit over the proposed assessment of personal–social development. The scheme was badly thought out and badly designed; if the job was to be undertaken at all, it should be done by the Schools Council.[302] In 1981 the Union strongly opposed the proposed West Indian survey. While they were in favour of monitoring the performance of children of different ethnic groups, they were against the APU doing it; they would prefer surveys by the HMI which could take all the relevant factors into account. In addition, they did not wish their teachers to have to identify West Indian children for testing as this would damage good race relations in schools.[303]

Of the other teacher associations, the NAS/UWT had most to say publicly. In 1978 the assistant general secretary gave a 'progress report' on the APU in the Association's journal. He outlined the Assocation's attitude towards the work of the APU: assessment was acceptable just as long as the procedures were sensible and the use of results appropriate. On light sampling, matrix sampling and anonymity he reported that the APU's plans should allay any fears about problems stemming from invidious distinctions between pupil and pupil or school and school. The APU's plans thus far were acceptable; however, there were serious reservations about the Unit's proposal to test in the area of personal–social development.[304] In early 1981 it was reported that the NAS/UWT too were concerned about teachers being exposed to criticism if they had to select children for the West Indian survey.[305] In mid-1981 the deputy general secretary commented on the poor dissemination of reports among teachers. He agreed that this situation was not satisfactory because the reports contained much that was of importance for teachers. But, in their defence, he said there was little money around in schools for providing books for the children, let alone the staff.[306]

LEA advisers did not, as a body, have much to say publicly about the APU but one maths adviser did write two lengthy articles in the *TES*. In 1977 he criticised the Unit's lack of statistical awareness in areas like sampling design, testing methods and analysis.[307] In early 1980 he commented specifically on the first primary maths report. Though it contained much new and useful information about children's achievement in maths, particularly in practical work, it did not provide a baseline with which future results could be compared.[308] In mid-1981, however, the president of the National Association of Inspectors and Education Advisers, speaking as a private individual, called for some discussion and understanding between the Examination Boards and the APU. It would be undesirable if the APU were to measure national performance by one standard when students' performances were measured against a different standard. He voiced what many in secondary education probably feel, that since the exam boards exert a more direct influence at the secondary level the impact of the APU results might be limited. However, given the anxiety over the statistical methods used to analyse the results, there would be many who would not regret this limited impact.[309]

The Institute of Physics and the Institute of Mathematics and its Applications both commented at some point. The Institute of Physics, reacting to the science team's discussion paper in 1978 dismissed it as vague, threatening and jargon-ridden. They felt that it left out important facts about how testing would be organised, what the long-term objectives were and what action would result from the tests.[310] The Institute of Mathematics and its Applications commented in an article on the primary maths report entitled 'Scandal of the dunces'. A spokesperson for the Institute said that there was a basic weakness in maths in most schools at all levels of ability and suggested, in an apparent *non sequitur*, that schools should recognise that arithmetic ability included the ability to get the right answer.[311]

There has been some academic comment about the test material, the value of the findings and the APU's impact on the curriculum.* Early in the life of the surveys a mathematics educator wrote about the APU and the value to teachers of the maths tests. His conclusion was that it was right to be cautious about any increase in the amount of testing to which pupils were subjected, but that the APU surveys could provide useful information for the teaching profession. The test material, representing as it did a considerable advance on what had previously been available, could be useful in schools for diagnostic and remedial work.[312] In mid-1980 two academics voiced their concerns over the APU. One was concerned that the surveys as they stood would not provide the sort of information which would enable educators to interpret the levels of performance reached by various children and this was essential if the results were to be of any value. Ultimately however, in order to investigate cause-and-effect relationships in-depth studies and action research would be needed. The main fear of teachers to whom he had spoken was that the APU's testing programme would ultimately be used to define what should be taught in every school.[313] This concern was echoed by the other academic, who described how he thought this might come about. The route was an indirect one based on the connection between the APU test items and the NFER's LEASIB test items. The danger was that the APU's curriculum model might provide a framework for LEA assessment programmes and thereby a means for introducing an agreed curriculum. The danger lay in the

---

* Statisticians and researchers also debated the pros and cons of the Rasch model; this argument is covered in detail in Chapter 4 on the Statistics Advisory Group and is not repeated here.

narrowness of assessment programmes – a result of both the expense and the difficulty of monitoring in a wide range of subjects – which then specifies a curriculum of basic subjects and within them a specific and limited range of competencies.[314] The present director of studies for the Schools Council went so far as to call for the APU to be scrapped. He described both the APU and LEA testing schemes as a 'costly diversion' from the important task of assessment in which schools needed to engage. Resources were too scarce for such blatant misapplications to be countenanced, and teachers must be given a key role in assessment and decisions about any national curriculum framework.[315]

In 1981 a curriculum specialist published a book containing a chapter on the APU[316] which represented the most extensive critique of the APU at that time. In this he outlined how he thought the DES, via the APU, was set 'to achieve national curriculum control by stealth'. And how once set up the APU was unlikely to be closed down:

It is a characteristic of pluralist societies . . . that it is relatively easy to allow new organisations to come into existence, and almost impossible to get rid of them. As soon as they become institutionalised, their adherents form a political power base and what might at first have come about largely by chance suddenly appears to fulfil an irresistible purpose. Even if some future administration resolved to close down the APU, it would no doubt be argued that such an act would destroy educational standards.

Yet the APU does not deserve to survive. National monitoring has a meretricious attraction, and it has seduced a number of educationists as well as politicians. But at the end of the day its promises prove to be hollow . . .

To suggest that the activities of the APU and its teams will lead to improved educational activities in schools is 'like burning a farthing candle at Dover to shew light on Calais'. If education is to be improved – and there can be no other reason, in truth, for setting up the APU – then the way to do it is not by vain attempts to measure what happens, but by helping teachers to define and solve curriculum problems.

I have argued that the APU has no educational value in its own right and is, indeed, likely to do more harm than good. But this would be an inadequate reason for putting an end to it, since it has considerable political value . . .

The APU has clearly come a long way in five short years: from an innocent inquiry into ways of helping disadvantaged pupils, it is seen by the present party of government as its major weapon in a 'back to basics' movement.

Working Relationships with the APU

The criticisms which have been levelled at the APU are aimed not only at the efficiency of its programme and its monitoring methods, but also at its assumed intentions and likely effects. The suspicions behind these criticisms have much to do with the fact that the APU is seen to be part of the DES and hence, to some, a possible agent for an undesirable influence upon the school curriculum. Yet the Unit was given its initial impetus in collaboration with members of the HMI, a body which maintains a great degree of independence from the DES. So what is the exact nature of the relationship between these three bodies, the DES, the APU and the HMI?

When the APU was set up in 1974 it was placed firmly within the DES. The reasons seem largely to do with control and speed of action, but entailed the drawback that there might be suspicion of its motives. There had been other possibilities, though to what extent the Department considered these is not clear. One possibility had been to use existing bodies as a base for the Unit and an obvious candidate was the Schools Council. However, there was a growing disenchantment in the DES with the Council at that time. Another possibility would have been an independent unit. The economic vulnerability of a completely separate unit may have been a reason for not following this course. For example, the Centre for Educational Disadvantage which was based at Manchester was a quasi-independent body and this was closed down while the Educational Disadvantage Unit, located within the DES, survived (see Chapter 2). Indeed, the Schools Council itself will now be closed down. The NFER, however, would have been a strong candidate and the solution finally adopted, which was to keep the APU within the DES but use the NFER's expertise for the monitoring, may be viewed as a reasonable compromise.

The APU's position and function within the DES is that of a department working to an Under-Secretary.* Its work comes under the scrutiny of Policy Group B within the Department and is also evaluated – on an informal basis – by the HMI. How then does the APU formulate ideas and views? Policy matters concerning the larger issues, such as ages at which to monitor, are decided by the Minister on the advice of the Consultative Committee. The Committee's view is 'interpreted' and turned into categorical options by the Assistant Secretary in charge of the APU, and other members of the Unit. The APU does put up ideas, an example being the feasibility study to look at surrogates for home support variables and the seminars on Rasch and trends over time. The APU formulates ideas like these through a management team which consists of the head or heads of the APU plus the chairmen of the groups.

The DES is essentially a body of administrative expertise; for professional expertise it relies heavily upon the HMI. Therefore, the APU was bound to involve the HMI in its work and, in fact, the Unit has always had a senior HMI as head or joint head. From one point of view

---

* We should make it clear that the view of the DES outlined here is essentially an 'outside' view; clearly there are more levels of interaction within the DES than are discussed here.

this early involvement of the HMI was pragmatic: an HMI was brought in to run it initially because the DES needed someone relatively quickly. Given their perceived professional expertise, however, the HMI involvement has been important for the success of the whole APU enterprise and undoubtedly the high profile of the HMI has helped on the public relations side of the APU. Although there were gains for the DES in securing this engagement of the HMI in the APU, it is not apparent that the HMI had similar, or reciprocal gains in prospect. When HMI were seconded to the APU they ceased to be HMI. Though some were appointed on a part-time basis, they were not regarded as HMI when doing their APU work. This was adhered to even to the extent of removing the subscript HMI after the names which appeared on APU documents while they were part of the secretariat. But this strictness of separation is usually not clear and, therefore, not appreciated by observers.

Over time there have been three major periods in the APU's work which are broadly coincidental with changes in leadership. The first was a time of establishment and generation of ideas; the second was more clearly developmental; the third and present period is one of on-line production when administration of the four testing programmes is increasingly important. The early contributions of the HMI have been described as 'philosophical and intellectual' to do with areas of the curriculum, the types of instrument required, specifying frontiers and acting as professional advisers. The change of APU leadership from HMIs only to the inclusion of DES administrative personnel can be seen as reflecting the change from developmental to administrative emphasis within the APU. But it can also be seen as freeing the hands of the HMI in order that they might more freely make use of the Unit's findings and advances in test development and feel able to offer independent evaluation of the APU's work. When, and if, the APU's tests are released to LEAs the opportunity will be presented to exploit this material and survey findings through in-service work. Though the HMI have always been closely linked with this, they are aware also that it is easier to become aligned with exploitation if they are not involved in the actual development.

There seems to be a further reason for the changing role of the HMI in the APU. There may be a danger to the HMI of being so definitely linked with the APU and identified with a programme of government monitoring. The independence of the HMI from the DES has given advantages to both sides. Ultimately, however, the Inspectorate depends upon the opinion of the outside world to maintain its credibility and independence. Recently this independence has not been as self-evident as the HMI perhaps would wish. Commenting on arguments for reshaping the HMI's function and organisation in the light of the

Rayner review, an ex-HMI wrote:

A first priority would be the establishment of independence from any other body. It would more accurately be a re-establishment, since the original terms of reference ensured this, and the prefix 'HM' has remained a gentle reminder of it ever since (though the terms 'government' and 'ministry' inspectors are frequently seen.[317]

The APU is viewed differently from most other parts of the DES because of the appointment of HMI as its early leaders and because the Unit works with a level of public consultation through the Consultative Committee that is unusual within the DES. While the HMI have been employed to provide the Unit with professional expertise and to lend a more publicly acceptable face in the critical early period, there are signs that the HMI may draw back from such close identification with the Unit. This comes at a time when the early hopes of being able to measure changes in 'standards' over time look like being frustrated. The HMI role would then be much more one of disseminating and helping LEAs to exploit the APU survey findings and tests in a programme of in-service training. The head of the HMI, Sheila Browne, has already expressed doubts about the present status of testing:

It is arguable that time for testing of one kind or another should not be taken from teaching and learning unless it can be shown to be to the profit of the pupils. In quantity and kind, testing must serve the pupils' interests without swaying their teachers . . . Testing would be more profitable if the different types of assessment and their appropriate instruments were better understood . . . In some cases the uses are slight or even questionable – as in the weight sometimes attached to a single score . . . One has to ask, is it all worthwhile or wise?[318]

Thus, the HMIs now seem to have a clear view of their role. They are to interpret and advise on the works of the APU to the educational world, within the wider framework of testing at LEA and school level.

The other all-important bodies with which the APU has to deal are the teacher unions. The APU's relationship with the NUT has been far more in evidence than that with other teacher unions. The NUT is the largest of the teacher unions and has the greatest number of representatives on the Consultative Committee (five, as opposed to one from each of the AMMA, NAS/UWT, SHA and NAHT) which enables them to form a bloc, and to dominate discussions. The other union representatives act more as individuals, in that they seem to interpret their role as reporting back to their union rather than acting in any particular way on its behalf.

In the section on the Consultative Committee (Chapter 3) the role that the NUT played within this group, and therefore in the APU's consultation process, is explained in detail. Suffice it to say here that they were an important factor in blocking the assessment of personal–social development, the measurement of home background variables, and a separate study of West Indian children (Chapter 2). The NUT's fears over personal–social development, in which they were not alone, centred on the difficulty of the value judgements involved in the assessment and the problems this would cause teachers. Likewise their opposition to the West Indian survey was based on both its political sensitivity and the sheer difficulty of doing it well. The reasons for its opposition to the collection of home background variables seemed to rest with its concern over the burden on teachers and the threat to teacher–parent relationships.

The Union had agreed to become involved with the APU for two reasons. First, at the time that the Unit was set up there was pressure for testing from many quarters and fears that LEAs might set up unsuitable testing programmes; in this atmosphere the NUT supported the APU because it was their way of showing that they wished to be involved in responsible testing. Secondly, the terms of reference included those magic words 'resource allocation' so they wished to monitor the Unit's work. They were sceptical about the resource allocation part ever coming to anything, particularly so since the closure of the Centre for Educational Disadvantage which could have carried out the practical side of this task, that is, giving advice on resource allocation based on information provided by the APU. The Union's view was that the APU should not expand into other areas of the curriculum; it should concentrate on the testing it had already started. The Union's grounds for not having a wide programme were twofold. First, the wider the testing programme the less valued become the subjects not tested. Second, maths and English are taught in all schools so testing these will not affect the curriculum, whereas if other subject areas are included there is more likely to be an effect on the curriculum.

Thus the NUT has been closely involved in the APU's consultation process and in return has guaranteed its members' co-operation. In effect the NUT has supported the work of the APU in return for a limitation of the APU's role. Its effectiveness in preventing the West Indian survey and the assessment of personal–social development may well have saved the APU, in the long run, from two embarrassing failures.

As for the exam boards, the only link between them and the APU is that each of the boards is automatically sent copies of APU publications. The boards do not have any formal representation on the APU committees although Nuttall was appointed to the Statistics Advisory Group when secretary of the Middlesex Board. Within the DES there is some linkage since both the APU and public examinations come under Schools III Branch but this link is not one that is open to public view, nor is there any obvious indication of it. Part of the minutes of a meeting of the Statistics Advisory Group in 1978 indicates the APU's attitude towards the exam boards (which has never been made explicit):

The Chairman (of the Group and then head of the Unit) referred to a letter received from the Welsh Joint Education Committee commenting on the Consultative Document 'Assessment of Scientific Development'. The WJEC had drawn attention to the vast assessment experience of the examining boards and had commented that the APU had appeared to make very little use of this. The Chairman explained that he had replied to the WJEC, pointing out that the activities of the APU and the examining boards were complementary to each other, but were not similar in nature.[319]

There are more recent signs of exam board involvement, however. At the June 1981 seminar on 'trends over time' several exam board researchers were present.

Finally we turn to an examination of the APU's relationship with the NFER, its major test developer. In December 1976 the head of the Unit told the Consultative Committee that:

The NFER has been selected as the centre for both (maths and language) projects because of its considerable general experience of assessment and monitoring and its previous involvement in the DES Reading Surveys and the TAMS project. Centres that might be suitable to undertake research and development work in other curricular areas would be less easy to identify.[320]

Clearly, there was never any real intention that the maths and language monitoring should go anywhere other than the NFER and this may seem reasonable given their experience of national testing.

The NFER's involvement in the APU exercise can be traced back to 1970 when the then Deputy Director was a member of the DES Working Group on Measurement of Educational Attainment (WGMET) (see Chapter 1). An academic who was asked by this group to make a survey of tests suitable for a national monitoring programme later became the Director of the NFER. Item banking, on which APU monitoring was based, was introduced to the WGMET by the then Deputy Director of the NFER, and it was at this point that the Rasch technique was introduced into discussions; it had first made an appearance in England in an article by an NFER researcher in *Nature* in 1968.[321]

Thus the NFER played a key role in the adoption of the concept of item banking. Of course, the NFER had carried out reading surveys for the DES since 1948 and was an obvious contender for the first APU monitoring programmes for several reasons: first, for the role it had always had in national monitoring, secondly for the expertise that was at the NFER as a result of this, and thirdly because, being supported financially by the LEAs, it embodied LEA interests and therefore had good links with them. With the first two APU projects based at the NFER, however, there seems to have been a feeling in educational circles that to avoid charges of nepotism the DES should fund the next project within a University. Thus, science testing went outside the NFER, although the modern language monitoring again went to the NFER.

Apart from the battles over statistical techniques (for a full description of the APU's role in this see Chapter 4 on the Statistics Advisory Group) the relationship between the NFER and the APU may seem to the outsider to have been a typical one of contractor/researcher with the researcher concentrating on fulfilling the terms of the contract rather than shaping the overall programme. Thus the NFER researchers, as we show in Chapter 4, have felt constrained by the APU because they could not pursue in-depth studies or offer interpretations of data. This latter decision meant that they were forced to produce bland reports which were very far from what they would have wished to produce, and they have, over the years, tried to persuade the APU to change its thinking on this issue. However, the inside picture is rather different and the relationship between the APU and NFER is clearly more interactive than might appear. The NFER has had three members on the influential Statistics Advisory Group out of a total of ten, in contrast to the science team which waited until 1981 to get a member and a voice onto this group. The NFER has also had representatives on the Co-ordinating Group and the Consultative Committee. Moreover, it has continued to have strong links with DES personnel through its many DES-funded research projects.

A further important link is the LEASIB project which was set up by the NFER in 1977 to develop item banks in maths and language in response to requests from LEAs for test materials:

the NFER was constantly being approached by LEAs who wished to calibrate their own assessment programmes to the results of APU monitoring. The Monitoring Group at the NFER had accordingly been given overall responsibility for both ventures, so as to ensure as far as possible that the results could be related and that a consistently high standard of test material would be used; in this context it was essential for LEAs to realise that the results of their own tests could *not* be compared with those of the APU unless they were compatible. There would, however, be no question of marketing APU tests as such; this was one reason for using item banks as opposed to producing set tests.[322]

Though the Department supported the NFER's LEASIB project, they encouraged the NFER to limit its availability just to those LEAs which agreed to use the tests in a 'reasonable' way. By this they meant not to use it on a blanket basis and not to use the same test two years running so that the effect on the curriculum, or 'backwash', would be minimal. The Department also agreed to a cross-calibration with the APU items so that LEAs could compare their performance with national figures. Behind these decisions was the aim of preventing LEAs from doing something less desirable on their own behalf, and the Department felt that this was possible if the item banks were used properly.

In 1980 the relationship between APU and LEASIB test items was explained by one of the Unit's heads:

I must emphasise that the link between the APU item banks and those of the NFER's LEASIB project is minimal, and relates solely to the calibration of the items in the LEASIB banks with those in the APU bank so that the results from LEASIB testing will be expressible in terms broadly comparable with APU results. The banks of material are quite separate and consist of totally different items, i.e. items developed for use by the APU are not included either in their original form or in a modified form in NFER banks. The APU items are necessarily confidential. To make them available to local education authorities would inevitably compromise their value for the purposes of repeated national monitoring, and thus destroy the possibility of comparing results over time. In addition, if APU test items were to be freely available to local education authorities, there would be a possibility, as you recognise, of schools beginning to 'teach to the test', and this we are anxious to avoid. However, a number of APU test items will be published for illustrative purposes in survey reports and we could have no objection to those items being used either by the NFER or by other educational publishers interested in developing material of this kind.[323]

During the autumn of 1981 the APU reached a decision in principle to allow LEAs to use APU items, although details have yet to be worked out. In order not to jeopardise the integrity of APU tests, it is unlikely that the banks will be thrown open before the five-year annual surveying period is over and monitoring drops to being once every five years. At about the same time the NFER decided to run down LEASIB. Two of the reasons behind this decision were that it had become too expensive to develop and that the technical problems associated with the analysis of items from banks had proved to be more intractable than at first envisaged.

It seems that the NFER/APU relationship will continue to be strong and the APU will remain reliant on the NFER for much of its expert advice. This relationship, which is a continuation of the NFER/DES relationship established well before the APU was set up, has obvious benefits for both parties but also dangers for them and for educational research as a whole. The dangers lie in a narrowing of vision and purpose, as illustrated by the Rasch debate, and the tendency to concentrate scarce funds for research in the hands of one body.

7 Conclusions

In this final chapter we have extracted what we see as the salient themes in the work of the APU. While earlier chapters have included some critical evaluation, the present chapter is more consistently evaluative. If it is not already clear, we hope it will become so in this chapter that while we have major criticisms and reservations about the APU, we believe that it could have an important role to play. Amongst other things it embodies a genuine desire to pursue useful knowledge and we see it as the start of potentially fruitful research. For this reason, at the end of the chapter, we have felt it worthwhile to make recommendations about the APU's future.

The Management of the APU

The composition of the Unit itself and its management style have emerged as key factors in the Unit's history. At the start, the Unit formed a Co-ordinating Group – to co-ordinate and plan ahead – yet these functions could just as easily have been taken on by the Unit itself. In fact, the Unit and the Consultative Committee did take on these functions, which left the Co-ordinating Group without much purpose and led to its demise. The Unit's apparent unwillingness to be seen to exert a powerful managerial role is consistent with a desire to operate in a low-key way. This may be conducive to political survival, but only at the cost of effective long-term planning. In addition, and perhaps more importantly, this unwillingness seems to have been a direct expression of the Unit's inexperience in managing a large-scale research project. The APU's subsequent method of management has led to some poor decisions. For example, there was no central co-ordination of the work of the teams, so that they had to arrange meetings among themselves outside the APU structure. This inevitably limited assessment across subject areas. More importantly, it sometimes led to confusion, delay and a clear lack of direction.

An important factor which must be held responsible for some of its weaknesses in management is the regular change in the Unit's personnel. The first head of the Unit was in post for less than three years, as was the second. No member of staff has been with the Unit since its inception. Thus, there is little collective memory, and perhaps little incentive for Unit staff to consider the longer-term perspective or to feel responsible for the long-term outcome. This contrasts with the management of most large-scale research projects where senior members, at least, tend to remain for the duration, as in fact has been the case with the APU monitoring teams.

The early 'facts only' position for published reports presumably stems from a belief in the 'objective' nature of test results, and is analogous to the existing departmental production of regular statistical reports on teacher qualifications, class size, etc. Such a position conforms to the normal mode of operation of government, where it is the task of Ministers and senior officials to give interpretations on the basis of facts supplied by more junior officials. Even if it is accepted that this actually works well in many areas of government policy, it is manifestly unworkable when applied to a major research programme – which effectively is what the APU is. Apart from anything else, the value judgements and interpretations built into the design of the monitoring instruments will make 'neutral' statements of results impossible. Despite a repeated emphasis by the APU that its business is monitoring rather than policy-related research, the logic of the programme does not support such a distinction. At all stages, from initial discussion of items to writing of final reports, traditional research issues have predominated. Attempts to keep out notions of research 'interpretations' have broken down in the face of opposition from those carrying out the work – themselves researchers. Perhaps more than any other concept in the collective minds of the APU, this attempt to keep to 'monitoring' has been the biggest constraint on its work. It has limited the usefulness of results for policy, frustrated the teams and failed to excite the interest of teachers and other educationists. Good research requires not only competent workers, in which respect the APU has been fortunate; it also requires research experience and knowledge from those who direct it.

The APU Now
The APU seems to be largely unaffected thus far by cuts in educational expenditure. Recently, modern language assessment, the fourth assessment area, has been commissioned; this is a large project and will cost £750,000 at 1981 price levels for piloting and three annual surveys. For the well-established maths, language and science testing, annual monitoring will continue until five surveys have been completed. This will

be in 1982 for maths, 1983 for language and 1984 for science. The teams will be expected to report fully on four of the five years, so that the research teams will be freer during one year to analyse existing data in more detail. Each team will also produce a retrospective view over all the surveys. As for the future beyond the five annual surveys, it has now been decided to monitor once every five years in each area while pursuing data analysis and other work between surveys. We discuss the implications of this in the final section of this chapter.

As for in-depth studies, the only funds at the moment have gone to a small project to look at trends over time using data from the primary maths surveys. The teams themselves hope to do some in-depth analysis of interesting findings during their year off from reporting, and it now seems likely that in-depth studies will be encouraged in the periods between the five-yearly surveys.

Dissemination of findings among teachers is an acknowledged priority for the future. To this end the APU started a new round of regional conferences in July 1982. It has commissioned the first of a series of occasional papers and there are regular newsletters. It is thinking about obtaining independent evaluations of reports, and there has recently been a softening of the early stance on the neutral reporting of results.

Concerning relational variables, which would be of help in interpreting data, several school-based measures are in use by the maths and science teams. The former, however, have published little in this area yet, while the latter have found that this information is less useful than they had hoped:

> The (science) team . . . had found little variation in performance by school variables and were now reconsidering whether a questionnaire was the most appropriate way to collect information on these variables.[324]

With regard to home-based measures, in March 1982 the Consultative Committee agreed to set up a small group to consider again the collection of information about home background. Meanwhile, the outcome of the work based at Leeds to look for a 'surrogate' measure of home background is awaited.

As explained in Chapters 4 and 6, calibrated banks of items linked to APU items will not be available to LEAs via the NFER's LEASIB. Instead it seems to be planned that the APU's own items will be available once the five-year round of annual monitoring in each subject is over. This is in line with one school of thought about what the APU's future should be, namely that the Unit should concentrate on making more use of the information that is available by opening the item banks, making data available to interested researchers, and improving dissemination among teachers rather than expanding into new fields.

The Curriculum

It seems that in the early 1970s there was increasing concern within the DES that it was excluded from involvement in the curriculum, despite funding the education system and ultimately being held accountable for it. Setting up the APU became for the DES a means of obtaining both a direct evaluation of the performance of the system and a way, however indirect, of achieving some say in curriculum content. That it may have been an inefficient way of affecting the curriculum, and that the APU is now no longer the DES's sole way of attempting to gain some control over the curriculum (as discussed later in this chapter) are both true. Nevertheless, curriculum impact was a part of the early thinking about national monitoring.

There are two ways in which the APU could have a global impact on the curriculum. One is that by limiting the monitoring to maths, language, science and modern languages the curriculum will become narrower and undue emphasis be placed on these subjects. The other way is that the APU might shape the content of the curriculum in these areas via the general curriculum models adopted by the test developers. The possibility of this impact is not denied by the teams, and they have concentrated accordingly on operating with a wide curriculum model. Though there is only limited evidence of advisers propounding curricula built around the APU tests, and though the worst fears of those who warned about the imposition of centralised control of the curriculum have not been realised, it would be surprising if the APU's work did not affect the curriculum in some way. The extent to which this has happened so far is limited, largely because of the low take-up of reports and the APU's adherence to the policies of light sampling and matrix sampling. It is, however, too soon to make a pronouncement about the APU's impact on the curriculum and the next few years will be vital in indicating how much of an effect there will be. At this point we can say only that early fears about domination of, and imposition on, the curriculum have not been realised. Indeed, with no public examinations link, the impact of the APU on the curriculum at secondary level will inevitably be minor. Moreover, such curriculum effects as there are may be good rather than bad: some early circumstantial evidence from LEAs and schools suggests that the results may be to widen what is taught in the areas being tested.[325]

It will be interesting to see whether the APU moves in the same direction as NAEP, in accepting that a curriculum effect is inevitable and then deliberately setting out to see how it can be managed.[326]

Already, as we report in Chapter 5, there is some feeling along these lines in the science team, and the APU will need to take this more seriously if it is not to find itself once again, through lack of purposeful forward planning, overtaken and perhaps embarrassed by events.

The cross-curriculum model never really came to anything (see Chapter 3). Certain vital areas, for example personal–social and physical development, have been dropped while within the areas chosen for assessment there has been little attempt, indeed little time and little incentive, to write items which are not subject-bound. The science team have attempted to make some progress in this area, but on the whole, the teams seem to view this as a future development.

The APU as a Tool of Accountability

As we have described, the idea of a national monitoring system as a means of accounting for education had its origins in the late 1960s and was refined by the mid-1970s when the 'standards' debate had gained momentum.

In all the deliberations of the APU and its committees we have found little mention of accountability *per se*. It seems that the notion of the APU as an accounting instrument, once accepted initially, simply lay undisturbed in the background waiting to be made functional by the results themselves. The published reports do not discuss the relevance of the results to accountability. The reason is perhaps simple enough: if schools are to be accountable through the achievement of their children, then more is required than a simple comparison of different types of schools in different parts of the country classified by type of child. What is required is a plausible means of attributing differences between components of the educational system to the components themselves rather than to some latent characteristic over which they have little control. Thus, it is of little interest for accounting purposes (although it may be useful when allocating resources) to know that children in schools which have a high uptake of free school meals, have lower than average test scores. This does not prove that such schools are necessarily educationally 'worse' than others, rather that they have a different intake of children who for other reasons will tend to have lower than average test scores. In other words, just like the simple presentation of exam results, monitoring achievement is of little help unless it is backed up by detailed research which attempts to uncover the reasons for variations in performance. Though the further analysis of existing material or related in-depth studies might be steps in that direction, at present the APU cannot be described rationally as an instrument of accountability.

How Far Has the APU Achieved its Aims?

Tasks

To appraise existing instruments and methods of assessment This task seems largely to have been a formality, new testing instruments being the order of the day, except in the case of the maths team who always intended to base their work on an assessment of the TAMS material. The language team, following Bullock, would never have used existing tests, and as for the science team there was really nothing suitable for them to consider using.

To sponsor the creation of new instruments and methods of assessment In dealing with this task the APU has had its biggest success. There is no doubt that the teams have produced some interesting new material and done pioneering work in the assessment of practical skills in maths and science. There are high hopes too of the oracy assessments from the language team. The APU has also broken new ground in the assessment of pupils' attitudes.

To promote the conduct of assessment in co-operation with LEAs and teachers This is rather a puzzling task. If the DES had meant it to mean persuading LEAs to allow the tests to be carried out in their areas and teachers to administer them in the classrooms, then the Unit has certainly succeeded. It is hard to imagine how monitoring could have been organised otherwise. If on the other hand, as seems more probable, this task meant something more active on behalf of the LEAs, for example, a link between APU testing and LEA testing as outlined in the 1977 Green Paper, then this has not yet materialised in a workable form, though it could if large numbers of APU items become available to LEAs.

To identify significant differences of achievement related to the circumstances in which children learn, including the incidence of underachievement, and to make findings available to those concerned with resource allocation within the government departments, LEAs and schools A start has been made on looking at performance in relation to some background measures. However, many of the measures used, for example pupil/teacher ratio and region of the country, are really of little direct use to policy makers or indeed to LEAs or teachers. More relevant variables which would relate to the circumstances in which children learn, for example, size of teaching group, qualifications and experience of the teacher, resources available (particularly for science) and aims of the programme of work, have been used in the later surveys but useful information on these has not yet been forthcoming. It may be that at the end of their five-year periods the teams, on consolidating their data, will have something more positive to report. It is quite likely that they may, on the other hand, decide that this type of information is best not collected through large scale surveys but in studies of an in-depth type. What is quite clear is that any attempt to look at underachievement, particularly of ethnic minority groups, certainly will have to be via in-depth studies and, as we have shown in Chapter 2, the Unit has so far made no progress in this part of Task Four. As we document in Chapter 1, the underachievement task was brought in for political reasons and it was only later that the difficulties associated with measuring it were realised. The Unit in any case means 'low achievement' rather than 'underachievement,' and the confusion over terms has diverted effort and wasted time. The monitoring teams have ideas about what areas of low performance they themselves would like to pursue, but whether they will have the time or manpower to get far with these while keeping up with their heavy timetables is not clear.

As for making findings available to those concerned with resource allocation, as they stand the findings are of little value to policy makers or LEAs. That the usefulness of the results for policy makers is limited was made obvious when it transpired that, out of the policy questions put forward by the APU itself in June 1981, many could not be answered by the current APU programme. There is a definite feeling within the DES, however, that there is a considerable amount of valuable data, some yet unpublished, which needs to be 'mined' for its lessons for teachers. Indeed it may well be that the APU's assessment material, capable in many cases of promoting a widening of the curriculum, will come to be seen as its greatest achievement, rather than any direct contribution to the debate on standards or account-ability.

Standards and measuring change over time
There has been little progress on the Unit's other aims which are outlined in their publicity material rather than in the terms of reference (see Chapter 1), namely to provide information on standards and to monitor changes in performance over time. By January 1983, the Unit had published 12 reports: six on maths, three on language and three on science. These do give information on levels of performance in terms of the percentages of pupils able to answer questions, for example on decimals, able to read and understand certain types of narrative or dialogue, etc. But it is not easy to see how useful this is to teachers and policy makers when the reports offer hardly any interpretation or judgements about educational significance and the tests themselves are not publicly available. One of the problems is that measuring standards and monitoring changes in them over time are related and no consensus

has been reached on how to analyse trends in performance over time (see Chapter 4). At the end of each five year period of surveying the teams are expected to produce composite measures of performance over the five years which will serve as a baseline (or standard) with which to compaie any performance measured subsequently. By then, the question of how to analyse trends in performance over time may have been answered in part. Certainly the Unit, although it said much about standards in the early days, for example: 'The first task of the APU is to identify and define standards of performance pupils might be expected to achieve through their work at school',[327] has not attempted to define 'standards' in the sense of acceptable or looked-for performance. Instead, it will rely on describing measured performance over a period of years – a less contentious task.

To sum up then, the conclusion on the APU's progress must be that it has had partial success. It has succeeded in test development, it has persuaded LEAs to co-operate in the surveys, and it has made a start on the study of circumstances in which children learn, although the outcome here is uncertain. On the other hand it has failed on underachievement and has not yet had any success in describing changes in performance over time. The Unit's achievements, given the scope of the task and the newness of the ground to be covered, should not be undervalued. Nevertheless our view is that, given a clearer structuring of early plans, a different style of management, and more careful forward planning throughout, the Unit could have made more progress than it has.

Arguments for Expanding or Contracting the Monitoring Exercise

Decisions about whether to extend the monitoring programme will be based on three factors: feasibility, cost and effects on the curriculum. The decision will be essentially a political one and will be taken at ministerial level, though recommendations about whether or not to monitor in the particular subject areas will be made by the APU secretariat guided by the opinion of the Consultative Committee.

Arguments for expanding the monitoring exercise into other curriculum areas hinge on the premise that, by testing only certain areas of the curriculum, the areas which are not tested may be devalued. The alternative view is that national monitoring exerts undesirable control over the curriculum and that therefore it should be limited to only the most basic skills. Of course the APU's programme has, by including science and modern language, already gone beyond the very basic skills of reading, writing and arithmetic, so that it has fallen part way between the 'test as little as possible' and the 'test everything' schools of thought. By testing language, maths, science and modern languages it has now come as close to testing a core curriculum as its early critics, who saw it as an agent of curriculum control, feared. It is clear, however, that the programme is unlikely to become as comprehensive as the American NAEP programme because of the response to the proposals to monitor personal–social development. The final decisions about expanding the programme, for example, with technological development may well be based on, or put forward as being based on, financial considerations – particularly if the Department looks at the APU exercise in terms of value for money so far. The cost of the exercise (see Appendix 3) is largely undiscussed but in an era of cuts the Department can no longer be blind to this argument.

The other possible argument against expanding the programme is a pragmatic one based on timing. 1982 sees the end of the five-year cycle of annual surveys in maths, 1983 in language, 1984 in science; testing in new areas yet to be commissioned would fall far behind testing in established areas, perhaps unacceptably so. Finally, there is a strong argument that whatever funds are available should be concentrated on the data already gathered and their updating. The pay-off from further exploitation of the maths, language and science monitoring would seem to outweigh any advantages from a similar expenditure on expanding the scope of the monitoring.

The Future

In these final few paragraphs we set out, tentatively and in the barest outline, some suggestions for the future course of the APU. The APU has had seven years of active existence; it has passed through a troubled and uncertain infancy, but its infancy is over and it is time for it to recognise and rectify its past mistakes.

First and foremost we believe that the DES and the APU need to revise their views about research and monitoring and to recognise that their own research expertise is limited. They should be aware that if anything of real use to policy makers is to emerge then it will do so as the result of a high-quality research effort rather than a narrowly conceived monitoring exercise. They need to appreciate that they have created a large and expensive research enterprise with considerable potential for answering a wide range of interesting and important questions. That the APU has shown some signs of moving in this direction is largely due to the efforts of the research teams it has engaged and we would hope that a more positive response to their efforts will be forthcoming.

While policy-related research such as that of the APU needs to have clear guidelines and direction, the present strong control exercised by the Unit through its groups and committees is, in our view, counter-productive and needs to be relaxed. The work of the research teams, concentrating on the exploitation of existing materials, should allow those involved to have the freedom to pursue their tasks according to the necessities of the research itself, consistent with the teams fulfilling the objectives and terms of their contracts. Naturally, in research of this kind, the DES would wish its views to be represented by means of advisory or steering groups, but these could well operate in the more normal research mode rather than in the heavily directive mode as at present.

Much of the value of the APU's results will be lost without better dissemination. Useful as it may be, a newsletter will not be enough. What is required is a means of informing teachers and others and discussing with them the implications of the APU's work within the context of the curriculum and different methods of assessment. The HMI, in conjunction with LEA advisers, would seem to be the body to do this and indeed seems prepared to do so. Inevitably, such an activity will be expensive, but it would seem to be well worth spending money on it.

Such shifts in outlook and operation inevitably will entail a redefinition of aims and tasks. To some extent, of course, these have been modified anyway over the years. The present programme has not allowed pronouncements to be made about standards; it is not concerned with underachievement; it has not yet been able to say anything useful about trends over time, and has thus far failed to set up major in-depth studies. Even as recently as June 1981 a list of questions of interest to the APU contained many that were unrelated to the actual monitoring programme (see Appendix 2). It seems high time that the *de facto* objectives of the APU were set out so that the Unit's future directions could be charted more clearly. The inevitable corollary of all these negatives is that the APU has not, to date, served policy makers very well.

We have already raised the issue of whether or not the APU is doing harm to the education system. If indeed such harm has come about, for example through a narrowing of curriculum content, it is still too early to assess it. Nevertheless, it seems to us that the DES does have a responsibility for systematically and openly evaluating such possible harmful effects and this is as much for the sake of the DES's credibility as for the health of the curriculum and other aspects of the system. Such issues as teaching to published test items or conscious decisions by schools to drop subjects not covered by monitoring programmes are amenable to empirical study, and it would be perfectly feasible to carry out such an evaluation.

On the success side, the APU's test development programme has been most notable. The effects of this on testing in general deserve to be widespread. The APU materials have broken new ground and explored many curricular areas further than ever before. At the moment the potential for alerting teachers to weaknesses in teaching content and method is not being realised, but with changes of emphasis in the Unit's work towards interpretation and dissemination of findings, this potentially beneficial influence upon schools could be released.

Finally, the recent decision to move to a five-yearly monitoring cycle is welcome. It will allow the existing teams to be retained, albeit at a reduced level, in between surveys so that they will be able to explore the data, carry out in-depth studies and have adequate time to develop efficient survey designs. It also provides a good opportunity for a relaxation of the hitherto strict managerial control of the teams and for a more open attitude to the use of the data by other educationists and researchers. Indeed, further exploration of the data and the development of in-depth studies could be enriched greatly by the allocation of funds for this purpose to independent researchers outside the teams. In the press release[328] announcing future plans for the APU it is stated that the new monitoring programme 'will be sufficient for identifying changes or trends in levels of performance while releasing resources for further interpretation and exploitation of the material collected'. Thus the DES wishes to be seen to be maintaining its interest in monitoring 'standards' over time while also making better use of the data already collected. Nevertheless, coupled with proposals to give LEAs more access to APU test items, this decision may point to a shift towards the LEAs assuming a significant, and perhaps major responsibility, for large scale monitoring. They could build upon the achievement of the APU and furthermore, they could draw upon the continuing expertise available in the further exploration and development supported by the DES. We have suggested that one of the original reasons for direct DES interest in monitoring was that it was one way of having a say in the school curriculum. In 1983 this motive seems less important, particularly after the recent decision[329] to abolish the Schools Council. This organisation has been replaced by two bodies, one for curriculum and one for examinations, with nominees appointed by the Secretary of State for Education, thus giving the DES a more direct, and presumably much more effective, influence on curriculum policy. The APU is no longer needed to fulfil this role.

References

Chapter 1
1 APU(CON)(82)3.
2 DES (1976), *The APU – an Introduction*.
3 DES (1980), *The APU – What it is – How it Works*.
4 DES (1974), *Educational Disadvantage and the Educational Needs of Immigrants*, Cmnd 5720 HMSO. Reproduced with the permission of the Controller of Her Majesty's Stationery Office.
5 Kay, B.W. (1975), 'Monitoring pupils' performance', *Trends in Education 2*.
6 Central Advisory Council for Education (England) (1967), *Children and their Primary Schools* (The Plowden Report), HMSO.
7 Maclure, S. (1978), Chapter 1, in Becher, A.R. and Maclure, S. (eds), *Accountability in Education*, NFER.
8 Peaker, G.F. (1966), *Progress in Reading 1948–1964*, Education Pamphlet No 50, HMSO.
9 Start, B. and Wells, K. (1972), *The Trend of Reading Standards*, NFER.
10 DES (1975), *A Language for Life*, (Bullock Report), HMSO.
11 ILEA (1976), *The Auld Report*.
12 Blackstone, T. and Wood, R. (1981), 'Education, accountability and testing', *New Society* 24.12.81.
13 *TES* 22.10.76.
14 Maclure, S. (1978), op. cit.
15 DES (1977), *Education in Schools: A Consultative Document*, Cmnd 5720 HMSO.
16 Paper by Byatt (referred to in WGMET Report 1971).
17 Cox, C. and Dyson, A. (1968), 'The fight for education', *London Quarterly Society*.
18 DES (1971), 'Report of the Working Group on the Measurement of Educational Attainment'.
19 DES (1975), op. cit.
20 Lawton, D. (1980), *Politics of the School Curriculum*, Routledge & Kegan Paul.
21 DES (1974), Cmnd 5720 op. cit.
22 DES (1972), *Education: A Framework for Expansion*, Cmnd 5174 HMSO.
23 DES Press Notice, 'A new unit on educational disadvantage' 28.8.74.
24 Kay, B.W., (1975), op. cit.
25 DES (1976), op. cit.
26 DES (1977), *Assessment – Why, What and How?*
27 Marjoram, D.T.E. (1977), 'Patience Rewarded', *TES* 14.10.77.
28 DES (1980), op. cit.
29 APU(CON)(78), 3rd meeting minutes.
30 Broadfoot, P. (1979), *Assessment, Schools and Society*, Methuen.
31 For example, Holt, M. (1978), *The Common Curriculum*, Routledge & Kegan Paul.

32 Wood, R. (1977), 'Charting the depths of ignorance' *TES* 2.12.77.
33 DES (1978), 'Assessment in schools', *Reports on Education* No. 93.
34 Simon, J. (1979), 'What and who is the APU?' *Forum* 22 1 Autumn 1979.
35 Pring, R.A. (1980), *APU and the Core Curriculum*, Curriculum and Resource Centre, Exeter University School of Education.
36 Owen, J. (1980), 'Is it a DES plot?' *Education* 4.7.80, and Taylor, W. (1980), 'Quality control in education', paper given at BEAS Conference 1980.
37 Burstall, C. and Kay, B.W. (1978), *Assessment – the American Experience*, DES.
38 Owen, J. (1980), and Taylor, W. (1980), op. cit.
39 APU(SC)(75) 1.
40 Kay, B.W. (1975), op. cit.
41 Lawton, D. (1980), op. cit.
42 Burstall, C. and Kay, B.W. (1978), op. cit.
43 Black, P. and Marjoram. D.T.E. (1979), 'National and State Assessment in the USA', DES/APU.
44 DES/APU (Autumn 1981), *Understanding Design and Technology*.
45 APU(COG)(79) 7.
46 APU(COG)(79) 18, revised.
47 Dennison, W.F. (1978), 'Research report: the APU – where is it leading?' *Durham and Newcastle Research Review* Vol 8 No 40.
48 Quoted in Lawton, D. (1980), op. cit.
49 Kay, B.W. (1977), *A Programme of Work for the APU*, DES. (quoted in Lawton, D. (1980), op. cit.)

Chapter 2
50 DES (1974), Cmnd 5720 op. cit.
51 DES Press Notice 28.8.74, op. cit.
52 APU(COG)(76), 3rd meeting minutes.
53 Ibid.
54 Ibid.
55 *Education* 4.7.80.
56 *The Teacher* 26.9.80
57 *TES* 16.1.81.
58 *Education* 13.3.81.
59 *TES* 26.4.74.
60 APU(COG)(75), 1st meeting minutes.
61 APU(COG)(76), 1st meeting minutes.
62 Minutes of the 'Monitoring Change over Time' Seminar, 23 June 1981.
63 APU(COG)(77), 2nd meeting minutes.
64 APU(CON)(78) 28.
65 APU(COG)(78), 2nd meeting minutes.
66 APU(COG)(79), 19, revised.
67 Brown, J. (1980), *Journal of Curriculum Studies* 12 1.
68 APU(COG)(76), 3rd meeting minutes.
69 APU(STAT)(77), 2 revised.
70 APU(STAT)(78), 4th meeting minutes.
71 APU(CON)(78), 3rd meeting minutes.
72 APU(CON)(78) 28.
73 APU(COG)(79) 21.
74 APU(COG)(79) 6.
75 Note of APU Seminar, 23 June 1981.
76 APU(LG)(77) 25.
77 APU(COG)(77), 4th meeting minutes.
78 APU(CON)(78) 28.
79 APU(CON)(79) 17.

80 APU(CON)(78) 28.
81 Letter to NUT from Jean Dawson, dated 12 May 1980.
82 NUT notes of the June 1980 DES meeting to discuss proposed West Indian Study.
83 Extracts from the Report of the West Indian Study Group, APU/DES 1980.
84 Ibid para 13.
85 Ibid para 36.
86 West Indian Study Group (80), 5th meeting minutes.
87 West Indian Study Group (80), 3rd meeting minutes.
88 Conclusion, Report of West Indian Study Group.
89 APU(CON)(80), 2nd meeting minutes.
90 APU(CON)(80) 22.
91 DES Press Notice, 'Achievements of West Indian pupils', 29.12.80.
92 'Dilemma over testing West Indians', *TES* 9.1.81.
93 'Why are some ethnic groups underachieving?' *Education* 2.1.81.
94 'Set back for APU over West Indian survey', *Education* 16.1.81.
95 'West Indian testing runs into storm' and 'Too many promises', *TES* 16.1.81.
96 'NUT attempt to block survey plan', *Education* 6.3.81.
97 'APU urged to abandon West Indian survey', *Education* 13.3.81.
98 APU(CON)(78) 28.
99 'Protest after Rampton is sacked', *TES* 22.5.81.
100 APU(STAT)(81) 11, 'Proposed Survey of West Indian Pupils'.
101 Fifth Report of the Home Affairs Committee, Vol 1 para 133, HMSO (1981).

Chapter 3
102 Kay, B.W. (1975), op. cit.
103 APU(CON)(76), 1st meeting minutes.
104 APU(CON)(76), 2nd meeting minutes.
105 APU(CON)(77), 3rd meeting minutes.
106 APU(CON)(76), 2nd meeting minutes.
107 APU(CON)(76), 3rd meeting minutes.
108 APU(CON)(77), 1st meeting minutes.
109 APU(CON)(78), 1st meeting minutes.
110 APU(CON)(78), 3rd meeting minutes.
111 APU(CON)(80), 1st meeting minutes.
112 APU(CON)(80), 2nd meeting minutes.
113 APU(CON)(81) 4.
114 APU(CON)(82) 2.
115 APU(CON)(77), 1st meeting minutes.
116 APU(CON)(77), 2nd meeting minutes.
117 APU(CON)(78), 3rd meeting minutes.
118 APU(CON)(78) 28.
119 APU(CON)(79), 4th meeting minutes.
120 APU(CON)(81), 1st meeting minutes.
121 APU(CON)(81), 2nd meeting minutes.
122 Wirtz, W. and Lapointe, A. (1982), *Measuring the Quality of Education: A Report on Assessing Educational Progress*, Washington: Wirtz & Lapointe.
123 APU(CON)(82) 5.
124 APU(COG)(76), 1st meeting minutes.
125 APU(MISC)(78) 9.
126 APU(COG)(79), 2nd meeting minutes.
127 APU(COG)(79), 3rd meeting minutes.
128 APU(COG)(80), 1st meeting minutes.
130 APU(COG)(76), 3rd meeting minutes.
131 APU(COG)(78), 2nd meeting minutes.
132 APU(COG)(78), 3rd meeting minutes.

133 APU(COG)(79), 2nd meeting minutes.
134 Jean Dawson letter to Maurice Holt 9.6.80, quoted in part in Holt, M. (1981), *Evaluating the Evaluators*, Hodder & Stoughton.

Chapter 4
135 APU(STAT)(77), 1st meeting minutes.
136 APU(STAT)(80) 8.
137 DES (1975), op. cit.
138 Start, B. and Wells, K. (1972), op. cit.
139 Wood, R. and Skurnik, L. (1969), *Item Banking*, NFER.
140 Lawton, D. and Lacey, C. (Eds) (1981), *Issues in Evaluation and Accountability*, Methuen.
141 APU(STAT)(77) 2.
142 APU(STAT)(77) 6.
143 APU(STAT)(77) 17.
144 APU(STAT)(77) 8.
145 APU(STAT)(77) 19
146 APU(STAT)(79) 11.
147 APU(STAT)(79) 4.
148 DES (1980), op. cit.
149 APU(STAT)(80) 2.
150 APU(STAT)(80) 7.
151 APU(STAT)(80) 19.
152 APU(STAT)(80) 24 and 25.
153 APU(STAT)(81) 2 and 6.
154 APU(STAT)(81), 6th meeting minutes.
155 APU(STAT)(80) 29.
156 APU(STAT)(81) 25.
157 APU(STAT)(80) 23.
158 APU(STAT)(77) 8.
159 APU(STAT)(77) 14.
160 APU(STAT)(77) 19.
161 APU(STAT)(77) 23.
162 APU(STAT)(77) 24.
163 APU(STAT)(77) 27.
164 APU(STAT)(78) 12.
165 APU(STAT)(78) 14.
166 APU(STAT)(79) 16.
167 APU(STAT)(80) 13.
168 APU(STAT)(78) 6.
169 APU(STAT)(80) 11.
170 APU(STAT)(80) 30.
171 APU(STAT)(79) 16.
172 APU(STAT)(77) 6.
173 APU(STAT)(77) 2.
174 APU(STAT)(77) MISC 1.
175 APU(STAT)(77) 12.
176 APU(STAT)(77) 22.
177 APU(STAT)(78) 1.
178 'Scepticism as APU maths tests get under way', *TES* 12.5.78.
179 APU(STAT)(78) 20.
180 Lawton, D. and Lacey, C. (1981). op. cit.
181 Dobby, J. and Duckworth, D. (1979) 'Objective assessment by means of item banking', *Schools Council Examinations Bulletin*, No 40, Evans/Methuen.
182 'Magic Testing', D. Nuttall (letter), *Education* 11.5.79.
183 APU(STAT)(80) 5.

184 Goldstein, H. (1981), 'Dimensionality, bias, independence and measured scale problems in latent trait test score models', *British Journal of Mathematical and Statistical Psychology* 33, 234–246.
185 APU(STAT)(80) 13.
186 APU(STAT)(80) 18.
187 APU(STAT)(81) 1.
188 'Pupil Testing may be unsound', *TES* 27.2.81.
189 Shavelson, R.J. and Webb, N.M. (1981), 'Generalisability theory: 1973–1980', *British Journal of Mathematical and Statistical Psychology* 34, 133–166.

Chapter 5
190 APU(SC)(75), 2nd meeting minutes.
191 APU(SC)(76), 4th meeting minutes.
192 APU(SC)(75), 1st meeting minutes.
193 APU(SC)(76), 4th meeting minutes.
194 APU(SC)(77), 1st meeting minutes.
195 APU(SC)(77), 2nd meeting minutes.
196 APU(SC)(77), 3rd meeting minutes.
197 APU(SC)(76), 1st meeting minutes.
198 APU(COG)(78) 2.
199 Fairbrother, R.W. (ed.) (1980), *Assessment and the Curriculum*, Chelsea College London.
200 Pring, R.A. in Lawton, D. and Lacey, C. (1981), op. cit.
201 Talk by Dr R. Driver at AEB 3 October 1980.
202 Ibid.
203 APU(SC)(79), 1st meeting minutes.
204 APU(SC)(80), 2nd meeting minutes.
205 Based on 'Science Progress Report 1977–78', APU (1979).
206 APU(SC)(76), 1st meeting minutes.
207 APU(SC)(78) 17.
208 APU(SC)(81), 1st meeting minutes.
209 ETSP schools survey (reported in *Testing Children*, Heinemann, forthcoming).
210 APU(STAT)(77) 14.
211 APU(SC)(78) 17.
212 APU(SC)(78) 2.
213 APU(SC)(78) 19.
214 APU(SC)(78), 5th meeting minutes.
215 APU(SC)(78), 6th meeting minutes.
216 APU(SC)(78) 25.
217 APU(SC)(78) 31.
218 Wirtz, W. and Lapointe, A. (1982), op. cit.
219 APU(SC)(80) 9.
220 'Science Progress Report 1977–78', APU (1979).
221 APU(SC)(80), 4th meeting minutes.
222 APU(SC)(78) 9.
223 APU (1981), *Science in Schools: Age 11 Report No 1*, HMSO.
224 APU(MA)(76), 1st meeting minutes.
225 APU (1978), *Monitoring Mathematics* p. 2.
226 Ibid.
227 APU(MA)(78), 4th meeting minutes.
228 APU(MA)(76), 1st meeting minutes.
229 APU(MA)(77), 2nd meeting minutes.
230 APU(MA)(76), 2nd meeting minutes.
231 APU(MA)(76) 3rd meeting minutes.
232 APU(MA)(77), 8th meeting minutes.
233 Based on APU (1982), *Mathematical Development: Secondary Survey Report No 3*,

HMSO, reproduced with the permission of the Controller of Her Majesty's Stationery Office.
234 APU (1980), *Mathematical Development: Secondary Survey Report No 1*, HMSO.
235 APU(MA)(78), 4th meeting minutes.
236 APU(MA)(78), 8th meeting minutes.
237 APU(MA)(78) 40.
238 APU(MA)(78), 8th meeting minutes.
239 APU(MA)(79) 2.
240 APU(MA)(79), 2nd meeting minutes.
241 APU(MA)(78), 3rd meeting minutes.
242 APU(MA)(78), 3rd and 4th meeting minutes.
243 APU(MA)(78), 3rd meeting minutes.
244 APU(MA)(80) 3.
245 APU(MA)(80) 18.
246 APU(MA)(81), 4th meeting minutes.
247 APU(STAT)(77), 14.
248 APU(MA)(80) 3.
249 APU(MA)(81), 1st meeting minutes.
250 APU(MA)(79), 3rd meeting minutes.
251 APU(MA)(79), 4th meeting minutes.
252 APU(MA)(79) 22.
253 APU (1980), *Mathematical Development: Primary Survey Report No 1*, HMSO.
254 APU(MA)(80), 5th meeting minutes.
255 APU(MA)(80), 6th meeting minutes.
256 APU (1981), *Mathematical Development: Secondary Survey Report No 2*, HMSO.
257 APU(MA)(81), 1st meeting minutes.
258 APU(MA)(78) 7.
259 APU(MA)(80) 2.
260 APU(MA)(80), 5th meeting minutes.
261 Peaker, G.F. (1966), op. cit.
262 Start, B. and Wells, K. (1972), op. cit.
263 DES (1975), op. cit.
264 Ibid. Para 3.26.
265 APU(LG)(75), 1st meeting minutes.
266 APU(LG)(76), 4th meeting minutes.
267 APU(LG)(75) 1.
268 APU (1978), *Language Performance*.
269 APU (1981),*Language Performance in Schools: Primary Survey Report No 1*, HMSO.
270 *Primary Education in England: A Survey by HMI*, HMSO (1978).
271 APU(LG)(76), 5th meeting minutes.
272 APU(COG)(77), 1st meeting minutes.
273 APU(LG)(76), 7th meeting minutes.
274 APU(LG)(77), 2nd meeting minutes.
275 APU(LG)(80), 2nd meeting minutes.
276 APU(LG)(78) 1.
277 APU(LG)(78), 1st meeting minutes.
278 APU(LG)(78), 2nd meeting minutes.
279 APU(COG)(78), 3rd meeting minutes.
280 APU(LG)(79), 3rd meeting minutes.
281 APU(CON)(76), 2nd meeting minutes.
282 APU(LG)(77), 1st meeting minutes.
283 APU(LG)(77), 16, and APU(LG)(78) 18.
284 APU(LG)(79), 2nd meeting minutes.
285 Gorman, T., 'Measured Performance', *TES*, 18.9.81.
286 Based on Gorman, T. (1982), *Monitoring Language Performance* (unpublished).
287 APU(LG)(76), 4th meeting minutes.
288 APU(LG)(76), 6th meeting minutes.

289 APU (1978), op. cit.
290 APU(LG)(78) 13.
291 APU(LG)(78), 3rd meeting minutes.
292 Letter from D. Carter, *TES*, 27.6.80.
293 Letter from D. Barnes, *TES*, 1.8.80.
294 Sheila Browne SCI, 'Language Assessment: to what end?' NFER Members' Conference 20.10.81.
295 APU(LG)(78), 2nd meeting minutes.
296 Burstall, C. and Kay, B.W. (1978), op. cit.

Chapter 6

297 Wood, R. and Gipps, C. (1982) 'An enquiry into the use of test results for accountability purposes', in McCormick, R. (Ed.), *Calling Education to Account*, Heinemann in association with Open University Press.
298 DES (1978), op. cit.
299 Roy. W. (1977), 'National testing: the teachers' role', *Secondary Education* November 1977.
300 Winters, D. (1977), 'The APU: the game of testing', *Primary Education Review 3*.
301 Roy, W. (1978), 'Should we monitor standards in our schools?' *Junior Education* March 1978.
302 'Testing of pupils' personal growth to be opposed by the Union', *The Teacher* 12.1.79.
303 'Union refuses to back survey of West Indians', *TES*, February 1981.
304 Smithies, F. (1978), 'A further progress report on the APU', *Schoolmaster and Career Teacher*, January 1978.
305 'West Indian testing runs into storm', *TES* 16.1.81.
306 Letters: 'Performance unit', *TES* 31.7.81.
307 Leonard, M. (1977), 'Art of the impossible', *TES*, 17.6.77.
308 Leonard, M. (1980), 'Platform', *TES*, 8.2.80.
309 Evans, I. (1981), 'Does assessment do its job?' *TES*, 29.5.81.
310 'Proposals "jargon-ridden" and "vague" say scientists', *TES* 17.3.78.
311 'Scandal of the dunces', *Daily Express* 22.1.80.
312 Bell, A. (1977), 'The APU and the 1978 Maths Survey', *Mathematics Teaching* No 80, September 1977.
313 Nuttall, D. (1980) 'Will the APU rule the curriculum?' *Education* (supplement) 6.6.80.
314 'Professor Pring's worries about the APU and the core', *Education* (supplement) 6.6.80.
315 'Government assessment unit should be scrapped', *The Teacher* 18.9.81.
316 Holt, M. (1981), op. cit.
317 Hopkins, R. (1982), 'Inspecting the inspectors again', *TES* 8.1.82.
318 Report of the Annual Conference of the NFER, *Education* 3.10.81.
319 APU(STAT)(78), 3rd meeting minutes.
320 APU(CON)(76), 3rd meeting minutes.
321 Choppin, B. (1968), *Nature* Vol 219, No 5156, 870–872.
322 APU(COG)(77), 3rd meeting minutes.
323 Jean Dawson letter to Maurice Holt 9.6.80, quoted by Holt, M. (1981), op. cit.

Chapter 7

324 APU(SC)(81), 5th meeting minutes.
325 Wood, R. and Gipps, C. (1982), op. cit.
326 Wirtz, W. and Lapointe, A. (1982), op. cit.
327 DES (1976), op. cit.
328 DES 30.11.82 Press Notice 'Assessment of children's performance to continue'.
329 *TES* 30.4.82.

Appendix 1   A Brief Chronology of the APU

1970
* The National Foundation for Educational Research commissioned to conduct a national survey into reading attainment at ages 11 and 15.
* Working party to look at educational measurement set up at the DES. This Working Group on Monitoring (WGMET) included two HMIs, two members of the planning branch of the DES and four educationists: Jack Wrigley, Director of Research at the Schools Council; Alan Little, Director of Research for the ILEA: Douglas Pidgeon, Deputy Director of the NFER and Bill Taylor, Research Adviser for the DES.

1971
* The Working Group on Monitoring reported that 'there is much to be gained from national assessment but care must be taken over backwash'.

1972
* Committee of Inquiry into the teaching of reading and other uses of English set up under the Chairmanship of Sir Alan Bullock.
* *The Trend of Reading Standards* by Start and Wells published. This reported on the last of the NFER reading surveys carried out in 1970/71.

1973
* The Tests of Attainment in Mathematics Project (TAMS) funded at the NFER.

1974
* Early in the year the Permanent Secretary at the DES, in evidence to a House of Commons subcommittee, hinted that the Secretary of State's position on the curriculum must be clarified.
* *April*: Mr Reg Prentice MP, Secretary of State for Education, in a speech to the National Association of Schoolmasters' Conference talked of underachievement as 'the greatest educational challenge of

the 70s and 80s'. He announced the setting up of a special unit, the Educational Disadvantage Unit, at the DES to look at educational underachievement, which would try to isolate educational reasons for underachievement from the social causes.[1]
* *May*: Publication of Community Relations Commission Report, *The Educational Needs of Children from Minority Groups*.[2]
* *August*: The White Paper *Educational Disadvantage and the Educational Needs of Immigrants* was published.[3] It announced the establishment in the DES of the Educational Disadvantage Unit (EDU); one of its terms of reference was to identify, with the help of the also newly established Assessment of Performance Unit, 'the incidence of successful practice in meeting the needs of all those suffering educational disadvantage'.[4]

1975
* *June*: Brian Kay HMI, Head of the APU, published an article 'Monitoring Pupils' Performance'.[5] In this he highlighted the growing interest in assessment of pupils' performance which was related to anxiety about standards. He also stressed the need for cross-curricularity and outlined the six main areas which should be tested.
* *June*: The Bullock Report was published under the title *A Language for Life*.[6]
* *September*: Science Working Group's first meeting. The group was chaired by the Head of the APU and included another HMI, two academics, one teacher and one LEA adviser. The composition of the working group was 'intended to represent a microcosm of the world of science teaching'.[7]
* *October*: First meeting of Co-ordinating Group (COG). The group was chaired by an HMI. The Head of the APU defined COG as the 'body which monitors and directs the progress of the working groups and which has a professional membership'.[8]
* *October*: Language Working Group's first meeting. The Head of the Unit was in the chair and the group included two HMIs, three teachers, two academics and one member of an LEA.

1976
* *March*: The Deputy Director of the NFER and the Head of the APU went to the USA to study the National Assessment of Educational Progress (NAEP).
* *April*: Consultative Committee's first meeting: 'a Committee representative of the major teacher and local authority associations and acting in an advisory role'.[9]
* *April*: Mr James Callaghan became Prime Minister and Mr Fred Mulley was appointed Secretary of State for Education. The DES produced the so-called 'Yellow Book', a discourse on 'School Education in England – Problems and Initiatives'.[10]

* *October*: Mathematics Working Group's first meeting. The group was chaired by an HMI and the membership comprised another HMI, two academics, four teachers, two LEA advisers and two representatives of the NFER. The Head of the APU explained that the establishment of this group had been deferred to await the completion of the Tests of Attainment in Mathematics in Schools (TAMS) project, the existence of which would give the group some pre-organised material.
* *October*: Personal and Social Exploratory Group's first meeting.
* *October*: Mrs Shirley Williams took over as Secretary of State for Education.
* *October 18*: Mr Callaghan gave a speech at Ruskin College Oxford:

> There is no virtue in producing socially well adjusted members of society who are unemployed because they do not have the skills . . . the basic purposes of education require the same essential tools. These are basic literacy and numeracy, the understanding of how to live and work together, respect for others, respect for the individual. This means acquiring certain basic knowledge, skills and reasoning ability.[11]

1977
* *January*: D T E (Tom) Marjoram succeeded Brian Kay as Head of the APU.
* *January*: Statistics Advisory Group's (SAG) first meeting. The meeting was chaired by the Head of the APU who explained that the group had been established to 'provide the Unit as a whole with expert advice on all matters concerned with statistics, sampling and item banking'.[12]
* *June*: Aesthetic Development Exploratory Group's first meeting.
* *June*: Physical Development Exploratory Group's first meeting.
* *July*: Green Paper *Education in Schools* published.[13] Section 3.6 referred briefly to the APU and the terms of reference were set out in Annex 3, section 3.10: the major function of the APU was assessment of individual pupils only as members of a representative sample. Tests suitable for LEA use in monitoring performance were likely to come out of the work of the APU. 'The Department's concern is that there should be consistency within local education authorities and wherever possible between authorities'.
* *October*: APU leaflets published.

An Introduction
Everyone wants to raise educational standards. But how do we know what educational standards are? How do we measure standards in education? How can we monitor progress?

There is not enough information available at present. There is plenty of hearsay, hunch, opinion. There are plenty of tests about but there are many important things these tests don't measure. And most of them are designed to give information about individuals, not to paint a picture of pupils' achievement nationally.

The last ten years have seen changes in school organisation and curriculum. We need to be able to monitor the consequences for children's education in school. We need to know how the schools are serving the changing needs of children in society.

The first task of the APU is to identify and define standards of performance pupils might be expeccted to achieve through their work at school.

Language Performance

Language is not simply something that belongs to the English lesson. It is fundamental to all learning. Every subject of the curriculum both uses and creates language skills.

The leaflet describes the four modes of language: writing, reading, listening and speaking. The group aims to test reading and writing and in the future listening and speaking.

Monitoring Mathematics

Mathematical performance involves an understanding of basic concepts, the exercise of a variety of everyday skills and the insight to apply mathematical knowledge to everyday problems.

The leaflet gives information on how the group intends to monitor mathematics.

Assessment: Why? What? How?

The APU gathers information that will.

- help determine policy including decisions on the development of resources,
- help teachers in planning the balance of pupils' work in schools, without an attempt at national level to define detailed syllabus content.

The leaflet stresses the cross-curricular model developed by Brian Kay.

* *December*: Lord Alexander resigned from the Consultative Committee over a disagreement over whether the APU should assess personal and social development.
* *December*: First seminar on the Rasch Method of statistical analysis.
* *December*: Foreign Language Working Group's first meeting.
* *December*: Shirley Williams, Secretary of State for Education, made a

speech at the NFER Conference. Backing from the LEAs was the first requirement of national monitoring. The role of the APU was to provide better information about achievement at school – not to promote curricular patterns. There was concern that there should not be backwash and there was to be no identification of individual schools or LEAs used in the APU surveys.

1978
* *January*: 'Assessment – The American Experience.' A report on NAEP by the Head of the APU, Brian Kay, and the Deputy Director of the NFER Clare Burstall, after their 1976 visit.

> The lesson for the APU is, we feel, clear, if it is to avoid the criticims levelled against the NAEP. On the one hand it needs to ensure that its findings are of interest and concern to the teacher, not because of what can be reported about an individual school (for that is outside the sphere of the APU) but because of what can be said about the overall pattern of education. The interests and involvement of these bodies, such as the subject associations, need to be engaged so that they will take advantage of its findings and use them to further desirable curriculum developments.[14]

* *April*: APU leaflet published.

Facts and Figures About Monitoring
The APU's task is to provide a national picture of pupil performance in certain agreed aspects of the curriculum and an indication of how performance is changing over time. It will not produce and is not concerned with information on the attainment of individual pupils or schools.

The leaflet outlines the official APU policy of light sampling.
* *May*: Surveying began: first primary maths survey.
* *May*: APU booklet *Language Performance* published. The publication outlined the basis for testing language and how the research team envisaged the monitoring process. It was meant as a discussion document inviting response.
* *August*: APU leaflet *Reporting on Performance* published. The format of the APU reports was discussed. They would contain descriptive material as well as statistical data and reports would need to be supplemented at a later date by further analysis.
* *August*: Publication of DES Report on Education No 93, *Assessing the Performance of Pupils*. This was a more detailed report on the APU than the publicity leaflets. It described what it is, its terms of reference and tasks etc. It warned that regular 'blanket' testing by LEAs wasted resources and could have an adverse effect on the curriculum.
* *October*: First secondary maths survey carried out.

1979

* *January*: The Consultative Committee opposed the monitoring of personal and social development, largely because of the vote of the NUT and the LEAs.
* *February*: Technology sub-group's first meeting.
* *May*: Language monitoring began with the first primary language survey.
* *May*: Secondary primary maths survey carried out.
* *June*: John Graham HMI and Jean Dawson DES took over from Tom Marjoram as joint heads of the APU.
* *August*: Conservative Party election manifesto included a mention of the APU: 'The Government's APU will set national standards in reading, writing and arithmetic monitored by tests worked out with teachers and others'.[15]
* *October*: The West Indian Study Group set up to look at the feasibility of an in-depth study of the achievement of West Indian children.
* *October/November*: First secondary language survey carried out.
* *November*: Second secondary maths survey carried out.
* Autumn issue of *FORUM* Vol 22 No 1 Special Issue: 'The APU Threat? Self Evaluation is the Answer', eight articles on accountability, the APU and self-evaluation:

What and who is the APU?	Joan Simon
The world of APU	Edgar Stones
The mystification of assessment	Harvey Goldstein
Accountability – a contagious disease?	Joan P Shapiro
A constructive response to the APU	Maurice Galton
The case for school self-evaluation	John Elliott
Self-assessment at a London comprehensive	George Varnava
A year of evaluation	A R Delves & John Watts

1980

* *January*: West Indian Study Group's first meeting.
* *January*: Reporting began with the publication of *Mathematical Development: Primary Survey Report No 1*.
* *March*: Seminar held to discuss methods of assessing listening and speaking skills.
* *April*: The assessment of personal and social development was shelved at a Consultative Committee meeting after discussion of a paper 'Assessment of Personal and Social Development – Is it desirable? Is it possible?'[16]
* *April*: Six-day conference on assessment at Nottingham. School-based assessment, examinations and the APU methods of assessment were discussed and speakers included the leaders of the APU

monitoring teams. A report of the conference later published under the title *Assessment and the Curriculum*.[17]

* *May*: Science monitoring began with the first primary science survey.
* *May*: Second primary language survey carried out.
* *May*: Third primary maths survey carried out.
* *June*: Last meeting of the West Indian Study Group.
* *June*: Second seminar organised by the DES to discuss the Rasch model.
* *July*: APU publicity leaflet *APU: What It Is, How It Works* published. The leaflet looks at testing and reporting, reiterating what has been said before.

As years go by the APU's monitoring programme will produce increasingly accurate and useful data. It will trace changes in performance; it will draw attention to features that will have cause for satisfaction as well as concern.

* *September*: APU publicity leaflets published: *Monitoring Mathematics*, an update of the October 1977 leaflet, stressing in addition the item banking system and random sampling which reduces curricular impact; and *Monitoring Language* which classifies the different modes of writing, e.g. for teachers or for strangers, and describes the problems of testing these. There are also different modes of reading, for example, skimming and scanning, which involve different levels of comprehension. The APU is concerned with the national picture and not the performance of the individual.
* *September*: *Mathematical Development: Secondary Survey Report No 1* published.
* *November*: First secondary science survey carried out.
* *November*: Second secondary language survey carried out.
* *November*: Third secondary maths survey carried out.

1981

* *February*: First science survey of 13-year-olds carried out.
* *February*: The NUT rejected the West Indian survey:

It is the considered view of the NUT, after much heart searching, that the educational needs of ethnic minority students will not be met by the APU's proposed study of West Indian pupils, and accordingly the Union recommends that its members do not participate in the survey. Moreover, the Union strongly urges the APU to reconsider its recommendations to the Secretary of State and hopes the government will not proceed with the survey in the face of opposition from the NUT in particular and a large section of the teaching profession in general.[18]

* *May*: Second primary science survey carried out.
* *May*: Third primary language survey carried out.
* *May*: Fourth primary maths survey carried out.
* *May*: Proposed West Indian Study finally abandoned.
* *June: Mathematical Development: Primary Survey Report No 2* published.
* *June*: 'Measurement of change over time' seminar. Jean Dawson, the administrative head of the APU, presented a paper 'The APU: measuring changes in educational performance over time', and affirmed the Unit's desire to fulfil its terms of reference.
* *July*: Aesthetics and Physical Working Groups wound up after submitting their reports.
* *August*: Survey of provision for teaching design and technology funded.
* *August*: NFER Research Information Leaflet 25, *Monitoring Performance in French, German and Spanish* published. Monitoring in first foreign language should start in 1983.
* *September: Language Performance in Schools: Primary Survey Report No 1* published.
* *November: Evaluating the Evaluators* by Maurice Holt published. Contains a major attack on the APU.
* *November*: Second secondary science survey carried out.
* *November*: Third secondary language survey carried out.
* *November*: Fourth secondary maths survey carried out.
* *December: Mathematical Development: Secondary Survey Report No 2* published.
* *December: Science in Schools Age 11: Report No 1* published.
1982
* *March: Language Performance in Schools: Secondary Survey Report No 1* published.
* *April*: Publication of APU Newsletter Number One. It is the first of a twice-yearly series intended to disseminate APU findings in a concise format. It contains articles by the monitoring team leaders, the chairman of the Consultative Committee and 'A Message from the Heads of the APU'.
* *May: Mathematical Development: Primary Survey Report No 3* published.
* *September: Language Performance in Schools: Primary Survey Report No 2* published.
* *September: Science in Schools Age 13: Report No 1* published.
* *October*: APU Newsletter No 2 published.
* *December: Mathematical Development: Secondary Survey Report No 3* published.
* *December: Science in Schools Age 15: Report No 1* published.

182 *Monitoring Children*

References

DES Press Notice 18.4.74, 'Special unit to study educational underachievement'.
2 CRC Publication, May 1974, London.
3 DES (1974), *Educational Disadvantage and the Educational Needs of Immigrants*, Cmnd 5720 HMSO.
4 Ibid.
5 Kay, B.W. (1975), 'Monitoring Pupils' Performance', *Trends in Education* 2.
6 DES (1975), *A Language for Life*, HMSO.
7 APU(SC)(75), 1st meeting minutes.
8 APU(COG)(75), 1st meeting minutes.
9 APU(MA)(76), 1st meeting minutes.
10 Quoted in Lawton, D. (1980), *Politics of the School Curriculum*, Routledge and Kegan Paul.
11 Transcript of 'Towards a National Debate', speech made at Ruskin College by Prime Minister James Callaghan, *Education* 22.10.76.
12 APU(SAG)(77), 1st meeting minutes.
13 DES (1977), *Education in Schools: a Consultative Document*, Cmnd 6869 HMSO.
14 Burstall, C. and Kay, B.W. (1978), *Assessment – The American Experience*, DES.
15 Conservative Party Manifesto, May 1979.
16 APU(CON)(80), 1st meeting minutes.
17 Fairbrother, R.W. (Ed.) (1980), *Assessment and the Curriculum*, Chelsea College London.
18 NUT (1981), *Comments on the Proposed APU Survey of the Achievement Levels of West Indian Pupils*.

Appendix 2   List of Questions to be Answered by Monitoring

These questions were presented to the June 1981 seminar by the head of the APU (Revised version, APU(CON)(81)(26)).

1 What are the characteristics of a school which would appear to have some relation to a pupil's level of performance?
2 Is there any relationship between the locality in which a child lives and his/her level of performance?
3 Do children perform better in schools of a particular size?
4 Is the size of the teaching group a relevant factor?
5 Is there a discernible connection between 'resources' and 'output'? Does the provision of additional teachers, equipment, laboratory space, etc. lead to a measurable improvement in levels of pupils' performance?
6 Are there any distinct variations in the patterns of children's performance in different parts of the United Kingdom?
7 What differences are there in the performance of boys and girls? Are these equally discernible at all the ages at which testing takes place? And in all the curricular areas tested? Can the monitoring data indicate why such differences, if there are any, exist and/or develop?
8 Does the language background of the pupil affect performance?
9 What connection, if any, is there between the pupils' level of performance and their home background – e.g. parental education, parental occupation, ethnic origin?
10 Are there particular areas of the curriculum, or particular categories of tasks or knowledge within individual curricular areas, which appear to call for special investigation?
11 Are there any changes in pupils' performance as tested in different modes of teaching? Can observation of pupils' performance in practical work illuminate the learning process?
12 What light can the tests throw on the effectiveness of different teaching skills?

Appendix 3   The Cost of the APU

How much does the APU cost? At a time when the education service as a whole has been made to suffer cuts in real terms in expenditure, the question is a legitimate one. Certainly Michael Brown MP thought so because in March 1980 he addressed the following parliamentary question to the Secretary of State for Education and Science, as reported in Hansard.

> . . . what is the function of the Assessment of Performance Unit; how many people it employs; and *what is the total cost to public funds per annum?* (our italics)

In his reply on 28 March[1] Dr Boyson said:

> The Assessment of Performance Unit promotes the development of methods of assessing and monitoring the achievement of children at school, and seeks to identify the incidence of underachievement. The unit itself consists of five full-time and five part-time staff. It commissions universities and research bodies to undertake the development of test materials and the administration of surveys on its behalf.
>
> The unit is an integral part of my Department, and it would not be possible separately to determine the total cost of its operations without undue expense. The total salary bill of the unit's staff is currently about £60,000 per annum. Expenditure on monitoring surveys varies, but in 1980 surveys in mathematics and English language – both at age 11 and 15 – and in science – at age 11, 13 and 15 – are expected to cost about £700,000.

Christopher Price MP, in February 1981, sought more precise information:

> . . . what were the operating costs of the Assessment of Performance Unit during the last financial year, including payments to research teams, the

salaries of the full-time staff of the Assessment of Performance Unit, the cost of providing papers and publicity material, the cost of running regional conferences and the expenses paid to the Assessment of Performance Unit committee and group members.

Dr Boyson's answer – on Monday 9 February 1981[2] – repeated the earlier proviso about the APU being an integral part of his Department so that it was not possible to separate out the total cost of its operations in any financial year. He continued:

> For the same reason it is not possible to identify the cost of providing papers. The cost in the financial year ending 31 March 1980 of the other items on which this information is sought was:

Payments to research teams:	£480,450
Salaries of full-time APU staff:	£30,000 (approximately)*
Publicity material:	£16,000
Regional conferences:	£6,900
APU committee and group members expenses	£12,300

Simple arithmetic shows a large discrepancy in the total sums implied in the two parliamentary answers. There are several reasons for this. The answer to Christopher Price gives cost based upon *actual* expenditure in the financial year 1979/80. The answer to Michael Brown is an *estimate* which relates to the financial year 1980/81 and includes an increase due to the introduction of science monitoring. The two answers also contain a mixture of price levels. Part of the expenditure in 1979/80 will have been incurred nearly two years before the end of the period 1980/81 covered in the estimate and inflation will have had its effect.[3] However, by combining the information from these two parliamentary answers it is possible to move towards an estimate of the cost of the APU's activities which makes some distinction between anticipated recurrent expenditure on the APU within the DES, and on survey administration and test development expenditure.

To aid in these estimates there is another source. Each year the DES lists the current educational research projects it supports.[4] The APU-linked projects are included, in each case together with the cost, starting date and duration. On 1 January 1981 the existing projects were as given below:

---

* The previous answer costed salaries at £60,000 and included 5 part-time as well as 5 full-time staff.

TEST DEVELOPMENT COSTS

Project and base	Cost £	Start	Duration
Language main project, NFER	491,981	April 1977	5 years
Maths main project, NFER	443,027	April 1977	5 years
Practical mathematics, NFER	128,145	April 1977	5 years
Science, Leeds University	600,721	September 1977	5 years
Science, Chelsea College	741,214	September 1977	5 years
A test validity investigation, NFER	67,616	April 1977	2¾ years
Aesthetic development – desk study Leicester Polytechnic	770	October 1980	3 months
Administrative services connected with the monitoring, NFER	287,860	April 1977	5 years

These amounts are as agreed by contracts at 1 January 1981 and comprise expenditure incurred up to that date together with forecasts to the end of the contract period.[5] Thus the average annual research/ development costs on the three major areas of language, mathematics and science are approximately £480,000 per annum according to estimates on the basis described above.

Since these figures were prepared by the DES it has been decided to go ahead with a programme for monitoring the performance of children at age 13 in their first modern foreign language.

. . . the cost of the work at present contracted is expected to be in the region of £750,000 at 1981 price levels. This will provide for an initial two years' work developing the assessment model and devising and piloting test materials, followed by three annual surveys in French (in June 1983, 1984 and 1985) and one survey in German and Spanish (in June 1983). The cost includes the involvement of Wales and Northern Ireland in the monitoring of performances in French only.[6]

Recurrent expenditure – central and survey administration
Under recurrent expenditure the APU would expect to continue to pay the salaries of the Unit's staff; the expense of the administration of the monitoring programmes; some conference costs; publicity costs; and expenses to APU committee and group membership. On a 1979/80 base for costing, the figures for recurrent annual expenditure are shown opposite.

In the near future it is unlikely that there will be savings under any of the headings listed here. On the contrary, expenditure is likely to rise – and not only because of inflation. As the number of surveys being conducted increases, the cost of the survey administration rises commensurately. The NFER 35th Annual Report 1980/81 shows the 1980/81 cost to be £116,337 – a 78 per cent rise on 1979/80. In addition we know that there is to be an increased emphasis on dissemination of

APU RECURRENT ANNUAL COSTS – ESTIMATES AT 1979/80
PRICES

Heading	*Annual Cost £*
Salaries of central APU staff	60,000
APU committee and group members' expenses	12,000
Publicity material	16,000
Regional conferences	6,900
Survey Administration – at the NFER	65,280[7]
	Total: £160,180

the results of the APU's work and thus the costs involved in this will
rise. Therefore recurrent annual costs are probably above £210,000 at
the time of writing (May 1982).

Test development costs

The DES list of research projects and the answers to the Parliamentary
Questions have shown that the annual research and development costs
for Language, Mathematics and Science combined were approximately
£480,000 in 1979/80. From 1981 approximately £150,000 per annum
will also go to the monitoring programme in Modern Languages – this
work will continue until 1985/86. Presumably, after the initial period of
research and development the annual costs will fall, but it is not
possible to say by how much. On the other hand, if the APU decides to
develop a monitoring programme in other areas such as technology,
there will be continuing high costs.

Summary

From 1977 to 1981 the APU's work has been costing, on average,
something of the order of £160,000 per annum for central and administration costs and £480,000 per annum for payments to survey teams,
that is £640,000 per annum. This is an average, however. Dr Boyson's
Parliamentary answer on 28 March 1980 referred to a total of at least
£760,000 expected expenditure in 1980. From 1981, with the Modern
Language monitoring getting under way, total costs per annum are
likely to rise well above £800,000 when allowance is made for inflation,
direct research and development costs and survey administration.
Decisions to initiate surveys in other areas could push the figure above
£1,000,000 per annum.

References

1 *Hansard* on the date given.
2 *Hansard* on the date given.
3 Information in this paragraph is based on a letter from the APU dated 27.4.82.
4 DES, *Current Educational Research Projects Supported by the Department of Education and Science, 1st January 1981*.
5 See (3) above.
6 Information supplied by the APU in a letter dated 2.2.82.
7 NFER 35th Annual Report 1980/81.

Appendix 4 People Interviewed by the Institute of Education Project Team

Mr R. Arnold HMI
Mr B.L. Baish
Mr J.F.T. Bartlett
Ms M. Beckett
Dr A.W. Bell
Dr A. Bishop
Mr T. Burdett HMI
Dr C. Burstall
Miss S.J. Browne HMI
Professor J. Dancy
Miss D.J. Dawson
Dr R. Driver
Professor S.J. Eggleston
Mr D.D. Foxman
Dr T.P. Gorman
Mr J. Graham HMI
Mr G. Hainsworth
Mr A.R. Hall
Mr P.H. Halsey
Sir James Hamilton
Dr W. Harlen
Mr A. Jarman
Mr B.W. Kay HMI

Professor A. Little
Mr S. Maclure
Mr D.T.E. Marjoram HMI
Mr D.J. Maxwell
Professor D.L. Nuttall
Mr J.G. Owen
Mr C. Parsons HMI
Dr D. Pidgeon
Professor R.A. Pring
Sir William Pile
Mr B. Rodmell
Mr G. Saltmarsh
Mr C.H. Selby HMI
Professor M.D. Shipman
Mr T.P. Snape
Dr B.E. Supple
Mr J.C. Taylor
Dr W. Taylor
Mr W.E. Thomas HMI
Mr G.M. Thornton
Mr P.C. Webb HMI
Mr J. Wight
Professor J. Wrigley

Appendix 5 Participants at the Institute of Education Seminar 21 April 1982

Professor J. Wrigley (Chairman)	Reading University
Ms P. Broadfoot	Bristol University
Dr C. Burstall	NFER
Dr R. Driver	APU Science Team, Leeds University
Mr A. Evans	NUT
Mr D.D. Foxman	APU Maths Team, NFER
Dr T.P. Gorman	APU Language Team, NFER
Mr J. Graham HMI	APU (retired)
Dr W. Harlen	APU Science Team, Chelsea College
Mr D. Hill	Heinemann
Mr C. Humphrey	CEO, Solihull LEA
Mr B.W. Kay HMI	APU (retired)
Professor M. Kogan	Brunel University
Professor D. Lawton	Institute of Education London University
Professor D. Layton	APU Science Team, Leeds University
Mr D.J. Maxwell	Adviser, North Tyneside LEA
Mr D.J. Noble	APU
Professor D.L. Nuttall	Open University
Professor R.A. Pring	Exeter University
Dr B.E. Supple	Christ's College Cambridge
Dr G. Sutherland	Newnham College Cambridge
Mr J. Wray	Inner London Education Authority

SSRC Project Team, University of London Institute of Education

Professor H. Goldstein	Professor T. Blackstone
Dr C.V. Gipps	Mr S.D. Steadman
Mr B.M. Stierer	Ms D. Head

Also present:	Dr E.A. Holdaway	University of Alberta
	Mr N. McGowan	Brunel University
	Ms D. Thom	Newnham College Cambridge

Index

ethical development, *see* personal–social
development
ethnic minority groups, 11, 28, 31, 32,
135, 162; *see also* Educational
Disadvantage Unit
Ethnic Minority Working Group, *see*
West Indian Study Group
ethnic origin, 32, 34n, 64, 69, 70
Examination Boards, 82, 86, 146, 152–3
expansion of monitoring, 163–4
Exploratory Working Group, 44; *see also*
aesthetic, personal–social, physical
and technological development
exposure, *see* Rasch model

feedback, 101, 121, 125, 134; *see also*
APU newsletter
findings of surveys, *see* results
forward planning, *see* planning; themes
free school meals, 70, 119, 160
future of the APU, 164–66

generalisability theory, 85, 86, 102
universe of items, 85n
Goldstein, Harvey, 63n, 81, 82, 83, 84
Great Debate, 3, 5
Green Paper 1977, 5, 12

Head of APU, 3, 14, 16, 27, 28, 31, 43,
51, 53, 55, 93, 110, 119, 122, 136,
153, 157
administrative, 1, 31, 33, 52, 56–7
professional, 1, 33, 49
head teachers, 139
Her Majesty's Inspectors of Education
(HMI), 49, 109, 120
credibility, 150
independence, 149
Primary Survey, 125, 144
relationship with APU, 148–151
role, 136, 151, 165
Secondary Survey, 97, 129
Senior Chief Inspector, 133, 151
see also head of APU; results, exploitation of
home background, 29, 30, 39, 41, 47,
50, 104, 120, 152
surrogate measure, 30, 48, 55, 73, 74
home-based variables, *see* home background
home, language of, 133
home support variables, *see* home background
House of Commons Select Committee,
40

in-depth studies, 11, 25, 30–32, 35, 40,
47, 59, 69–72, 74, 100, 119, 120,
126, 135, 158, 160, 162, 165, 166

in-service training, 46, 118, 121, 134,
136, 138, 141–4, 150, 151
independent schools, 78
Inner London Education Authority
(ILEA), 123
Institute of Education (London University), ix, 26, 42n
Institute of Mathematics and its Applications, 147
Institute of Physics, 147
interviews, viii, 43, 56, 141; *see also*
Local Education Authority
IQ, 28, 30, 72; *see also* cognitive ability
indicator
issues, 20–21, 41, 45–51, 54–5, 58–9,
100, 106, 118–21, 131–35, 138
item, banking, 13, 61, 62, 63, 79,
154–55, 158
core of, 13, 73, 80
clustering, 86, 114, 120
difficulty, 62, 80, 82, 86
homogeneity, 63
release of, 77, 86, 121
relevance, 82
validation, 98
see also Rasch model; testing, combined

Kay, Brian, 3, 9, 14, 15, 19, 42, 52, 93,
136

Labour
Government, 9
Party, 8
language, *see* monitoring team, steering
group
Layton, David, 93, 95, 103–4, 105
leadership of the APU, 150
LEASIB, 13, 77, 132, 140, 144, 154–55,
158
Leeds University, 1, 48, 91, 96; *see also*
monitoring team, science
Leonard, Martin, 82
literacy, 79; *see also* monitoring team,
language
Local Education Authority
advisers, 33, 120, 141, 146, 159, 165
APU impact, 12, 120, 138, 140,
141–44
Associations, 34, 35, 36, 42, 52
interviews, 138, 141
representation, 51, 93
survey of, 139, 141–44
testing by, 5, 12, 140, 147
use of APU items, 12, 77, 132, 144,
155, 161, 166
see also in-service training; LEASIB
light sampling, *see* sampling
low achievement, *see* achievement;
underachievement